W9-BYU-659

TC CO 1-29-57

THE MAKING OF MODERN BRITAIN

Wingate College Library

Title Page

London from the terrace of Richmond House, painted by Canaletto for the second Duke of Richmond, probably in 1746,

THE MAKING OF

Life and Work from

T. K. DERRY, M.A., D.Phil.(Oxon.) an

New Yor

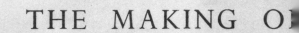

42.07
D

MODERN BRITAIN

George III to Elizabeth II

L. JARMAN, *M.A., B.Litt.(Oxon.), A.M.(Harvard)*

niversity Press

Wingate College Library

First published in England 1956
by Iohn Murray (Publishers) Ltd.

First United States edition 1956

©1956 by New York University
Library of Congress catalogue card number: 56-11980

Manufactured in the United States of America

PREFACE

This is a short book on a large subject, for social and economic history should include the whole record of how men have won their living, made their homes, and occupied their leisure. But, compared with political history, its outlines are less firmly established; sentiment and propaganda creep in even more easily. We feel therefore that there is room for an objective and up-to-date sketch such as we have attempted to give here, of the changes in British life during the past two hundred years.

We try to show, not only the growth of the Industrial Revolution down to our own time, but how the Welfare State has emerged from the individualistic society of the days of Arkwright and Adam Smith and the stages by which the rustic Englishman we meet in the pages of Woodforde or Surtees developed the character and way of life appropriate to an urban civilization in an overcrowded island. Only six generations divide the subjects of Elizabeth II from those of George III: yet the material circumstances of life have been altered far more radically in those six than in the forty generations which separate Gibbon, born the year before the king, from his beloved Age of the Antonines. A short book like this must then be remarkable chiefly for its omissions; but it will serve its purpose if text and illustrations together raise in the reader's mind a desire to know more of this fascinating subject. The highly selective Book List has been designed to encourage such further exploration.

The book was originally planned by the late E. H. Carter, who drafted the first chapters and began the selection of illustrations. He was advised on various points by Mrs. Mary Stocks, Mr. A. H. Ensor and Mr. H. C. Honeybone, to all of whom the authors would like to tender their most grateful thanks.

T. K. D.
T. L. J.

November, 1955

ACKNOWLEDGMENTS

Thanks are due to the following who have kindly permitted the reproduction of copyright illustrations:

The Duke of Richmond and Gordon (*title page*); Adprint Ltd. (*p. 2*); The Trustees of the British Museum (*pp. 5, 8, 18, 40, 54, 56, 86, 110, 114, 121, 126-7, 148*); Picture Post Library (*pp. 38, 62, 73, 79, 95, 132-133, 172, 225, 279*); Platt Bros. Ltd. (*p. 45*); The Director of the Science Museum (*pp. 48 77, 130*); Aerofilms Ltd. (*p. 66*); The Director of the National Portrait Gallery (*p. 116*); The London School of Economics (*p. 152*); Co-operative Union Ltd. (*p. 158*); British Railways (*pp. 164-165*); ; R. Weaver-Smith (*p. 177*); Labour Party (*p. 215*); Gernsheim Collection (*p. 224*); Central Office of Information (*p. 239*); Hodgson Advertising Ltd. (*p. 247*); London County Council (*pp. 256, 257*); The National Trust (*p. 266*); The *Daily Mail* (*p. 267*); Frederick Gibberd, Esq. (*pp. 280-281*).

The poem by W. H. Davies quoted in Appendix I, No. 7 is reproduced by permission of Jonathan Cape Ltd.

CONTENTS

Before the Great Changes

The Coming of the Machine

Early Social Changes

The Great Victorian Age

The Last Half-Century

ILLUSTRATIONS

BEFORE THE GREAT CHANGES

I

VILLAGE LIFE IN THE EIGHTEENTH CENTURY

LESS than two hundred years ago England was still mainly a land of countrymen leading country lives. Let us then begin by looking at the England of those days through the eyes of a countryman—the Rev. James Woodforde, a bachelor and the newly appointed parson of Weston Longeville in the county of Norfolk. His diary, happily preserved through a century and a half, enables us to observe the life of his own day and district, hum-drum and far from the madding crowd. The portrait (taken in the gown, bobwig, and bands appropriate to his profession) shows us the sort of man his parishioners were staring at: for the arrival of a stranger was a great event in a country village.

In the opening months of 1776, Parson Woodforde has been busy moving in to his Rectory; then, as now, a tiresome business—what with the buying of furniture, house repairs, and in this case the destruction of a plague of rats, requiring the services of a rat-catcher at what was then the high price of 10s. 6d. By early summer he appears to be settled, and on June 3rd two servant maids come and offer their services. He engages them—the more experienced for £5 5s. a year and tea twice a day, the less experienced for £3 3s. a year. Then there is a disagreeable interruption: he is racked with toothache. On June 4th he rises at 5 a.m. after a sleepless night: "Sent for one Reeves a man who draws teeth in this parish, and about 7 he came and drew my tooth, but shockingly bad indeed: he broke away a great piece of

1

Parson Woodforde, wearing a bob-wig and the gown and white bands of his profession

my gum and broke one of the fangs of the tooth: it gave me exquisite pain all the day after, and my face was swelled prodigiously in the evening and much pain. Very bad and in much pain the whole day long. Gave the old man that drew it, however, £0 2s. 6d. He is too old, I think, to draw teeth; can't see very well."

Next day he pays his bills for "2 cows, 3 Pigs, 3 pr. Shoes, Flour, Tea, Sugar, News Papers, Pipes, Candles, Pan, Tobacco, Beer, Mustard, Salt, Washing, Halters, Comb and Brush, Crabs, Bread, and Porterage," in all £14 9s. 3d. After that life goes more quietly. Like many other clergy in those days Parson Woodforde farmed his own land, the glebe, so in September he is busy with his harvest—mostly barley—and on September 14th he entertains his "Harvestmen with some Beef and some Plum Pudding and as much liquor as they could drink". That done, he goes for a pleasant jaunt to Yarmouth with his nephew. The fees at the turnpike gates[1] on the roads cost him 1s. 6d. They watch the Dutch herring boats come in. He notes that "The Dutch are very droll fellows to look at, strange, heavy, bad dressed People with monstrous large Trousers, and many with large wooden shoes." But the two holiday-makers have a very good time and are entertained "with Wine, Gin etc." on board a collier about to return to Sunderland.

Later in the autumn, Woodforde feels that he ought to do something about a local smallpox scare; and at 11 o'clock on November 3rd a Dr. Thorne comes to the house and inoculates two of the servants. This was a complicated business unlike our modern

[1] See page 53.

vaccination, involving careful dieting and physicking during recovery, and the Parson writes anxiously in his diary: "Pray God, my People and all others in the Small Pox may do well; several Houses have got Small Pox, at present 9 in Weston."

But the year ends well. There was generally a good congregation at church, and they seemed to like certain changes the new Rector had made. On December 3rd, his people come to pay him their tithes—one-tenth of the yearly farm produce, which was the proportion that had always been given to the support of the clergy. Parson Woodforde in return gives them a good dinner: "sirloin of beef roasted, a leg of mutton boiled and Plum Puddings in Plenty"—not to mention, later in the day, "Wine, Punch and Ale as much as they pleased; they drank of wine 6 Bottles, of Rum 1 gallon and a half, and I know not what ale." There were only seventeen of them, so they must have drunk plenty.

On December 10th he arranges for Mr. Chambers, the schoolmaster, to teach his two men-servants, Ben and Will, "to write and read at 4s. 6d. a quarter each." December 13th "was appointed a Fast on our Majesty's arms against the rebel Americans," and there was a full congregation that day, but their prayers were unavailing. As we know from other sources, those "rebel Americans" soon ceased to be British subjects and became citizens of the new United States.

Yet life at the village of Weston continued almost undisturbed by upheavals in the great world. On Christmas Day the Rector entertains seven poor old men to dinner. He gives to each a shilling, and to one an old black coat and waistcoat. In the afternoon he goes to church. "It was very dark at church." He could "scarce see". So, with the year moving to its end, let us there take leave of him—in a church where men still worship—reading the services still familiar to many, on one of those dark winter afternoons which are familiar to us all.

The Old Village

Most villages in England, and many in Wales and Scotland as well, have not only an ancient parish church but other buildings dating far back into the Middle Ages. Much of the past history of a village can also be learnt from the names and shapes of the old fields; we may even be able to trace in the rise and fall of the ground something of the strip system of farming[1] as it was in the days before modern methods of agriculture came into use. Broadly speaking, there is most to be seen from the old days in counties south of the Trent: southern and eastern England were then the most prosperous areas and the areas in which most people lived. Two hundred years ago the northern counties were thought of as a remote district of infertile moors and Wales as poorer still, while the Highlands of Scotland would be regarded by Parson Woodforde as almost entirely uncivilized.

Thus a sleepy village street somewhere in England south of the Trent, with one or two comfortable-looking, red-brick Georgian houses, some rows of thatched cottages, orchards, and gardens, represents the world that many, perhaps most, of our ancestors knew well. For the poor, who in those days hardly ever travelled more than a few miles from home, it was their only world. The Plate of Rural Occupations is an eighteenth-century design, intended as decoration for the three beautifully written Whitsuntide texts. It shows at the top a typical thatched farmhouse and busy farmyard; then the six main seasonal tasks familiar to the farm workers and, in the bottom right-hand corner, the water mill. The river turning the great mill-wheel to grind their corn would be the nearest thing these villagers knew to the power-driven machinery which frees us from their narrow life of toil.

The Manor House

But we must not forget the houses of the great. They are still one of the chief glories of the English countryside, those castles and mansions and manor-houses, in some cases built in the time of the Normans. Even nowadays, when their owners have been greatly impoverished by high taxation and other causes, these places more often than not still cherish, besides their excellence as specimens of architecture and historic buildings, the loveliest gardens, the finest furniture, and even the best pictures to be seen in their district. How much more true was this in the eighteenth

[1] See page 15.

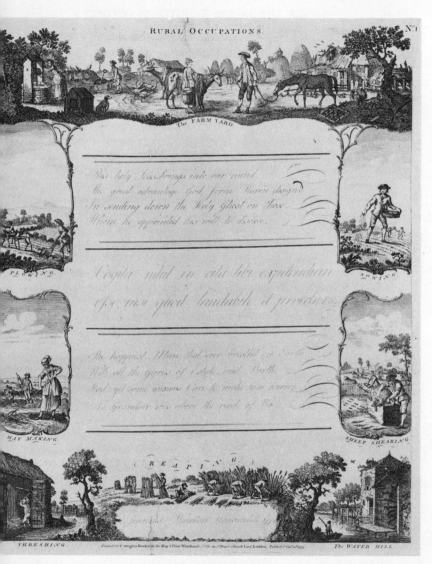

Plate of Rural Occupations.
The text was written by Joan Stainton in 1778

century! There were no newspapers for the masses, and the Sunday sermon in the parish church was the nearest thing the villager knew to all we get from broadcasting or television.

A nobleman's palace, like Chatsworth in Derbyshire or Woburn Abbey in Bedfordshire or Knole in Kent, used to be the centre from which ideas about politics, society, arts and manners would spread through a whole county. As for the "big house" in the village—the Hall or Manor where the squire (and still more important, often, the squire's lady) resided—it was the one link with the outside world. A Georgian wing, or even a couple of bow windows, added to the mansion would spread the sound knowledge of structural proportions which made eighteenth-century buildings of all kinds so satisfying to the eye. A landscape gardener, called in to make the park or gardens more "natural" in accordance with the new eighteenth-century taste, would create years of discussion for the frequenters of the local inn. The contents of the picture gallery or the library, new styles of furniture and new patterns of china, even the costlier kinds of food and drink—these things, which were not bought locally but came from London or the larger towns, had some effect, at least through hearsay, in making country life as a whole less isolated and brutish than we might suppose.

It was, of course, an age of class-distinction, when everybody in the village "knew his (or her) place"—or was constantly reminded of it. But it was also the age of "Merry England", as people called it after it was over. The eighteenth century was the time when fox-hunting, which gave pleasure as a spectacle and an excitement to thousands who could not afford a horse, became established as the fashionable winter sport of the English countryside. It was also the time when cricket matches began to be of more than local interest[1] and it saw the start of professional boxing (bare-fist)—two interests which, even more than the meet, brought together all classes to share a common pleasure. The people who in 1740 first sang the strains of "Rule, Britannia!" were very far from regarding themselves as slaves or their island-home as a prison.[2]

[1] See page 262.
[2] Crabbe's contemporary account of *The Village* emphasizes other sides of its life (see Appendix I, No. 1).

2

TOWN LIFE IN THE EIGHTEENTH CENTURY;
LONDON

LONDON, as the painter Canaletto saw it from the terrace of a nobleman's West End mansion on a bright morning in 1746, might well be called "the hub of England's universe".[1] Count the towers and spires of Sir Christopher Wren's churches, which belong to the rebuilding after the Great Fire of 1666; examine the fine buildings which line the river bank; notice the traffic on the river and the elegant costumes of the onlookers. There can be no disputing the greatness of mid-eighteenth-century London—its West End, where Robert Adam (architect to King George III) and his three brothers were about to create the fine terrace of houses known as the Adelphi, and other monumental works; the City, with the endless bustle of business in its ancient jumble of narrow, huddled streets; and the shipping of the Pool below London Bridge, that great medieval structure with both sides of its narrow roadway still lined by shops and houses.

In 1738 London had obtained its second bridge, at Westminster, near Parliament, the Abbey, and the Palace of St. James's, and it was indeed to the west of the City that most of the spectacular new building was done; east of Aldgate the houses of the poor were merely allowed to spread themselves without plan or comfort towards the green fields of Essex. The West End was admired by every visitor, as estate-owners and speculative builders joined efforts to extend the network of gracious squares and dignified streets northwards across Tyburn Road (that mournful road for condemned criminals) on to the Duke of Bedford's lands at Bloomsbury or in the direction of Marylebone Fields, and west-

---

[1] See Title page.

The north side of Cavendish Square, showing the mansion designed
for the Duke of Chandos in 1720

wards to Hyde Park, across which one could walk to Kensington
village with its royal palace.

It was indeed fortunate that this golden age of London "improvement" was also the age which produced the greatest of the
Georgian architects—and rich men with sufficient taste to employ
them. Many of the new houses were the town residences of country gentlemen; but others were occupied by City business men, for
it was now no longer so usual to live on the top of one's business
premises in the City. It was pleasanter to be within easy reach of
the West End parks: St. James's and Green Park and Hyde Park.
For those who sought more glamorous amusement, there were the
pleasure gardens of Ranelagh to the north of the river beyond
Westminster; or Vauxhall on the south bank beyond Lambeth
Palace. Both on summer nights were full of music and ablaze with
lights among the trees. Ranelagh was the great marvel of the age,
with its resplendent "Rotunda" (circular hall) and its ornamental
boxes where one could listen to the music, and eat and drink and
talk, and watch the people of rank and fashion meeting and
promenading and "quizzing" one another. It was indeed so popu-

lar in fine weather that on one occasion Horace Walpole—son of the famous statesman—had been held up for thirty-six minutes in a traffic block of four-horse coaches on the road from town.

Foreign visitors were naturally impressed with all this, but a little surprised at the wealthy Londoner's preference for living "vertically", in houses where rooms were built one on top of the other and connected by steep staircases. Foreign visitors might well be impressed, too, by the enterprise of public-spirited citizens who, since the Government would do nothing to help, had got together to begin schemes for policing, lighting and paving their neighbourhood. Cavendish Square, which was the first square built north of Oxford Street, is shown in our illustration with street lamps and a pavement. But the carriages are moving at a slow walk over the rough roadway, and the fact that the two pillared houses in the foreground were originally designed for a duke cannot altogether have made up for their hideous inconvenience. There would be no water on the upper floors and no proper sanitation; the domestic staff would be lucky if they were allowed to sleep in the attics (which are nearly hidden by the pediment).

The Life of the Poor

For the houses of the well-to-do, however, "Improvement" was in the air. But there was far more that needed to be done in the older parts of central London and the regions beyond Aldgate in the east. Men were still talking of the bad old days of unrestricted gin-drinking before the Act of 1751, which limited its sales and made it more expensive. They were reminded of those disreputable scenes by prints of Hogarth's famous picture, *Gin Lane*, painted in the same year as the Act. But there was still much heavy drinking, and all that goes with it of crime, poverty and disease. Yet the Bow Street magistrate of the time considered "the rabble much mended within the last fifty years, though still very insolent and abusive, sometimes without the least appearance of a cause." Certainly the London death-rate had fallen, and something was being done to keep foundlings and workhouse children alive.[1]

[1] See page 22.

London was surely a noble city, to which the rich went then in search of company and culture and the poor in search of service with the rich. To its busy river port came Welsh slates and Portland stone and Baltic pines for building, coal from Newcastle for domestic hearths and bakehouses and distilleries, sugar and tobacco from across the ocean, and much else for use or sale in London.

But it was not very safe to walk through the "rookery of St. Giles" (on the site of New Oxford Street) after nightfall, and all round the City there were streets and courts and alleys where open sewers and back-garden cess-pools bred disease. Nearer the river one shut one's window at low tide because of the stench of sewage which Father Thames was expected to carry to the sea.

There was as yet no L.C.C., no Metropolitan Borough Councils, no Ministry of Health, to challenge the onslaughts of sickness that come from dirt. Nor was there any Unemployment Insurance or National Assistance to help men to tide over the periods of trade depression, which caused great hardship to many groups of citizens, such as the big population of silk-weavers, who in those days still plied their craft—or rioted for more wages—in the congested district of Spitalfields, east of the City boundary.

Provincial Towns

So much for the "hub of England's universe". For London was then about fifteen times as large as the largest provincial towns, which were Bristol and Norwich—the great West of England port and the great centre of the East Anglian cloth manufacture. These two had held their proud position for hundreds of years, but in the eighteenth century they were beginning to be caught up by the towns we think of as the biggest. Birmingham, for instance, with its metal trades—chains, locks, bolts, nails, pins, buttons and buckles—in which much of the work was done by women and children in little home-workshops, was already something more than a quiet market-town. Birmingham also had a considerable industrialized hinterland in the Black Country. Liverpool and Manchester likewise grew fast from humble origins, Liverpool rivalling Bristol in trade with Africa and across the

Atlantic, Manchester beginning to expand a little later and helped by the money of the Liverpool merchants to develop the cotton industry of which it was to become the world-centre. Equally remarkable was the growth of Glasgow.[1] Up to the union of the English and Scottish parliaments in 1707 it was quite unimportant; the Union threw the trade of the colonies open to Scottish tobacco-importers and merchants of every kind, with the result that in the course of the eighteenth century the population of the town at the mouth of the Clyde was multiplied by six.

Nevertheless, to complete our general picture of where people mostly lived, before the modern industrial towns which most of us know so well had come into existence, we must emphasize the importance of certain traditional local centres, to which the well-to-do resorted for business and pleasure. Besides Bristol, which had a fashionable residential area at Clifton, well away from the busy river-side, and Norwich, with its famous cathedral, the best examples might be York, capital of the north even in the far-off days of Roman Britain, and Exeter for the south-west. But any county town was attraction enough for the squires and their families. Quarter sessions, military duties, the buying and selling of lands and houses could be pleasantly combined with dances, theatre visits, and concerts, so that there was often little desire to attempt a long and perilous journey over bad roads, possibly infested by highwaymen, in order to join in the pleasures of the London season.

The most important people went to London every year, when Parliament met, as a matter of course. Others, if they ventured far afield, were more likely to take the road to Bath, which since the beginning of the century had become increasingly famous as a holiday resort. In theory, people went there to drink the waters, which are good for various ailments; in practice, they found society and amusements there—it was a great place for courtships, and for duels. Scotland, too, had its special resort in the Edinburgh "new town", as they called the district of fine new houses and squares, worthy of the West End of London, which started to grow up about 1760 when Edinburgh was becoming a great centre for literature and learning. Even earlier in the century Edinburgh and

[1] See illustration, p. 29.

the other three Scottish university towns compared favourably as places of serious study with the Oxford, and even the Cambridge, of that period.

Like London, which for a long time depended on the steady flow of new arrivals from the country to maintain its population, the towns were all unhealthy by modern standards, though the smaller ones had the advantage of the breeze blowing in from the country to purify the tainted air and less difficulty also in getting rid of their refuse. But the death-rate was usually very high, particularly among infants and from the smallpox which so alarmed Parson Woodforde even in his little rural parish. It is therefore a most important fact that there was a widespread enthusiasm among charitable people in the eighteenth century for the establishment of hospitals.

Hospitals and Medicine

Out of the seven most famous hospitals in modern London, no fewer than five were founded in the years 1720–45: Guy of "Guy's", for example, was a bookseller of that period who had made a fortune out of Bibles. The provincial towns, led by Bristol, imitated London, which in 1769 added to its hospital system the first dispensary, forerunner of the modern clinic. Over the whole period 1700–1825 new hospitals and dispensaries were being founded at the rate of one a year. The doctors worked with primitive instruments and very few medicines; antiseptic surgery was unknown; nurses and midwives were not well trained. It remained something of an achievement to have managed to survive the first few years of childhood; but in fact year by year a good deal was being done to encourage survival.

Scotland was in advance of England, and Edinburgh University was the leading centre of medical studies, though knowledge came also from Holland and Italy. In London individual doctors and surgeons trained pupils, and apprenticeship of this kind was a common road to medical practice. From Scotland to London came a number of famous doctors, William Smellie (1697–1763), and the brilliant brothers William Hunter (1718–83) and John Hunter (1728–93). These men did much by their careful dissecting and teaching of anatomy, and John Hunter, famous for his writings and his museum of specimens, is regarded as the founder of scientific surgery. Not long before it had been part of "the art and mystery of barbers"; he made it a regular profession.

Results were to be seen in a considerably reduced loss of life in childbirth and a less unscientific treatment of infectious diseases: attempts were made to get smallpox patients into isolation hospitals. This deadly scourge was then being treated by the direct-inoculation process, a mild form of the disease being injected into the human body, which then develops its own organisms of defence. Lady Mary Montagu, the famous letter-writer, had introduced this to England from Constantinople in 1718. At the very end of the century, however, Dr. Edward Jenner, who was a pupil of John Hunter, discovered that inoculation with cowpox gives immunity from smallpox. This new process of vaccination proved so successful that within fifty years it had been made virtually compulsory—and deaths from smallpox had virtually disappeared. This is a small but dramatically successful example of the public services, which the crowding of population into towns made it both necessary and possible to provide.

Wingate College Library

3

EIGHTEENTH-CENTURY PEOPLE AT WORK

So far we have been picturing where people lived before the great modern industries began—in the south more than in the north, in villages rather than in towns, and if in towns then in a kind of town which was altogether smaller and quieter than the industrial areas of to-day. London alone was already big by modern standards. We can also form some idea of the houses they lived in: the country seats of the nobility and gentry, from which they moved for the season to their town houses in the newly built streets of the West End of London or some local centre; the solid-looking homes of the middle class, scattered about the larger villages but chiefly forming dignified streets in the middle parts of towns (and nowadays often converted into shops); the farmhouses and clustering cottages of the countryside; the lanes and courts and alleys where the poorer townspeople lived and worked in noisy crowds. But it is also important to picture what the men and women (and children) of those days did for their living, since without knowing this we cannot understand how modern Britain began.

Farming

The main occupation was agriculture, for Britain in those days produced all its principal foodstuffs, except sugar, and in fact not only grew enough corn for its own needs, but some to export to the Continent as well. Wheat and the darker rye were grown for bread, barley and hops for beer, and oats, the staple food of the Scots. The meat was also "home-killed", though beef and mutton were luxuries which seldom reached a working-class family; their meat came in one form or another from the humble pig or else they made do with cheese, of which nearly every county then pro-

14

duced its own variety—Cheddar, Cheshire, double-Gloucester, Wensleydale, etc. All this gave work in the thousands of villages and even in the smaller market-towns, which often had farms entangled among their streets; but it was work that was not very efficiently organized. New ideas, such as the sowing of seed in drills instead of broadcast or the growing of turnips for winter fodder, spread very slowly, because in the eastern counties and east Midlands, and in large patches elsewhere, the medieval three-field system still prevailed. That is to say, the farmer had his land scattered in small strips over three huge village fields, which were cultivated on a cropping plan agreed to by all the farmers, and his livestock grazed the common in company with all the livestock of the village. The north and west and the southern seaboard had more usually separate farms, such as we are familiar with to-day, but the soil being poorer for the most part those areas could not afford to try out new ideas. Another difficulty was the badness of the roads. To save the cost of transport corn was usually ground locally—every stream in those days had its mill—and sold in the nearest market-town. The meat supply might, indeed, come from farther afield, but the Scottish and Welsh cattle made their way along the old drove-roads leading to London on their own hoofs.

The badness of the roads had another effect—it compelled every village to make for itself many of the things which are now bought as a matter of course from shops in the towns or, if there is no town near, by mail-order purchase. In those days the village would be as likely to have its own carpenter and cabinet-maker, shoemaker and tailor, builder and harness-maker as it is now likely to have its post office or garage. Not only so, but a long list could be constructed of articles of everyday use which most village homes made for themselves—bread, sausages, and all kinds of preserves, the simpler kinds of furniture and the less stylish forms of clothing, such as smock frocks and flannel petticoats. And besides all this which the village produced for its own use, there was also the contribution its wool-spinners—this was the typical job for the unmarried woman or "spinster"—made to the great national export of woollen cloth.

The Bigger Industries

English cloth was sold all over Europe and as far afield as India, Africa, and America; it was also of course used in large quantities at home. Its manufacture for local use took place in almost every county where sheep were to be found, but the three main districts were East Anglia, the West of England, and the West Riding of Yorkshire. The last-named of these was famous for its small-scale organization, with master weavers whose wives spun their own wool, which the men wove on their loom, a piece at a time, and took for sale to the weekly market. But more commonly a rich merchant bought wool in large quantities, sent it round the villages for cottagers to spin in their homes, collected the yarn, employed the weavers (who received so much for each piece they wove), paid for all the finishing processes, such as dyeing, and finally sold the cloth wholesale. In some parts of the country cottages can still be seen with a large, well-lighted upstairs room or attic which was built originally to hold the loom. Hogarth's famous drawing shows two silk looms—indeed, the Spitalfields address can be seen on the quart pot which the Idle Apprentice keeps handy, as his employer has no doubt just observed: but the wool-weaver's equipment was very similar. The spinning-wheel, on the other hand, was much smaller and stood in a corner of the cottage kitchen during the rare hours when it was not in use.

But perhaps the most important things to notice, because of their bearing on later developments, are these. The cloth trade was a great source of wealth, making eighteenth-century England wealthier than many of her neighbours. It was a great source of employment, enabling women to earn money in their own homes by spinning, men to combine a smallholding with work at the loom, and even giving a job to reluctant children of four—the age at which they might be set to clean the wool by treading it barefoot in a tub. It was also one source of experiment in more modern methods of industrial organization, for sometimes a big employer had a weaving shed full of weavers working for him in what were almost factory conditions.

There were some industries, less important than the textile

manufactures (which included silk and linen and a little cotton as well as the great traditional trade in woollen cloth), where the nature of the work required a large workplace with a large number of workers. Such were the mines—of Cornish tin, Durham coal, and iron ore which was mined or worked in half the counties of England. They provided the material for the metal manufactures of Birmingham, Sheffield and elsewhere, in which people had found another reason to organize the work on a fairly large scale, namely the advantage of specialization.

A very famous writer on trade, Adam Smith, mentions this in 1776 in his book *The Wealth of Nations*, describing what had then been common for a generation or more. He writes about a pin factory—with the same sort of admiring enthusiasm that a twentieth-century observer might experience on seeing a Ford car assembled by a series of simple hand-turns on a moving conveyor belt. "One man (he writes) draws out the wire, another straightens it, a third cuts it, a fourth points it, a fifth grinds it at the top for receiving the head; to make the head requires two or three distinct operations; to put it on is a peculiar business, to whiten the pin is another; it is even a trade by itself to put them into the paper." Indeed he had actually seen a factory in which, by means of such organized division of labour, ten persons could make "upwards of forty-eight thousand pins in a day," though working with quite primitive equipment. Had they worked independently, he points out, they could not each of them have made twenty, or perhaps even one pin in a day.

Local Trade and Transport

So much for the bigger industries. But for the most part the boy who was apprenticed to a trade or handicraft in those days would be serving a small master who worked with his own hands, in a shop or workplace attached to his master's home, and most probably in what we should call a very small town. What would the trades of such a place be? There might be some luxury trades, which helped with the furnishing and equipment of the mansions of the nobility and gentry—cabinet-makers or carriage-builders,

The first of twelve Plates in which Hogarth contrasted the careers of Industry and Idleness, personified by the two apprentices of a Spitalfields silk weaver. The series was published on September 30th 1747; the originals were bought by Horace Walpole, the collector and letter-writer referred to above (p. 9)

upholsterers, bookbinders, saddlers, etc. There would also be many small firms which made things in a cheaper way for humbler homes. But chiefly the average town would live by the business of shop-keeping in the modern sense, selling the sugar and tea, which were the imported luxuries now in demand by all classes of the population, and everything else which the surrounding villages did not produce in their own fields and gardens. The shops were no doubt busiest on the weekly market day, when the country people came in with their eggs and fowls and butter and went away with their haberdashery or groceries. In a few favoured localities there was also a great annual fair, when people came

great distances to buy and sell on the fairground—and doubtless
to visit the shops as well.

But we must not paint too rosy a picture. If we were carried back
two hundred years to see our ancestors, what would strike us most
would be the terrible isolation of their lives. A good many villagers
never saw a town at all. In town and country alike it was difficult
for the poor to move in search of work from the parish in which
they were born, because the dreaded Settlement Law (1662) entitled the authorities to send them back again for fear they should
some day ask for poor relief in the new parish. And all trade and
travel was handicapped by the shocking state of the roads, already
mentioned. Parson Woodforde, for example, thought it a wonderful thing when (in 1774) he managed to travel from Oxford to
Somerset, "near 100 miles", in one day: it had taken him from
5.30 a.m. to 8 p.m. and the cost (by post-chaise) was nearly a
shilling a mile. The ill-constructed road-surfaces were churned into
thick mud by the four-horsed coaches which linked up the growing
centres of population (much as the motor-coach lines do to-day
but with markedly different time schedules); and by the herds of
cattle; and by the commercial travellers on horseback and the
gentry in their carriages; and again through the transport of
heavy goods (corn, pottery, textiles, coal, metal-work) in rumbling
covered wagons or by strings of heavily laden pack-horses picking
their way in single file among the pot-holes, splashing through the
puddles, and slithering along the ruts.

Thus without new ideas in transport and communications modern Britain could never have come into existence. In the early
eighteenth century a very few of the roads began to be improved
by the first Turnpike Trusts, which (as we shall see in a later
chapter) relaid a stretch of road and charged users a toll to pay
for it. But this was only just beginning, and for heavy goods like
coal and timber, bricks and building-stone it remained true, as in
earlier centuries, that they could be moved only by the coastal
shipping routes and up and down the rivers. That is why towns of
any importance were almost invariably situated within easy reach
of harbour or river bank—like Bristol on its Avon, Norwich on the
Wensum, and all the towns strung along Thames, Severn, and
Trent. But the river which flows slowly enough to be navigable

easily silts up. Far more important, therefore, than the first turn-pikes were the "new cuts" and the deepening and widening of old river beds, on which the more enterprising towns since about 1700 had been spending much money. These improved river channels were called "inland navigations", the men who dug them "inland navigators": with the introduction of this name, familiar in its shortened form of "navvy", we are approaching those tremendous labours of construction and reconstruction which since about 1760 have changed the face of Britain in achieving the Industrial Revolution.[1]

---

[1] Crabbe's description of Aldeburgh, where navigations were not improved, gives the social atmosphere of towns and trade before the "coming of the machine" (Appendix I, No. 2).

THE COMING OF THE MACHINE

4

WHAT WAS THE INDUSTRIAL REVOLUTION?
A BRIEF SURVEY

As we said at the end of the last chapter, the Industrial Revolution changed the face of the country. It had been changing slowly ever since men first began to cut down trees, drain swamps, plough fields, and build houses: but the change now became much more rapid—towns and sprawling suburbs, factories and mines and workshops, canals and docks and railways spread (and are still spreading) to make in less than two hundred years the Britain of to-day. To put it in another way, the same small island which then provided for 7 million inhabitants, of whom the great majority were by our standards very poor, now provides for 50 millions among whom the very poor are a dwindling minority.

Population Changes

The vast and rapid increase in population is in itself one of the most astonishing features of the Industrial Revolution; the increase in population was partly the result of industrial changes and at the same time the cause. If we consider western Europe as a whole, up to the seventeenth and eighteenth centuries its people had been thinly spread out and had increased but slowly, so far as we can tell. Agriculture, relying on primitive methods, could not support large numbers. When crops failed, there would be starvation for some and, more widely, under-nourishment. Under-nourishment brought physical weakness and encouraged disease. Death from starvation, plague and other diseases reduced the number of marriages and hence the number of children born, and also reduced the number of children who would grow up to become parents. War also was an ever-recurrent means of reducing population. Thus the death-rate tended to be very high, and this checked the growth of population. But with improved methods of agricultural production and industry, with longer periods of peace, and with the development of medical services, a great change set in.

The factors making for an increase in population applied, probably more strongly than elsewhere, in Britain. Internal peace and order was a basic condition; with improvements in agriculture and industry and the increase in scientific and medical knowledge the other conditions became increasingly effective. Eighteenth-century Britain took no census, but there appears to have been an increase in the birth-rate from about 1710 onwards, which reached its climax at about the year 1790. With the breakdown of apprenticeship and the demand for workers in new industries, cotton, coal and iron, men, and in some cases women, began to marry younger, and more children were born.

But probably more important than the increase in the birth-rate was the fall in the death-rate, which had always been high, especially among infants and children. Now infant mortality was reduced, and more mothers were saved—and lived longer to have yet more children. Thus, later on, the large family came to be characteristic of Victorian times: in fact, the rate of growth of our population did not begin to slacken until late in the 1870's.

How was the fall in the death-rate brought about? It was due to a number of causes working together. The growth of medical knowledge, the training of doctors, and a more highly skilled care for women in childbirth began to take effect in the eighteenth century, as a sequel to the two centuries in which the ideas of the Renaissance had slowly developed a spirit of scientific inquiry. Humanitarianism also played a part, not only through the establishment of hospitals, already mentioned, but through philanthropic work of many kinds. The Foundling Hospital was opened in London in 1745 through the efforts of Captain Thomas Coram, and saved the lives of thousands of deserted children. The work on behalf of children was continued by Jonas Hanway, who also exposed the appalling conditions and high mortality rate in prisons. The cause of the prisoners in turn was taken up by John Howard (1726–90), who from the study of jail fever went on to consider how contagious diseases in general might be prevented. This great English philanthropist and citizen of the world was in fact touring the military hospitals of Russia when his examination of a case of camp fever brought him to a distant grave. It is noteworthy that his successor, the famous Quakeress Elizabeth Fry (1780–1845), likewise interested herself in hospital as well as prison conditions.

There were other improvements, in town and country, less spectacular than the improvements which the nineteenth century was to bring—and therefore easily overlooked—which helped to make the people of eighteenth-century Britain longer-lived than their predecessors. The dietary of country people above the level of the labourer was probably more nourishing, with wheaten bread replacing a poor quality mixture of barley and rye, more use of vegetables, and—through the introduction of root crops—a more plentiful supply of meat. The towns, which seem to us to have been so pestilential and chaotic, were at any rate on the upgrade at the end of the century, when Parliament passed over 200 Improvement Acts in fifteen years, giving Improvement Commissioners in particular towns legal powers of drainage, streetcleaning, and so forth. At the same time cheap cotton clothing, which could be more easily washed than wool, gave a new impetus to the growth—disgustingly slow in all classes of society—of modern standards of personal cleanliness. Lastly, we may suppose that a more generous administration of poor relief, which was to make the name of Speenhamland (where it originated in 1795) later notorious, must have helped to keep more poor people alive.

Thus the population of Britain increased. How were the new mouths to be filled and the new hands employed? The adaptable Englishman, already eager in the pursuit of trade, achieved—or perhaps we should say stumbled upon—the solution which we call the Industrial Revolution. New techniques gave a livelihood to vastly increased numbers of people, first in this country and later elsewhere. For the Industrial Revolution which began in Britain about 1760 spread abroad into foreign countries, slowly at first but with increasing speed, so that to-day there is scarcely a nation in the world left unaffected by it. It has even been claimed by a recent writer that "The positive achievements of human ingenuity in the past 150 years overshadow all the previous achievements of mankind since the beginning of the New Stone Age 15,000 years ago."[1]

Changes in World Trade

Until the beginning of the nineteenth century, the industrial history of the vast majority of mankind was largely the record of the way in which they kept their animals, grew their crops, and sheltered their homes. Most of the peoples of the world got their food, clothing and housing material by the same simple means as their ancestors had done from time immemorial. In the more civilized communities some part of the population might live in large towns, but even they relied for their food and the raw materials of industry upon the work of countrymen in neighbouring villages and farms. Watermills and windmills were the most conspicuous, and often the most complicated, machines in common use.

During the nineteenth century—with the coming of the all-powerful machine, as we know it—all this was changed. To-day, far fewer men and women live under the simple conditions of earlier generations. Instead, many live in factory towns, and they draw their food and the raw materials of industry not from their immediate neighbourhood but from all parts of the world. Historians describe this vast and gradual social and industrial change as the "Industrial Revolution". The word "revolution" is no exaggeration, for social, political and industrial life is utterly different from what it was before the Industrial Revolution developed. The traditional emblem for Britain was John Bull, the corpulent and prosperous farmer shown in cartoons, but in the nineteenth century the emblem ought really to have been changed to John Bull and Co., since it was no longer the farm but the in-

[1] Professor Henry Hamilton, *History of the Homeland* (1947), p. 19.

dustrial firm which was typical of our new position as the workshop of the world.

Before the Industrial Revolution, moreover, world trade—that is, the exports and imports of every country—was both smaller in amount and different in its contents. Britain, as we have seen, exported cloth and hardware, but also corn; the bulk of the world's trade, however, was in luxury goods. These did not take up much space in the holds of ships which we should call tiny—spices and silks, coffee, tobacco and tea. Sugar, for which Europe then had no satisfactory home-produced substitute, was the only big food import. The Industrial Revolution changed all this. New raw materials like cotton, oilseeds, jute, rubber, skins and metals were brought across the world to the manufacturing countries; so were foodstuffs—wheat and meat, and fruit from the tropics, and eventually even dairy produce. Manufactures were sent in return, with the result that almost the whole world became joined together by a network of steamship routes and railway lines, and finally by airways, carrying the goods which distant countries now found it advantageous to buy from one another.

Changes in the Economy of Britain

If the whole world has been reorganized on a basis of trade, so also the industrial map of Britain has been almost completely transformed. There are many new industrial areas, such as the Lancashire cotton towns, Clydeside and Belfast with their shipyards, the South Wales coal-field, and the factory districts of outer London, which give employment to millions of men and women. In most cases the original reason for this density of population was the nearness of cheap supplies of coal and a convenient situation for transport. Early in the Revolution, canals were cut in order to distribute the raw materials and products of industry cheaply. Even more important changes came with the invention of the steam locomotive and the building of the great railway systems. These connected the factory towns with the docks at the greater ports, and thus made the distribution of food and raw materials imported into our country from overseas still easier and cheaper.

Following the example of Britain—where the Industrial Revolution began—other nations imported machines, built railway lines, and established steamship services, so that in the end they also became fully industrialized. But partly because, in Britain, coal and iron ore were found near to each other and could be cheaply mined, and partly because British inventors were the first to perfect the railway locomotive, Britain was fifty years ahead of her future competitors in applying machine power to manufacture and transport. And thus it was British engineers and workmen who started the Industrial Revolution in many parts of the world, and Britain usually lent the money with which foreigners bought the equipment to launch their industries. But during the first half of the Industrial Revolution, Great Britain was almost alone in the development of world trade, and this in turn meant that a large proportion of world trade was carried in British ships.

TABLE SHOWING GROWTH OF POPULATION AND
NATIONAL INCOME IN THE UNITED KINGDOM

Year	Population	Estimated National Income £	Income per head £ s. d.
1821	20,893,584	464,000,000	22 2 0
1841	26,709,456	515,000,000	19 2 0
1861	28,927,485	800,000,000	27 12 0
1881	34,884,848	1,160,000,000	33 2 0
1901	41,458,721	1,760,000,000	41 18 0
1911	45,221,615	2,060,000,000	45 16 0

Note. The first Census of Production was taken in 1907. For earlier periods, an estimate of National Income (i.e. the national product—profits, salaries, wages, etc.) gives only a rough indication of economic output and the "wealth of nations". The period illustrated is that in which Britain was continuously on the Gold Standard, but the figures are to be considered in relation to prices. Prices fell in 1821-45 and again in 1875-1900, and were rising in 1845-75 and in 1900-11: but the maximum variation does not exceed 20 per cent above or below the level of 1850, which (as regards retail prices) is almost identical with the level of 1914.

Thus the effect of the Industrial Revolution in these ninety years was to enable five people to live where two had lived before—and, *on an average*, to live twice as well.

Thus for a period of about a century the world situation result-ing from the Industrial Revolution suited perfectly the interests of our island people. We had the coal, the inventions, and the shipping. We took the lead, as farmers and planters, merchants and traders, engineers and industrial experts, in developing new countries overseas. As a result an endless stream of raw materials and foodstuffs was poured into the island, and the whole world bought our manufactures at prices which were advantageous to us, because we were then the principal large-scale suppliers of the cotton goods and hardware, coal and machinery which the rest of the world needed. Even the industries slowly developing in other countries added to our wealth, since a good rate of interest was paid on the capital which British investors lent to help them buy the machines to start with. The meat from the Argentine, for in-stance, was bought with the earnings of the railways in the Argen-tine built by British capital.

Competition had become serious by 1880, but it is chiefly the two World Wars which have speeded up the process of change and enabled those younger rivals, such as the Americans, who were bound to outstrip us some day (as youth always must overtake age), to outdo us as a manufacturing nation with a suddenness and completeness which seem decisive. Thus the Industrial Revolution has rather suddenly ceased to appear as a special gift of Provi-dence to the British people. But that is no reason why we should neglect the drama of the great changes which introduce us to modern Britain. In Act I a number of inventions and discoveries increase the output of our workers as though by magic. In Act II the people of the island find that as a consequence a rapidly ex-panding population can be maintained, with the help of imported food, at a slowly improving standard of life. In Act III our magic secret *and* our desire for an improving standard of life are both shared with other countries, which are therefore less eager to buy our industrial output or to sell us their food. The very size and solidity of our great towns, of which we have been so justly proud, begins to be a cause of anxiety. In Act IV—but that is the part of the play which the readers of this book must themselves help to devise and to perform.

5

HOW THE GREAT CHANGES CAME: TRADE AND EMPIRE

WE may now consider in more detail why the great changes, which (as we have seen) spelt wealth and growth of population and world leadership, came first to our small island and nowhere else. One great advantage which Britain enjoyed over other countries was the long-established internal peace. When George III became King in 1760, which is about the time when the changes in industry gathered enough speed for us to speak of a "revolution", England at least had lived without serious disturbance for exactly a century, while other nations had been torn and distracted by foreign invasion and civil war. There had been several great crises, such as the Revolution of 1688 and the change of dynasty in 1714, but Sedgemoor (1685) and Preston (1715) were the only battles fought on English soil and the march of Prince Charles Edward to Derby in the Jacobite rebellion known as the '45 was the only later occasion when the peace of London and the south-east was even seriously threatened. The Scottish record was rather different, what with the struggles of the Covenanters in the reign of Charles II and the devotion of the Highlanders to the Jacobite cause, but the work of pacifying the Highlands had been begun with the building of the first main roads and bridges by Marshal Wade's soldiers in 1726–37 and completed by the crushing of the clans on Culloden Moor in 1746. The growth of Glasgow and Edinburgh shows that the fear of the Highlanders, who throughout Scottish history had raided the Lowlands for plunder, was already disappearing.

Peace encouraged the growth of trade, and if the trade of our towns and villages was badly hampered (as we know it was) by the condition of the roads, it was helped by the fact that there were no

28

Glasgow from the north-east, 1760

internal customs barriers. In other countries, like France, town was separated from town and province from province by the charges which had to be paid for bringing goods of any kind across the boundary between two areas, whereas in this respect all parts of England, Wales, and Scotland were a single unit. The numerous spires and towers shown in our view of eighteenth-century Glasgow are evidence of its rapidly growing prosperity: the state of the road in the foreground reminds us that the prosperity was not due to better communications but to the fact that in 1707, thanks to the Act of Union, the customs barrier and all trade restrictions as between England and Scotland had been finally overthrown.

When Daniel Defoe, the author of *Robinson Crusoe*, travelled through Britain early in the century he was much impressed by the evidence of increased trade, the rapid growth of some of the towns, and the general prosperity of the country. It is all set down in his book, *A Tour through the Whole Island of Great Britain*. Defoe noticed that "the business of export and import in the Port of London is prodigiously increased". It had become a centre for the collection and distribution of colonial products, and it was also our chief corn market. He saw that corn came to London from the corn-growing districts of East Anglia and the south-eastern counties, much of it for export to European markets: other thriving ports included Newcastle with its coal trade, and Hull trading with the Baltic.

Besides "the business of export and import", internal trade also flourished in the eighteenth century, as the growth of towns provided new markets. Defoe has much to say regarding the transport of food: for instance, about the commotion made by the flocks of five hundred or even a thousand geese which he met on the road to London, and the quaint sight of other poultry sent to town in great four-storey wagons, with the driver sitting on the roof. More important, Defoe relates that "it took thirteen counties to dress the grocer's wife", and that travelling merchants were accustomed "to go all over England with droves of pack-horses and to call at the fairs and market towns over the whole land."

The Chartered Companies

Alongside this growth of internal trade, there had been a big increase of overseas trade by the early part of the eighteenth century, as a result of colonial expansion and the work of the Chartered Companies. These were trading companies, holding charters from the Crown which gave them special privileges as the only British subjects allowed to trade in certain areas. The greatest was the East India Company, founded in 1600 at the close of Elizabeth I's reign, which traded both with India itself and also with China and Persia. From China in 1660 the Company began to bring tea to England, and also "china" or cups and saucers of fine porcelain. From India came spices, perfumes, precious stones, silks and indigo for dyeing. Cotton goods—muslins, calicoes and chintzes—were also brought to England by the East India Company; but this particular import roused the jealousy of the English woollen workers and was therefore made illegal. The sailing ships belonging to the Company, and known as East-Indiamen, with their huge holds were the largest vessels afloat; and they had a dock to themselves at Blackwall on the Thames. The Company gradually developed settlements in India and employed a small force of soldiers, and they protected their property by fortifying the chief settlements, at Bombay, Madras and Calcutta. The French also had interests in India, and there was great rivalry between them and the British.

Of other early Chartered Companies the most important were the Merchant Venturers, who used to have the sole right of selling English cloth in Germany and the Netherlands. Then there was the Levant or Turkey Company which traded with the Near East and the Mediterranean countries, bringing wines and fruits to England, and finding a market for English cloth and wool as well as for sugar and tobacco from our West Indian colonies. Another Company, the Eastland, tried to capture the trade of the Baltic, formerly monopolized by the Hansa—the German League of Merchants—which had had its depot in London (the Steelyard) until the reign of Elizabeth I. West African trade was in the hands of the Royal Africa Company, founded in Charles II's reign; it was largely a trade across the Atlantic in slaves. The Hudson's Bay Company was also founded in Charles II's reign, under the presidency of his cousin Prince Rupert. It was favoured by the government because it was a direct rival to the enterprises of the French, who at that time held Quebec. The English had the advantage of plentiful shipping, and were able to use Hudson Strait and Bay, saving them a long overland route. The Company was mainly engaged in the fur trade, and acquired rights over a huge extent of land. These were retained until 1869 and then sold to the Canadian Government; but the Company still continued as a trading corporation and carries on its business at the present day.

Yet another chartered company was founded in 1710 to develop the commercial advantages which were being won by our successes in the War of the Spanish Succession. This South Sea Company received the monopoly of trade along the Atlantic coast of South America, and in the Pacific Ocean or South Sea (though in fact it never did trade there). In George I's reign, the Company offered, in return for further privileges, to take over the National Debt, then £51 million. The dazzling promises of enormous profits led to a rush for shares in the company, and the price of its stock rose to fantastic heights, £100 shares changing hands at £1,060. But the enthusiasm for the shares collapsed as quickly as it had risen; the "South Sea Bubble", as it was called, burst; and confidence in trading companies was badly shaken. The government

took back the burden of the National Debt, and although the
Company went on trading for another hundred years, its successes
were small.

Generally speaking, it was felt by this time that the Companies
had completed the pioneer work of opening-up new lands to
British trade, and from 1688 onwards Parliament was inclined to
encourage "interlopers", the name given to merchants who tried
to trade in the territory set apart for a Company to which they did
not belong. It was claimed that this kind of "free trade" was often
more profitable and varied than what the Company's regulations
permitted. In the end only the East India Company and, on a much
smaller scale, the Hudson's Bay Company were able to hold on to
their monopolies, the former up to 1813, the latter to 1869. We
may now turn to examine another factor which contributed to the
increase of British trade, namely the growth and development of
our colonial empire.

Colonies and Colonial Trade

Newfoundland, England's oldest colony, was claimed by
Cabot in 1497, but was for centuries the seasonal resort of the
men who fished the great cod banks rather than a place of settlement. The first attempt to colonize Virginia in the reign of Elizabeth I, associated with the great Sir Walter Raleigh, produced
nothing lasting except the name, given in honour of the Queen. It
was not until 1607 that Virginia was established as the earliest
permanent settlement under our flag, the leader of the venture
being Captain John Smith, whose life was saved by the Red Indian
princess, Pocahontas. Other bands of colonists (such as the Pil-
grim Fathers in 1620) also settled on the American seaboard, and
yet others in Barbados (which has the oldest colonial parliament)
and the Bahamas and Bermuda. Cromwell's war with Spain
brought the important island of Jamaica into the Empire, and the
Treaty of Utrecht in 1713, at the end of the long wars against
Louis XIV of France, marks the moment when Britain became at
last a leading colonial Power.

During the eighteenth century colonial trade was continually
expanding as the resources of the colonies and their population

increased. At first the colonies were valued mainly as sources of supply for goods not obtainable at home, but they became more and more important also as markets for British manufactures. In the eyes of our merchants, the most valuable colonies were the islands of the West Indies and the two neighbouring American mainland colonies of Virginia and Carolina. As these lay in tropical or sub-tropical regions, they could supply the homeland with increasing quantities of sugar, tobacco, rice and cotton, while the colonists, waxing prosperous, bought greater quantities of our woollen and (later) cotton goods, iron goods and pottery. A large number of slaves were annually transported, under shocking conditions, by British slave-traders from West Africa to the West Indian islands and also to the southern mainland colonies, where the slaves were employed on the plantations.

The exports of fish, timber and corn from the northern American or New England colonies might be shipped to any market unless they were required as stores for the Navy; but trade with the southern colonies and the West Indian islands was closely guarded. Certain goods, known as "enumerated commodities", including tobacco, sugar and dyes, had to be sold in Britain and nowhere else; re-exportation to the Continent of what had been brought from our colonies was one of the most profitable trades of all for the merchants of London and other ports, who handled it. Moreover, our old Navigation Laws of the mercantile age— before the days of free trade—allowed goods of colonial origin to be carried only in British or colonial ships, and ship-owners could be compelled to pay forfeits if they did not carry their cargoes to such places as were approved by the government.

During the middle of the eighteenth century England and France were again at war (the Seven Years War). Clive's victory at Plassey in 1757 and Coote's victory at Wandewash in 1760 destroyed the French power in India. General Wolfe's capture of Quebec in 1759 destroyed French power in North America, and by the Treaty of Paris in 1763 Britain gained the whole of Canada and also further advantages in West Africa and the West Indies. Thus the Empire reached a new stage of importance: it included eastern Canada and the whole Atlantic seaboard of North America as far as Florida; in India, the control of Bengal and other smaller possessions; many West Indian islands; slave centres in West Africa; and the Mediterranean key-points of Gibraltar and Minorca.

Growth of Liverpool

The growth of the port of Liverpool is a remarkable instance of the development of overseas trade in the eighteenth century. In 1700, the population of Liverpool was only 5,000; by 1773, it had risen to 35,000; by 1801, to 77,000. At first the trade of Liverpool was mainly with Ireland; but the opening-up of trade with the West Indies and the North American colonies, together with the development of the cotton industry in Lancashire, gave a great impetus to the growth of the town; and before it became the chief cotton port, it was already the greatest slave-trading port in Europe. Bristol, which shared prominently in the slave trade and had been for centuries the distributing and collecting centre in the West of England, got great profit from sugar and tobacco, but as the eighteenth century went on it was being rapidly overhauled by Glasgow.

To sum up, in the period 1720–60 British exports more than doubled in value; imports nearly doubled; and it seems safe to suppose that internal trade must have increased equally fast. But population during the same period, though growing, grew much less rapidly. Therefore the increase of trade meant that there was more work waiting to be done than there were workers available to do it. Therefore labour-saving inventions—that is, the sort of inventions which made the Industrial Revolution—were urgently needed and anyone with a practical idea of this kind would be encouraged to experiment. Moreover, the fact that many of our existing exports, such as woollen cloth, were not luxury goods but things which all the world wanted, safeguarded the future. For, as Britain developed her inventions, more rapidly expanding trade might be found to support a more rapidly expanding population.

6

HOW THE GREAT CHANGES CAME: CAPITAL AND BANKING

ONE of the main reasons why the great change-over to machine industry came first in Britain rather than in any other country was because there was more capital saved up in Britain. Without the help of capital new ideas could never have been developed on a commercial basis. The idea of an invention by itself achieves nothing unless there is the money available to pay for experiments, raw material, buildings, and workers' wages in the long period before the new thing can be sold in large enough quantities to be really profitable. In addition, the best chance of rapidly increasing sales is in a country where it is easy to make payments. In Britain this could already be done by means of notes or bills or even cheques instead of paying in gold or silver coins, which are heavy to carry about and tempting to thieves.

England, as we have seen, by comparison with other lands had for a long time been a very safe place, where it was worth while to save for the future and where thrifty people could lend their savings and earn interest on them without being afraid that they would lose it all in invasion or civil war. Hence the important part played by banks, in which savings were deposited for safety and convenience and to earn some interest: the banks in turn lent out the deposits to businesses which could not develop without capital, for which they would readily pay high interest.

In the Middle Ages Christians were officially discouraged from lending money at interest, so this was a business largely confined to the Jews. Later on, when the Italians were the chief traders in all Europe, they provided our first banks and gave its name to Lombard Street, which is still at the centre of London's banking system. Then for a time the goldsmiths looked after people's

35

money for them, as they had safes for their gold. Finally, towards the end of the seventeenth century, the most important landmark in our banking history was reached.

The Bank of England

William III was in desperate need of money for his wars against Louis XIV of France—for his army fighting in the Netherlands and for the upkeep of the Channel Fleet. His ministers advised him to raise a loan of £1,200,000—this was virtually the beginning of the modern National Debt. But only twenty years earlier there had been an occasion when the King refused to pay interest due on the money he had borrowed, so the public were not eager to lend, and it was realized that some special attraction must be offered in order to obtain the money. In addition to receiving 8 per cent interest, the lenders of the money were to be made by law into a joint-stock company which had the privilege of being sole bankers to the Government. The bait was successful, and the whole amount of the loan was subscribed within eleven days, June 21st–July 2nd, 1694. A few years later (1709) this "Bank of England", as it was called, was given a further privilege. In return for a reduction in the rate of interest it charged, and the making of a fresh loan, it came to be the only joint-stock bank allowed to issue bank-notes in England and Wales. Scottish joint-stock banks could issue their own notes (as they still do); so could private banks in England, but these were smaller concerns, backed usually by the wealth of a single family, therefore more liable to go bankrupt, in which case their notes would suddenly become worthless. The capital of a "joint stock", on the other hand, might be subscribed from all over the country and such a bank would have considerable resources.

Thus the Bank of England was given a position of superiority, and in the eighteenth century was doing three things of great importance for the growth of trade. The Bank accumulated wealth, which people deposited there instead of hoarding their money, etc., as before, because the Bank was felt to be safe; it lent out these deposits to big trading organizations like the East India Company, as well as to the Government; and its notes (in multiples of £10) were available to the smaller banks and to private individuals as a safe and easy means of keeping and paying out money. In 1734 the first of the present buildings was opened on the present site; the buildings have grown larger in the course of two hundred years, but their appearance still suggests security rather than show, and dignity rather than the opulence which we might expect of the premier banking institution of the world.

The eighteenth century also witnessed the growth of two other methods of solving the problem, so important for the growth of trade, of paying money without the transfer of coins or bullion from place to place. Private banks, of which the first was set up by a Bristol soap-dealer in 1716, spread so fast in the second half of the century that 230 could be listed in 1797; they made use mainly of Bills of Exchange. These promises to pay were sent from one district to another, and most often from the country to London; they were generally payable in three months, cash being obtainable sooner at a discount; and it was usually possible to cancel out Bills payable *from* a certain district against Bills for a similar amount payable *to* that district. Payment by cheque, on the other hand, which became very common after about 1850, developed slowly. The cheque began in the days of the goldsmith bankers as a letter telling the banker to pay a named sum out of the writer's account; but it was not until 1770 that the number of cheques used in London was big enough to start a Clearing House system. If two cheques required the transfer of sums from an account in Bank A to an account in Bank B and vice versa, it was obviously convenient for the banks concerned to arrange to transfer no more than the difference between the amounts named in the two cheques: the bank clerks originally met to "clear" all such transactions at a public-house in Lombard Street, already mentioned—close to the Bank of England, from which modern banks still draw the differences for transfer at their four daily clearances.

The facilities we have described grew up in the eighteenth century to make easier the business of payment, which grew more complicated with the growth of trade, abroad as well as at home. Abroad, there was the difficulty that no nation parted lightly with any of its stock of gold. But the high reputation of the Bank of England and the general stability of the country also made easier

The Threadneedle Street frontage of the Bank of England in 1797. The west wing, in the foreground, was built after the Gordon Riots (1780) on the site of a church overlooking the Bank; this was pulled down as a precaution against its use by future rioters

the business of payment in overseas commerce, for Bills of Exchange on London now began to take the place of Bills on Amsterdam, which was the traditional centre of European finance (and still held a part of our National Debt). But a still more important requirement for the development of British industry was the provision of capital.

Business Capital

It is probably true to say that the personal savings of the owner, his family, and friends were the main source from which businesses got the means to pay for buildings, machinery, raw material, and the wages of workpeople in anticipation of the profits that some new enterprise would eventually earn for them. But the early banks also played a part, by collecting people's savings, on which the bank undertook to pay interest, and then lending those savings—of course at a higher rate of interest—along with the bank's own "credit", to any new venture of which the bank approved.

For example, we know that money borrowed from the banks helped to build the first canal, paid for the earliest factory spinning machines, and kept the pioneer steam-engine at work.

Cash for wages was a special problem in this period. The coinage, based originally on the silver penny, which was 1/240th of a pound weight of silver, had been renewed in 1696, but there was a chronic shortage of small change. Farm labourers had been paid partly in kind and their numbers in any one place were small, but factory workers and others expected to be paid in cash, however numerous they might be. The shortage of coin became so great that some employers in the metal industries struck token coins of their own, which circulated locally and were exchanged for proper money if and when it became available. These pieces can still be found in second-hand shops, an interesting reminder of great names like "John Wilkinson, Ironfounder".[1] This difficulty over cash led to the prevalence of the Truck system. A "truck shop" was an establishment owned by the employer, where the employees were obliged to exchange their due wages for food or other things which they might or might not want, at prices which were often exorbitant. In 1701, a Truck Act was passed for the textile and iron industries, expressly forbidding the payment of wages in "clothes, victuals or commodities". Other laws followed, including a General Truck Act in 1831; but something of the system survived, though denounced by a Royal Commission in 1871–2, until the trade unions became really powerful. There were, of course, some industrial undertakings situated in very lonely places where the employer's shop was a necessity, but in the main "truck" provided a longstanding grievance for the workers.

The Gold Standard

Meanwhile in 1819, after the Napoleonic Wars, during which the pound sterling for a time lost half its value, Britain adopted the Gold Standard; that is to say, the currency was based entirely on gold, and silver ceased to be legal tender for sums over forty shillings. In 1817, a new coinage was issued, and the twenty-shilling sovereign replaced the twenty-one-shilling guinea. The Bank

[1] See page 85.

Charter Act of 1844 forbade newly founded banks to issue notes, and ordered the Bank of England to stock bullion of equal value to any increase in its note issue, so that it could always pay gold in exchange for bank notes on demand. Up to 1914, in spite of crises and trade depressions, the British organization of capital and banking worked with marvellous smoothness. Not only did we finance the development of our own industries, but loans from Britain financed the early stages of similar industrial developments in many other parts of the world.

At the present time, the Bank of England (nationalized in 1946) still does the banking business of the Government and normally holds the reserve funds of the other large banks—Barclays, Lloyds, the Midland, the Westminster, and the National Provincial. Each of these five powerful banking companies is the result of the union of many smaller banks, and they also have offices or agencies overseas in the Commonwealth and in some foreign countries. But there are also a number of small banks still surviving, some of which (such as the Merchant Banks) have specialized in certain kinds of banking. The key part which banks and the accumulation of capital still play in industrial development to-day is a reminder of their important function when large-scale industry was first developed. By being able and ready, against sound security, to lend large sums of money, banks have enabled business men to borrow capital for new and increased production, backing their judgment, sharing the risk, and thereby in the long run assisting the growth of the national wealth and welfare.

Token money made during the period of great financial stringency, 1797–8

7

THE REVOLUTION IN TEXTILES

IN 1760 Britain had four textile industries which wove four different materials—wool, silk, linen, and cotton. Wool was so much the largest industry of the four and had played such a great part in building up our national wealth that Daniel Defoe referred to it again and again as he visited the different districts in his famous *Tour through the Whole Island*. Thus he describes the prosperity of the Norwich "stuff-weaving trade by which so many thousands of families are maintained". He also states that in 1724 "there was not in all the eastern or middle part of Norfolk any hand unemployed if they would work; and that the very children after four or five years of age could every one earn their own bread". The West Riding of Yorkshire is described by Defoe as a "noble scene of industry and application". In one of the larger establishments Defoe saw "a house full of lusty fellows, some at the dye-vat, some dressing the cloths, some at the loom . . . all hard at work". In the smaller cottages, he saw the women and children all busy carding and spinning. He also visited the great cloth market at Leeds. Then there were the West of England weavers, who produced serges and other cloth, especially broad cloth. Exeter had a serge market to which came the produce of the looms of Tiverton, Crediton, Ashburton, and other towns. Defoe states that the serges sold at a single market were worth from £60,000 to £100,000.

An attempt to establish a woollen industry in Northern Ireland during the seventeenth (or Stuart) century was indignantly opposed by the English cloth-workers, and an Irish linen industry was set up instead. After a slow start this became the staple trade of Belfast and Londonderry. But what we think of as our biggest textile industry nowadays, the manufacture of cotton goods, was still at the early stages of its development in the first part of the eighteenth century. Cotton materials were originally imported from India, as we have already noticed, and it was the ban on these imports which gave home-produced cottons their first chance: but even then what was produced was mostly mixtures of cotton and wool or linen. From 1736 to 1774 there was still a law against the use of any goods made entirely of cotton, it being presumed that they must have been imported from the East.

Defoe in the 1720's had little to say of East Lancashire—nowadays a region of busy cotton mills—beyond describing the marshy condition of its extension towards the sea. He speaks of Manchester as "the greatest mere village in England . . . neither a walled town, city or corporation; they send no member to Parliament; the highest magistrate is a constable". But he noted that the population of Manchester was increasing and that it was making a cotton material called "dimity" (for bedroom hangings) as well as coarse "fustians" of cotton and wool. The Lancashire Defoe visited was mainly a county of poor farmers and cottagers, many of whom helped out their scanty earnings from the not very fertile soil by spinning and weaving the wool of the moorland sheep. But its textile workers were enterprising rather than conservative; they were already using and mixing together such varied raw materials as linen, silk, worsted, cotton, and mohair. The capital which would be needed for any big development was also accumulating fast through the expanding trade of the neighbouring port of Liverpool; and Liverpool could bring cotton in quantity from the West Indies and elsewhere. In these circumstances the jealousy with which the older woollen and silk industries regarded the growth of cotton could not prevent the last-named from seizing any chance for expansion that came along.

Spinning and Weaving

Accordingly it was in the new, and at first somewhat despised, cotton industry that the inventions which began the revolution in the textile industries were first widely used. Ingenious men experimented and improvised in the older woollen manufacture; the inventions were taken up and widely applied in the new cotton industry, bringing about radical changes in production by the use of machinery; and, more gradually, machine methods of production were adopted in the woollen industry also. It is a complicated story, and before mentioning any of the particular inventions, it will probably help to say a few words about the basic processes in the textile industry.

The word textile comes from the Latin *textilis*, which means "woven". To weave the weaver must first have yarn, which is prepared by spinning. Spinning and weaving are among the oldest of handicrafts, and have been developed in most parts of the world, so that various kinds of cloth have taken their names from places where they were originally developed, e.g. fustian from Fustat, the old name for Cairo, calico from Calicut in India, and muslin from Mosul in Iraq. The word cotton comes from Arabic and again reminds us of the eastern origin of cotton cloth.

First, the spinning of the yarn. The raw material has first to be cleansed and prepared—the wool has to be carded (from *carduus*, a thistle) or combed (to make worsted), and cotton has to be carded, these processes being different ways of separating and preparing the fibres for spinning. Then the fibre is spun. This was originally done by a hand spindle—a stick with a weight on the end is dangled by an attached fibre and rotated (i.e. spun) while other fibres are drawn out from the carded or combed bunch of raw material and attached by twisting until a continuous thread or yarn is formed. By the eighteenth century this process was carried out by a simple machine—the spinning-wheel. In this the spindle was mounted horizontally and turned by a wheel worked with a treadle.

Next, weaving. There are various forms of loom. But the basic process consists of the inter-crossing of two sets of parallel lines of yarn. The warp is a set of threads fixed to a frame, but fixed in such a way that alternate threads can all be raised together by means of attached cords so as to create a gap or "shed" in the warp. Through this shed is passed the shuttle carrying the weft, and the shuttle is passed backwards and forwards, as the threads of the warp are raised and lowered, until a stretch of cloth is woven. There are further processes such as the bleaching of cotton and fulling or felting and dressing of wool, and in many cases the material is also dyed; but spinning and weaving are the foundation of all the textile industries. The weaver was literally a manufacturer—a worker by hand. The inventions brought machines which would work much faster, and greatly multiply output.

The Flying Shuttle

First came the "Flying Shuttle", patented by John Kay in 1733, while working in his father's woollen business at Colchester. By pulling a cord, the weaver could send the shuttle carrying the weft to and fro through the "gap" or "shed" in the warp. This enabled a weaver, working alone, to weave broad cloth that had previously required two men at the loom; it also speeded up the work. Kay also made other improvements in textile machinery. New methods are often unpopular. Some weavers, fearing the new machines would throw men out of work, broke into Kay's house, in his native town of Bury in Lancashire, destroyed his machines, and burned and looted his property. Kay fled to France. He had suffered financial loss and may have been helped by the French Court, but very little is known about the end of his life.

His invention, intended primarily for the woollen industry, was taken up after some twenty years by the cotton weavers; sheds were built to house the larger loom which was needed with the new shuttle; and the immediate result was to create a famine in cotton yarn. A weaver now used up yarn faster than the spinners could supply it, and he often had to tramp three or four miles before starting his day's work, calling at the cottages of his spinners to collect enough yarn to keep his loom working. Men began to wish for a spinning-wheel which would spin more than one thread at a time.

Improvements in Spinning

It was not until thirty years after the invention of the flying shuttle that a Blackburn weaver, James Hargreaves, found a way to speed up spinning. His wife's spinning-wheel was accidentally overturned, and he noticed that the wheel continued to revolve while he held the thread in his hand. This gave him an idea and, being a carpenter as well as a weaver, he was able to work out a device for spinning several threads simultaneously. A number of

Water-frame used at Arkwright's mill at Cromford to spin thread
for cotton stockings

spindles set up in a row are rotated by a wheel, which also moves
a travelling carriage to and fro. As it moves to the right, threads
are drawn out from the rovings of cotton attached to the carriage;
as it moves back again, the twisted threads are wound onto the
spindles. His first machine, invented in 1767 (patented in 1770),
was a small one but even this could twist eight threads at once. It
perhaps got the name "spinning jenny" because it did the job
commonly done by women, or it may have been so called after
Hargreaves's wife. For a time, Hargreaves kept his invention a
secret, but other spinners noticed that his family produced great
quantities of yarn, and they broke into the house and smashed the
machines. Hargreaves then moved to Nottingham, where there
was a cotton-stocking industry. There he set up a small spinning
factory, and made machines which would spin sixteen, twenty, and
then thirty threads, and in due course a hundred and twenty

threads: but the "jenny" was a small and compact machine, which, like the spinning-wheel which it replaced, was normally used in cottages.

Hargreaves's invention practically coincided with Arkwright's spinning frame. Richard Arkwright was a barber and wig-maker of Preston, who became interested in spinning machinery as a money-making proposition and very probably "pirated" the work of an earlier inventor, Lewis Paul. Be that as it may, after some experiments he completed his spinning frame, bigger and heavier than the "jenny" and not capable of being worked by hand in a cottage room. This was able to produce thread strong enough for use as warp—which Hargreaves's machine had been unable to supply. Arkwright patented his famous machine in 1769 and set up a spinning factory in Nottingham. Two years later he entered into partnership with a firm of Nottingham stocking-knitters, and together they built a spinning-mill at Cromford in Derbyshire. Because the new machine was worked by water-power it became known as the "water-frame". A letter written thirty years after its first erection describes Arkwright's cotton mill as "a palace of enormous size, having at least a score of windows in a row, and five or six storeys in height". Like other inventors, he had his difficulties. One of his mills was completely sacked by rioters; others were attacked by mobs. But on the whole, Arkwright was the most successful of the early inventors. He became a millionaire and a baronet, and ranks in history as the founder of the modern factory system.

Although it was now possible to make textiles entirely of cotton without a linen or woollen warp, English cotton goods remained coarser than those imported from the East until another invention was made. This was a machine designed by Samuel Crompton of Bolton, who is said to have looked like a combination between the youthful Napoleon Bonaparte and one of the early Methodist preachers. After years of hard work and poverty, he made a machine in 1775 that spun finer and stronger thread than either Hargreaves's spinning jenny or Arkwright's water-frame—and as it was a cross between the two machines it was called the "mule" This machine enabled even fine muslins to be made in England instead of importing them from the East. Crompton was, however, very unfortunate. Jealous spinners broke into his house and tried to wreck his machine. Manufacturers took up his invention but avoided recompensing him; he died penniless. But with his "mule", spinning moved from cottage to factory and from village to town; the change was completed early in the nineteenth century, and an improved version of Crompton's invention, the self-acting mule, is still the basis of Lancashire's premier industry to-day.

These inventions speeded up spinning. Spinning-mills were built beside streams, where the machines could be worked by water-wheels such as were used to grind corn; these were known as "beck-side" mills. But the looms were still worked by hand, with the result that yarn was now being prepared faster than the looms could use it. Then Edmund Cartwright, a clergyman, became interested in the new machines. He visited the new spinning-mills, and suggested that weaving also might be done by a power-driven machine. His suggestion was laughed at, but he set to work, and made the first power-loom; it was a clumsy affair driven by a bull. About this time James Watt's steam engine,[1] which had been used for pumping water from mines and blowing bellows in blast furnaces, was being adapted for driving machinery. In 1789—the year of the French Revolution—Cartwright's factory at Doncaster was fitted with a steam engine. Two years later, a Manchester firm contracted to take a number of power-looms. Other inventors improved on Cartwright's work; and by the time of Napoleon's defeat at Waterloo in 1815 power-looms were beginning to come into wider use.

Steam now began to take the place of water-power, and some of the beck-side mills were deserted while factories were set up near the coal-mines. New towns sprang up to house the factory workers, who moved in from surrounding country districts. Meanwhile, some more inventions streamlined the production of cotton goods. The most important was the cotton gin for extracting the seeds from the cotton; this was introduced by the American Eli Whitney in 1793. Up to this time three-quarters of the raw cotton was imported from the British West Indies, the rest from Brazil, India, or the Levant: the American cotton plant had

[1] See page 78.

Calico-printing

very little commercial value because its seeds were too tightly em-
bedded in the fibres. The new machine, by replacing the costly
hand-picking, made the southern states of the newly established
U.S.A. a land of cotton: thirty years later they were supplying
three-quarters of the total British demand, which in the meantime
had multiplied itself eight times over.

Another important improvement was the use of bleaching pow-
der to replace the older bleaching processes which took months
to complete. Chloride of lime began to be manufactured for this
purpose in Glasgow, where cotton was now the main industry, in
1798. The production of calico was further helped by the invention
of Bell's colour-printing cylinder, with which one man could do
more work in a day than could be done by a hundred hand-
printers. Our engraving of an early calico-printing establishment,
even though the machines look clumsy and are tended by men in
tailcoats and knee breeches, shows clearly a forerunner of the
factory of to-day. Lastly, we may mention the lace-making
machine, which did work that had been thought too complicated
for anything but a skilful human hand. When artisans in 1816
attacked his factory at Nottingham, the inventor Heathcoat

removed to Tiverton in Devon; there he was able to invent a process by which the frames could be worked either by water-power or by steam, and he set up a lace factory which is still at work.

Results of the Inventions

The cotton industry of south-east Lancashire and neighbouring districts, and of Glasgow and Lanarkshire farther north, was the first to benefit from the new methods of manufacture. These areas had local advantages for this particular industry in their humid climate, which facilitates spinning, and pure water available for bleaching and cleaning processes. An almost unlimited supply of raw material came readily to hand from overseas. The market for the finished goods, consisting chiefly of calico and others of the simpler and cheaper forms of cotton cloth, was likewise virtually inexhaustible.

It is no wonder that in the early nineteenth century cotton became firmly established as the first and greatest machine industry. Thereafter, for over a hundred years, it dominated all other export activities. By 1880 it had made Lancashire the most populous county in Britain and the richest in revenue from all sources, carrying on two-thirds of the cotton trade of the world.

For a time the woollen industry largely despised the new machines, but gradually the wool workers also introduced machines adapted to their special needs. Machinery driven by water-power could readily be installed by Yorkshire cloth-workers, for there were many streams in the hilly districts of the West Riding. But in Norfolk, with its flat countryside, this was not possible; by the end of the eighteenth century, all that remained of the East Anglian woollen industry was the preparation of wool. However, Cartwright invented a combing machine on the same lines as his power-loom, by imitating the movements of the hand. Actually it was not until 1850 that the combing machine ("Big Ben") became efficient enough to oust entirely the hand industry over which their patron saint ("Bishop Blaize") had long presided. But already the Norfolk wool-combers were singing this dirge:

Come, all ye Master Combers, and hear of new Big Ben,
He'll comb more wool in one day than fifty of your men
With their hand-combs and comb-pots and such old-fashioned
　　ways;
There'll be no more occasion for old Bishop Blaize.

When steam-power took the place of the water-wheel, Yorkshire again had the advantage of coal-mines close at hand, while Norfolk had to bring coal by sea. So the centuries-old East Anglian cloth trade came to an end just at a time when the distress which followed the Napoleonic Wars was most acute. Many families, unable to make a living, moved to the new industrial towns on the Yorkshire coal-field. Others emigrated to Canada or the United States to find employment in the new lands.

As we have seen, the introduction of new methods in textiles was unpopular, chiefly because of the dread of being out of work. One writer complained that "the employment of machinery was one of the greatest evils that ever befell the country". The setting-up of new machines often led to riots by bands of machine-breakers. The best known are those who in 1811–16 called themselves Luddites—perhaps after Ned Ludd, a half-witted lad of Leicestershire, who, being unable to catch someone who had been tormenting him, destroyed some stocking-frames in a fit of rage. The Luddites in various districts vented their rage on the particular kind of machinery which seemed to threaten their employment. In Nottingham, they attacked the stocking-frames because the master hosiers began to reduce wages and make stockings on wider machines. In Lancashire, the Luddites were hand-loom weavers; they succeeded at the third attempt in burning a steam-loom factory at Westhoughton, in April 1812. In Yorkshire, it was the "croppers" who were Luddites—these were skilled workmen who cropped the nap on the cloth to give it a smooth surface; they objected to the use of the shearing-frame, which replaced their work. As a result some rioters were hanged, and others transported to Botany Bay in Australia. But their demonstrations and violent acts of protest against the changes, though bound to fail, were not altogether unreasonable, and we may be glad that the Luddites won the sympathy of the poet, Lord

Byron: for it was true that people were being thrown out of work by the machines and were not at once re-employed elsewhere. This caused terrible suffering. But it is also true that in the end the use of machinery increased the demand for labour: the machine-produced goods were much cheaper and were sold in much larger quantities, so their manufacture *in the long run* found work for far more people than could ever have been employed under the old system.

8

THE REVOLUTION IN TRANSPORT

INCREASE in trade made it essential for traders to have better means of transporting their goods. Coastal shipping had long flourished and it continued to expand: until the close of the nineteenth century it carried a greater weight of cargo than made up all our exports. But for many centuries the English roads had been in a very bad condition, and it was not until the latter half of the eighteenth century that any great progress began to be made.

Arthur Young, an agricultural expert who made tours at that time through nearly all parts of England, tells us that the roads were often little more than bridle-paths, quite unfit for any kind of wheeled vehicles. He advised travellers to avoid the roads around Newcastle, which "must either dislocate their bones with broken pavements or bury them in muddy sand". The Norfolk roads he described as "ponds of liquid dirt", while the Essex roads were "so narrow that a mouse cannot pass any carriage". In winter, the road between Kensington and London was an "impassable gulf of mud". King George II and his Queen once spent a whole night on the road when going the eight miles from Kew Palace to St. James's Palace, and once the coach overturned in a ditch. It is little wonder that highwaymen found easy prey on such roads. Though the four horses were changed at every town, it took four days for a coach from London to reach Manchester or York, while the journey from London to Edinburgh took ten to fourteen days.

Turnpike Trusts

The great obstacle to improvement lay in the fact that the up-keep of the roads was a parish responsibility: they were renewed, improved, and repaired to the extent and by the methods which suited the needs of the people who lived there. The needs of long-distance travel and transport—except for horse riders and trains of pack-horses, which could get round the holes and unsafe stretches of highway—were simply ignored. The solution was the Turnpike Trust; we hear of them occasionally as early as the reign of Charles II, but it was the difficulty of moving the army northward to meet the Jacobites in 1745 which caused the need for them to be generally recognized, and 1773 is the date of a law which made it easy to administer them. Each Trust consisted of local people who were willing to invest their money in improving a stretch of main road in their own locality. Having improved it and arranged for its upkeep, they were empowered to recover their expenditure by a toll on every vehicle or beast driven along their road. Soon the turnpike gates on the high roads were almost universal: on leaving London, for instance, the traveller bound for Oxford would pass through one near the modern Marble Arch and a second at what is still called Notting Hill Gate. If the caricaturist Rowlandson is to be believed, such a gate was a very lively place and its corpulent keeper had a busy time enforcing his placarded list of tolls on coaches, carriages, and horse- and donkey-riders. The erection of turnpike gates and the vast improvements with which they were associated, ushered in the age of the flying coach and the private post-chaise, racing to Bath or Brighton or Gretna Green at nearly twelve miles per hour. For humbler purposes, too, pack-horses began to disappear when covered wagons could move more easily.

Roads and Bridges

But the Turnpike Trust itself was merely a way to raise money for the roads: its importance was that it gave scope for inventive minds to introduce better gradients and drainage and more durable and smoother surfaces. Towards the end of the eighteenth century three great road-makers were at work—John Metcalf ("Blind Jack of Knaresborough"), Telford, and MacAdam. For nearly thirty years Metcalf—blind through smallpox at the age of six—was at work superintending the making of roads in Yorkshire, Lancashire, and Derbyshire. He invented a smooth, durable

Turnpike at Hyde Park Corner, by Rowlandson

road surface, made by pounding small stones together, and he tested the surface and slope of a road by walking to and fro, tapping the road with his hollow stick. The second famous eighteenth-century road-maker and engineer, Thomas Telford, became road surveyor in Shropshire. He advocated solid foundations, with a firm, moderately cambered surface. His chief work was in Scotland, where, between 1803 and 1821, he constructed 920 miles of road and more than 1,200 bridges. As a result of his work traders and travellers were enabled to move freely between England and Scotland; this helped to bring a new era of prosperity to North Britain. In southern Britain, Telford's best-known work was the great London to Holyhead road, along the line of the old Roman Watling Street, which he furnished with new bridges and extended from Shrewsbury through the Welsh mountains to the Menai Straits and beyond.

An even more famous road-maker was John Loudon MacAdam (1756–1836), a Scotsman, who found a way of making roads as good as, but less expensive than, those of Telford. Even when a boy at school, MacAdam made a model section of a road. As a youth he went to New York, and there became a successful merchant. Later, back in this country, he experimented at Falmouth, and was able to put his ideas into practice, first as surveyor-general of the Bristol roads (1815) and finally, in 1827, as general surveyor of roads for the Government. He realized, like Metcalf, the need for well-drained subsoil. If the subsoil were well drained and the road raised above the general level, then the subsoil would be strong enough, without the solid foundations of Telford, to bear the weight of the road surface and the traffic passing over it. His method was to make the top layer of the road of small broken stones, which the pressure of the traffic would crush and weld together into a hard smooth surface. To ensure that the stones for the road surface were not too large, he used to tell the stone-breakers: no stone should be larger than can go comfortably in the mouth. On one occasion MacAdam is said to have expostulated with an old man who was breaking the stone into too large pieces, only to have the old man pop a piece easily into his mouth. But the mouth was large and toothless!

In various parts of England he helped to plan, repair and build a great network of roads, on many of which the mail coaches[1] could travel at an average rate of eleven or twelve miles an hour, a speed that would have been thought impossible thirty years earlier. Visitors to this country from Germany and France were highly impressed by British roads. Whereas in 1706 the coach from Newcastle to London took eight days, in 1820 on the good roads the journey could be made in forty hours. The coaches had been immensely speeded up. But this was true only of the best and most rapid passenger transport. To send heavy goods might take weeks; normally they would go by sea where possible. It was this slowness of goods transport which stimulated the construction of railways and, earlier, of canals.

MacAdam's plan for road-making is still in use, though in these days of motor traffic what were once called "macadamized roads" are reinforced with tar, and the surface is now known as "tarmac".

The construction of bridges was a problem which had to be faced by some road-makers. The old method of building a bridge

[1] See p. 182.

Nequicquam Deus Abscidit Prudens, Oceano dissociabili Terras, si

The Most Noble Francis Egerton, Duke of Bridgewater
and Marquis of Brackley.
Seu Navis Brittannæ Magister.
Magnificum pretiosus emptor.

was to sink either large boulders, or baskets filled with stones, into the bed of the river as foundations to support the arches. The old London Bridge was built in this way, stood for centuries, and supported rows of houses. But the art of bridge-making did not make much headway until the late eighteenth and early nineteenth centuries. Then progress was rapid, owing to the work of famous bridge-builders and engineers, such as Smeaton, Telford and Rennie. John Smeaton (1724-1792), who attended Leeds Grammar School as a boy and became a Fellow of the Royal Society before he was thirty, had studied the canals and bridges of the Netherlands. His most famous bridge, 900 feet in length, was built across the River Tay, in Scotland. Telford's Menai Suspension Bridge, which carried his Holyhead road across to Anglesey, had the central portion supported by chains, so as not to interfere with the navigation along the Straits below. Rennie built the old Waterloo Bridge in 1817, and his son built a new London Bridge in 1831. When bridges for railway traffic were built, even greater strength was required; but the main problems had been solved by these great pioneers in civil engineering. Smeaton founded the first society for the profession, from which the Institution of Civil Engineers was developed in 1818, with Telford as president.

Canals

The bad roads of the eighteenth century made the carriage of heavy goods—such as coal, iron, clay, pottery, and machinery—very difficult and sometimes impossible. River traffic was important, as we have seen, but the course of rivers is often irregular, and they may suffer from droughts and floods. In the second half of the eighteenth century, canals or artificial waterways were made. The first English canal-maker was James Brindley, a Derby-

---

The Duke of Bridgewater, who was only 25 when the Worsley Canal was opened, pointing to Barton Bridge, the 40-foot aqueduct over the River Irwell, and a line of coal-barges bound for Manchester. An appropriate inscription—*Perrupit Acheronta Herculeus' labor*—marks the mouth of the tunnel by which the canal emerges from the underground workings of the mines at Worsley

shire cottager's son. Brindley was largely illiterate, but possessed high ability. He became a wheelwright by trade. From 1759 he was employed by the Duke of Bridgewater to construct a canal from the Duke's colliery at Worsley to Manchester, eleven miles away.

Brindley began by cutting a tunnel (or adit) straight from the coal workings. He invented water-tight embankments to carry the canal through bogs; and finally brought it across the River Irwell by an aqueduct at Barton Bridge which was regarded as a great triumph of ingenuity. Brindley trained his workmen or navvies, and fitted up special boats as forges and carpenters' shops, which were floated along each section of the canal as it was made. The canal proved a great success, and the cost of coal in Manchester was halved. The Duke then had the canal extended to Runcorn, thus connecting Manchester with the Mersey estuary and so with Liverpool. When the whole canal was completed, it was so much used in preference to the bad roads, both for goods and passengers, that the tolls paid for its use brought the Duke a large fortune.

Brindley next undertook a greater piece of work, the Grand Trunk Canal, which, when completed, extended southwards from Runcorn through the salt and pottery districts to join the Trent at Wilden Ferry. The first sod of this canal was cut by Josiah Wedgwood, the potter, one of the chief promoters, in 1762.[1] The canal, with all its branches, had a total length of 139 miles, and brought great benefit to the important pottery industry. Large quantities of clay, lime and coal had to be fetched from some distance; and the finished goods were bulky, brittle, and difficult to carry by road. The Grand Trunk Canal reduced the cost of carriage on clay and other materials from 30s. a ton to 13s. 4d. It also made bread cheaper by reducing the carriage on a quarter of wheat from 20s. to 5s. for a hundred miles.

During the four years from 1790 to 1794, no fewer than eighty-one Acts of Parliament granted permission to cut canals. Among the other famous canal-makers was John Smeaton, who constructed the Forth and Clyde Canal in Scotland. Another Scottish canal, the Caledonian Canal through the Great Glen, was the work of Telford and financially a failure. His best work in this field was

[1] See illustration, p. 92.

the Ellesmere Canal, famous for its two aqueducts, which forms part of the Shropshire Union network linking the Mersey, Dee, and Severn. In general the canal was a perfect example of a labour-saving device. A *General History of Inland Navigation*, published in 1792, described canals as "roads of a certain kind on which one horse will draw as much as thirty horses on an ordinary turnpike road, or on which one man alone will transport as many goods as three men and eighteen horses usually do on common roads".

Canals had their defects: they were a rather slow means of transportation at best, and there were often delays at the locks; through-traffic was also seriously impeded by the absence of any standard width of water-way. But the development of England during the Industrial Revolution of the late eighteenth century and the early nineteenth century owed much to the canals. The pottery towns of Staffordshire, for example, trebled in size within a generation of their coming into use. Ports also benefited enormously by being brought into direct communication with the industrial districts. Lastly, canal transport helped farmers, who were provided with a wider market for their crops as well as a cheaper means of obtaining manure and other bulk supplies. Thus the canals are one factor which is common to the industrial and agrarian revolutions.

9

THE REVOLUTION IN FARMING

The deepe and dirtiest lothsome soyle
Yeldes golden grayne to careful toyle.
(Norden, in Elizabeth I's reign.)

WHILE the invention of new machines was bringing about an Industrial Revolution, important changes were taking place in the eighteenth century in agriculture—through the enclosure of the open fields to form compact farms where better farming could be practised.

Clover and deep-rooted lucerne for cattle food had been introduced in the seventeenth century, but their value for improving the soil and breaking it up with their long roots was not at first understood. The horse-drill for sowing seeds, and the horse-hoe for weeding, had been invented by Jethro Tull in the very early years of the eighteenth century; his method of sowing seeds in rows some distance apart actually produced a strike of labourers who believed the right way must be to scatter broadcast as in Biblical days! Nevertheless, Tull persevered, and eventually produced a book, *Horse-hoeing Husbandry*, with diagrams showing how easily his machine could be made.

Among other pioneers of eighteenth-century farming was the 2nd Viscount Townshend, who began farming in 1730, and by his constant praise of turnips as a crop earned the nickname of "Turnip Townshend". At his estate of Raynham in Norfolk, he introduced a new rotation of crops known as the Norfolk system of four courses, namely: turnips, barley or oats, clover, wheat. Thus he was able to keep all his land in use instead of letting a third of it lie fallow (or uncropped) each year, as under the old system of the Middle Ages. His new rotation of crops not only improved the land itself, but root crops and clover meant winter food for cattle—and therefore fresh meat for people during the winter. His soil at Raynham was light and sandy, and in earlier days "two rabbits had fought for every blade of grass", but under the new cultivation it was greatly improved.

Coke of Holkham

Another Norfolk farmer, Squire Coke of Holkham, inherited in 1776 a badly cultivated, unproductive estate. He applied new techniques, often with more care than their original inventors had shown, and at the end of a long life—he died as Earl of Leicester in 1842—had multiplied his rent-roll by ten, while his tenant farmers prospered with him. By draining and manuring the light soil, Coke succeeded, to everyone's surprise, in growing corn. He also did much to improve the breeds of cattle and sheep; he studied grasses to find out which kinds were best for the animals. Every year, beginning in 1778, Squire Coke had a meeting at sheep-shearing time to which he invited farmers—sometimes 7,000—from all parts of the country to discuss agriculture. "Everybody made use of expressions towards Coke which affectionate children used towards their parents"—wrote Cobbett, a farmer and journalist who did not, as a rule, have much to say in favour of the landlord class.

Meanwhile another farmer, Robert Bakewell, of Dishley, Leicestershire, experimented in scientific cattle-breeding. Taking advantage of the improved feeding provided by root crops and clover, he produced a breed of sheep, "New Leicesters", nearly three times the weight of the long-legged, bony creatures previously reared. He then turned to cattle with equal success, and provided such good beasts that other farmers began to take more interest in cattle-breeding and so improved the meat supply. His work was continued by the Colling brothers, who after a visit to Dishley began to develop the modern breed of shorthorn cattle on their own farms near Darlington.

King George III—"Farmer George"—set up a model farm at Windsor, and even wrote articles for the *Annals of Agriculture*, a monthly publication which was continued for twenty-five years (1784–1809) by Arthur Young. Young's *Tours* of agricultural in-

Coke of Holkham

vestigation have already been mentioned; in 1793 he became
secretary of the newly founded Board of Agriculture. This was
not the direct ancestor of the modern government department
of that name, but a national society for collecting facts and figures
and reports about new methods, and it offered prizes for essays on
farming and for inventions of benefit to agriculture. This propaganda, as we should call it, was very necessary because farmers
were slow to change, having always provided for themselves and
for a local market in traditional ways and without being exposed
to much competition. The result was a series of further improvements, which came slowly into use. New methods of draining the
land were preached in Warwickshire and perfected in Perthshire.
In 1813 Sir Humphry Davy published his *Elements of Agricultural Chemistry*, from which the modern use of artificial fertilizers
eventually grew. A Scotsman (Meikle) invented a threshing machine as early as 1786, which came quickly into use in the Lothians:
but in 1830 this machine, through which the steam engine was

harnessed to perform an agricultural task, was still a novelty in most parts of England.

These new methods brought prosperity to wealthy landowners, able to spend money on experiments, on machinery, and on new breeds of cattle to improve their stock. For example, in the background of the scene in which Thomas Coke is proudly inspecting his Southdown sheep, Holkham Hall appears—the magnificent mansion he built with his farming profits. But it was impossible to practise the new farming on the old large "open" or unfenced fields divided into "strips". At the beginning of the eighteenth century, as we have seen, much of the land was cultivated in the old style as it had been throughout the Middle Ages. But as long as his land was not fenced off, a farmer could not grow turnips or clover on his strips—they would be eaten and trampled on by other men's cattle when they were given the run of the common fields after harvest. A man might see that his land could be improved by drainage, but where could he carry the water without making a neighbour's land sodden? If a man tried to produce a better breed of cattle, as Bakewell was doing, the beasts had to mingle with the ill-kept village herds, usually infected with footrot, scab and other diseases. Again, it was difficult to keep one's own crops free from weeds when a careless neighbour's strips were overrun by thistles. Further, much time was wasted in going from strip to strip; and the land itself was wasted in the balks and pathways separating the strips.

Enclosure Acts

In his tours over England, Arthur Young saw that if agriculture was to prosper it must make use of new methods. He also realized that as these methods could not be used on the old open fields, the latter must go, and the land of the unenclosed villages be redistributed. While some enclosures were carried out by general agreement among all concerned, the usual method was for each village to obtain its special Act of Parliament. A few such Acts had been obtained under Queen Anne and George I, and over two hundred during George II's reign; but even at the accession of George III in 1760, the open-field system still existed in about half the counties of England—in a roughly triangular area on the east side of the country, bounded by the East Riding of Yorkshire, Norfolk, and Wiltshire.

From about 1760 onward it became more evident that efforts must be made to increase the food supply of the country. The population of England and Wales was almost certainly growing rapidly in the later decades of the eighteenth century; this growth was very marked in the towns. Another reason for increasing the agricultural output was the series of wars with France, which made it impossible to import much corn from abroad. With bigger demand came bigger prices; and this made many farmers anxious to make better use of their land, and if possible to acquire a greater acreage. The number of enclosures therefore increased. During George III's reign some 3,200 Enclosure Acts were obtained, including in 1801 a General Enclosure Act which simplified the procedure.

The actual process of enclosure, after an Act of Parliament had been passed, was carried out by Commissioners. They were generally named in the original petition asking for the Act, and their appointment was ratified by the Act. They were often three in number, and might be peers, gentlemen, clergymen, or farmers; sometimes they acted without fee, but usually fees and travelling expenses had to be paid. The Commissioners generally held a public meeting in the district, and then appointed a valuer and surveyor. Each holding of land had to be valued and measured—and this was no light task. The Commissioners had to allow for the roads, either public thoroughfares or private roads leading to individual farms, and they could make regulations as to drainage. But the main task was the redistribution of the land in the district: the claims of the lord of the manor and all owners of land in the common fields, and of all who had legal claim to meadow, pasture, or use of the common had to be considered. It was a most intricate and complicated business. At the end, when the reallotment of land was finished, each landlord or farmer would have, instead of his former scattered strips and his right to a share in the common, a compact allotment of land, a farm or farms, where he could work and carry out improvements untrammelled by his neighbours. Next came the expensive task of fencing or hedging the newly allotted farms. Boundary fences for each total share had to be put up, and payment for them was exacted from each farmer in proportion to the size of his allotment of land. The interior fencing of fields was left to the farmer as he chose. The whole business was most costly, from the beginning, when the petition had to be drawn up and presented to Parliament, until the final work of the Commissioners. Lawyers had to be paid, there were visits to London with travelling expenses and delays which also cost dear. Between the passing of the Act and the completion of the Commissioners' work of reallotment five or six years might pass. During that time there was uncertainty and confusion, and the land might be badly farmed in consequence until the change-over was settled.

Effects on the Poor

On the face of it, the system was a fair one. Parliament did not pass the Bill unless the owners of four-fifths of the area of property to be enclosed were in favour; it sent, as we have seen, Commissioners to settle the redistribution; and every strip belonging to the old open fields was replaced by an equivalent area. But the small man was nevertheless at a great disadvantage because the compact piece of land which he received had not only to replace his arable strips but also the use he had formerly had from the common—the untilled land where he (like his neighbours) had kept his horse and cows and a few sheep and geese and hens, to say nothing of the free timber and firewood on which he had always relied. And the poorest class, the cottagers, who had no arable strips but picked up a living from the common did not, at least if they were newcomers to the village, necessarily receive any compensation at all. Sometimes the freemen of an ancient town still share an unfenced common, such as the Port Meadow at Oxford; more often it is a little village green which survives to remind us of what was lost when the compact modern farms with their hedged fields came into existence.

The hedges or fences, too, cost money and, together with the proportion of the cost of the award which had to be paid by each person who benefited, were another thing which made it harder for the small farmer to keep his farm. Many peasants sold their bit of land to a more fortunate neighbour. They became landless men and worked as whole-time agricultural labourers: the big new farms were mainly arable and would need more men. But the fact that their families no longer had any "stake in the country" was one strong reason for a movement of "surplus" population away from rural areas into the new industrial towns or overseas, which continued all through the following century. In this way the cultivation of the land passed mainly into the hands of men with capital. Small freeholders, who had been the most independent type of yeoman (because, being actual owners of their land they need obey no squire), kept their farms as long as prices were high. But at the end of the French Wars many of these had to sell up their possessions and go to the towns. In the end nothing was left of the ancient system of agriculture but the one or two unenclosed villages, such as Laxton (Notts), which still stand out, as seen from the air, in strange contrast to their neighbours.

Even Arthur Young, who had for years advocated enclosure, was forced to acknowledge the "knavery of commissioners and

Air view of open fields under strip cultivation at Laxton, Notts, a few miles west of the Great North Road

attorneys" acting under the Enclosure Acts, and owned that "by nineteen out of twenty Enclosure Acts the poor are injured, and most grossly". Oliver Goldsmith in his poem, *The Deserted Village*, lamented that

> . . . *a bold peasantry, their country's pride,*
> *When once destroyed can never be supplied.*

The hardships of the villagers were increased during the Industrial Revolution by the gradual loss of their other means of livelihood, hand-spinning and part-time weaving. The spinning-wheel, in particular, had been a regular source of income, for under old conditions it required six or eight pairs of hands to prepare and spin the yarn needed by one weaver. But by the end of the century, wool was being spun in factories, so the women and children of the countryside lost their small earnings. The menfolk also found that, when the power loom began to spread, the hand loom could no longer be brought out to supplement the profits of a small holding. Then there were the incredibly harsh Game Laws—seven years' transportation was the penalty for being found by night on open land in possession of nets for rabbiting. But the most unbearable thing of all was the knowledge that the great agricultural changes, which enormously increased the nation's stock of wheat and meat, had brought no improvement at all to the lot of the landless rural worker, who eked out a miserable existence on inferior bread, potatoes, and cheese, washed down with weak beer or weaker, unsugared tea.

Other Considerations

Nevertheless, the future lay with the large compact farms, where the farmer had capital for purchasing machinery and stock and for improving the land. One of the reasons which led to a great increase of enclosures was the desire of men who had made a fortune in trade or industry to become landowners. As early as 1724, Daniel Defoe had noted that on estates near London families of local gentry were being displaced by families enriched in business; and Cobbett, the writer who admired Squire Coke of

Holkham, felt very differently about the people from London whom he termed "the Squires of Change Alley". The possession of land had political and social as well as economic value. Until the reform of Parliament in 1832, nobody but landowners was entitled to vote in county elections, and even later every candidate for Parliament was nominally supposed to prove himself to be a substantial landowner: the landed interest was the basis of political power. Parliament was controlled by landowners. The possession of land also conferred social distinction, for the lord of the manor or squire was the local magistrate or Justice of the Peace. But beside political and social distinction, the keen business man who invested money in land would expect profitable returns. He wanted to bring as much as possible of the open fields and the "common" under his control to farm according to modern methods for profit; or he might let the land after enclosure to tenant farmers at a high rental.

It is now clear that, though much distress was caused by enclosures, they were essential to work the improved methods of agriculture, and without them it would have been impossible to feed the growing population in the factory areas. It is possible, too, that the hardships of the poor have been exaggerated by some writers: Goldsmith is said by Lord Macaulay to have introduced into his English 'Deserted Village' conditions characteristic only of Ireland. For it must be remembered that waste land also was enclosed, particularly during the Napoleonic war, and this bringing of new land into cultivation to meet the increased demand for food meant *more*, not less, agricultural employment. During the wars, too, tenants often took advantage of high profits to buy their holdings. During the years 1800–50 no English county, however rural, showed an actual decline in population, though London and the counties containing the new industrial areas showed by far the greatest increase.

10

OUR HERITAGE OF COAL

FOR centuries wood had been the principal fuel for household use —except in the districts where outcrop or surface coal was easily obtainable. Wood had also been used in great quantities (in the form of charcoal) for smelting iron ore. Two loads of wood were required to make one load of charcoal, and two loads of charcoal were needed to smelt a ton of iron ore. In the seventeenth century, the forests and woodlands of England were dwindling, and Parliament began to fear that ship-builders would be short of timber at a time when there was an increasing demand for new ships for trade and defence.

One result of the shortage of wood was to increase the mining of coal to provide fuel for domestic and industrial purposes. This led to a rapid opening of coal seams in Northumberland and Durham. Coal was sent from Newcastle to London by sea, and so it was known as sea-coal. At the time of the Civil War in Charles I's reign, the coal-pits of Northumberland and Durham were so valuable that some people suspected the Scottish army of planning to gain permanent possession of them. Apart from corn, it was already the chief article of internal trade.

Transport of coal otherwise than by water was difficult on account of bad roads. Until the cutting of Brindley's canal from Worsley to Manchester in 1759–61, coal was carried in baskets on pack-horses. The usual load was 280 pounds, and the cost of carriage doubled the price of coal. The digging of the canals not only assisted the development of the Lancashire coal-field, which up to the middle of the nineteenth century was second only to north-east England in importance; it also started the coal industry of the South Wales valleys, with iron ore close at hand and convenient sea communications from Cardiff.

Owing to the increased demand for coal, the surface outcrops were used up, and miners had to dig down. At first they made pits thirty or forty feet deep, and worked over a small radius from the bottom of the shaft. More than half the coal was left in the form of huge pillars to support the rocks above. Lower seams had been reached by 1776, and pits as much as 600 feet in depth were being worked. These deep pits presented great difficulties—drainage, raising the coal to the surface, ventilation, and the danger of explosive gas. As the mines went deeper the danger of flooding increased, and pumps were set up, worked by various contrivances such as tread-mills, wind-mills and water-wheels.

Power provided by wind and water is unreliable, and this led to the introduction of Savery's primitive steam pump, which had been patented in 1698 as "an engine to raise water by fire". Newcomen improved on Savery's engine, and Newcomen's engine was in use in many coal-mines during the earlier part of the eighteenth century. The way in which this was developed into the modern steam engine, which could raise the coal as well as pump up the water, will be described in the next chapter.

Raising the coal to the surface was another problem which had to be faced as mines became deeper. In most collieries some kind of mechanical apparatus came into use, either a simple windlass or horse gin or crane. The winding tackle served also to lower and raise the miners. But some pits had no mechanical gear, and the coal was carried to the surface by means of ladders in baskets slung over the shoulders of women and children, the distance climbed being equal, in at least one case, to the height of St. Paul's Cathedral. Even after the steam engine came to be used for haulage, there was still the difficulty of finding a rope strong enough to take the strain; the wire cable was not invented until 1839.

Prevention of Mining Accidents

The problem of ventilation was equally difficult. Most coal-mines contain harmful gases, and are only made fit to work in by having pure air forced through. The first method adopted was the provision of two shafts on different levels, the air rising in one and being drawn down the other. The air from the down shaft was conducted through the mine workings by a system of trap doors which were opened and closed by boys and girls. This method was not sufficient for deep mines, and towards the end of the eighteenth century a mining engineer, John Buddle of Wallsend, invented an exhaust fan. This drew the foul air out of one shaft by suction, which caused a current of fresh air to be drawn down the second shaft.

Upon the ventilation of the pit depended the miners' safety from dangerous gases. In the smaller pits "choke-damp", or carbon dioxide, was the chief danger; but in the larger and deeper pits there was sometimes "fire-damp", or methane. Fire-damp was the more dangerous, for the flame of the miner's candle caused it to explode without warning, while choke-damp usually put the candle out before its suffocating fumes took effect on the miner himself, thus giving him time to escape.

Fire-damp made the lighting of mines a serious problem. The usual method was by the naked flame of a candle or by a lantern. Explosions were frequent, and caused great loss of life. A clergyman, the Rev. John Hodgson, who once lost over ninety of his parishioners in a colliery disaster, became the pioneer of a movement to establish societies for the prevention of mining accidents. The first of these societies was started in Sunderland in 1815. At about the same time the old North of England practice, by which mining disasters were exempt from coroners' inquests, was at last abandoned; it had taken two laws (1775 and 1799) to abolish the still more shameful Scottish custom of compelling miners to serve for life in the same pit as "bondsmen", punishable if they ran away.

Thus public attention was directed to the need for greater safety in mines, and by 1815 an important step forward was made. After careful experiments, Sir Humphry Davy (1778–1829), one of the leading scientists of the time and a pioneer in chemistry, invented a safety lamp in which the flame is shielded by a cylinder of metal gauze fine enough to let the light through. But the conductivity of the gauze disperses the heat of the flame throughout the cylinder, so that the temperature is not high enough to ignite any gas outside, as the naked flame would have done. The lamp proved very useful. When told by a friend that he ought to patent the lamp as it would bring him a small fortune, Davy nobly replied: "I never thought of such a thing. I am only too happy to have been able to help our miners. That is my reward." In more recent years electric lighting has been introduced into the main galleries of the mines, and portable electric lamps are used in other parts; but as late as 1926 half a million Davy lamps were still carried in British mines, so that the "cap" of burning gas within the gauze might give its warning of the presence of fire-damp.

As the Industrial Revolution progressed, coal became more and more important to feed the ever-increasing steam-engines, for the iron manufacturer, and for millions of new domestic hearths. In the first seventy years of the eighteenth century the output may have doubled to reach an estimated total of six million tons. Between 1770 and 1816 the six million became sixteen million, which in turn was nearly doubled by 1836, and the 1836 figure more than doubled by 1854, the date when accurate coal statistics began.

Deeper shafts were sunk to reach lower seams of coal. By the end of the eighteenth century, wooden props were being used to support the roofs of the galleries in the mines, instead of leaving pillars of unworked coal. But, because of the cheapness of child labour, boys and girls were still employed in coal-mines: some dragging the trucks of coal through the low, narrow tunnels, others crouching for hours in the dark by the side of the trap doors which they had to open and shut as the trucks passed. It was not until many years later that reformers denounced the hardships endured by these children, and steps were taken (in 1842) to forbid work underground for females of any age and boys under ten.

Modern Developments

Since then governments have ceaselessly tried to improve safety and working conditions in the mines. An important law in 1850 established the principle of control, by officially listing coal-mining as a dangerous trade and requiring all mines to be inspected. Miners' earnings were next safeguarded against fraud by an Act of 1860 which gave them the right "at their own cost to station a person (being one of the persons for the time being

Sketch by sub-commissioner, reproduced from 1st Report of the Children's Employment Commissioners: Mines and Collieries (Cmd., 21st April 1842): "Hurriers at Elland Colliery (near Halifax) being drawn up cross-lapped upon the clatch-iron. As soon as they arrived at the top the handle was made fast by a bolt drawn from the upright post; the woman then grasped a hand of both at the same time, and by main force brought them to land. The corve [coal-container which the children 'hurried' along the underground workings] on these occasions is detached from the hooks to render the load lighter."

Hauling up child workers from a coal-mine

employed) to take account of the weight measure or gauge of coal", and the position of check-weighman, as he is called, was strengthened by two later laws. An Act of 1872 raised the age at which boys might be employed to twelve years; it was again raised in 1900 to thirteen years; in 1911 to fourteen years; and in 1944 to fifteen (to be raised later to sixteen). An act of 1881 gave the Home Secretary the right to hold inquiries into the causes of accidents in mines, while another Act in 1896 regulated the use of explosives in blasting. The record of beneficial legislation is almost endless. But even at the present day, though it is no longer ill-paid or un-regulated, the work of the miner at the coal face continues to be hard, cramped, dirty, and above all dangerous.

Up to the First World War our output of coal grew continu-ously, though as early as 1865 a well-known economist (Professor Stanley Jevons) had written a gloomy book on *The Coal Question*, i.e. what was to happen when it was all used up. But in the first ten years of the twentieth century the annual total was 242 million tons, about four times the figure for the 1850's, and this was sufficient to provide both for all our own needs and for three-quarters of the total weight of British exports to all destinations. Well might Kipling write, as he did:

> *Oh where are you going to, all you Big Steamers,*
> *With England's own coal, up and down the salt seas?*
> *We are going to fetch you your bread and your butter,*
> *Your beef, pork and mutton, eggs, apples, and cheese.*

II

THE STORY OF THE STEAM-ENGINE

THE steam-engine was the key invention which made the Industrial Revolution possible, and after a century and a half is still one of our main sources of power: even in the days of jet aircraft the steam locomotive seems to keep its fascination. Let us trace the story from the beginning—a long story, since the wet, white cloud we wrongly call "steam" must have attracted attention as soon as early man placed the first pot of water on the first fire. What is popularly called "steam" is really the little drops of water condensed from steam by the cooler air surrounding it, steam itself being an invisible gaseous substance which is formed when water changes into vapour. Steam expands, that is, it takes up more room than water. When the water in a kettle boils and turns into steam, the lid of the kettle begins to shake and rattle—because the steam is expanding. It is this expanding power of steam that has made it so useful to mankind.

Nearly 2,000 years ago a Greek named Hero, living in Alexandria, who had invented a number of curious machines, experimented in the use of steam. He placed water in a globe with an opening at the top; in the opening were two tubes. When the water was heated the steam passed out through the tubes and kept a ball turning round and round on two pivots. This apparatus was just a curious toy, but it showed that steam might be made to do work.

Through the centuries men continued to experiment with steam, trying to make it useful. In the seventeenth century an Italian physician named Branca, and a French scientist named Papin made useful experiments. Papin discovered a way of using steam in a cylinder, so that none of its power was lost. But it was not until 1698 that an English military engineer named Thomas Savery made use of steam for an important practical purpose.

75

At that time the coal-miners (as stated in the last chapter), having worked out many of the seams of coal near the surface, were trying to reach lower seams. As they dug deeper into the earth water collected in the pits and there was danger of flooding. Savery invented what he called a "fire engine" for pumping water out of mines by filling a cylinder with steam, condensing the steam by means of cold water so that there was a vacuum, or space, in the cylinder, and then allowing the cylinder to fill with water by means of the pressure of the air. This engine was called the "Miners' Friend" because it drained the pit without the hard work of pumping by hand and baling with buckets. Several of Savery's engines were set up in mines, and enabled miners to work at a greater depth; but the engines were slow and used a lot of coal.

In 1711 Savery's original patent was improved by his partner, Thomas Newcomen of Dartmouth, an ironmonger or blacksmith by trade. His first engine was used in a coal-mine, where they were most needed; they were also used in the Cornish tin-mines. They had many faults, and were wasteful of fuel, but remained in use for over seventy years—especially in coal-mines, where fuel consumption was of no importance—and during that time doubled the depth to which the miners could go. A Newcomen engine developed $5\frac{1}{2}$ h.p., and it could raise 50 gallons of water a minute from a depth of 156 feet, which seemed no small achievement—until Watt set to work on it.

James Watt

James Watt (1736–1819) was a largely self-educated young Scotsman who was employed as mathematical instrument-maker to the University of Glasgow. He had already interested himself in the subject of the steam-engine when, in 1764, he was given a model of a Newcomen engine to repair. He became absorbed in its improvement, and after many failures he succeeded in making a model for an engine which would be greatly superior to Newcomen's.

But Watt had neither the money, nor the materials, nor the workmen to make a full-size engine which he could show to mine-owners and others, and no one in Glasgow took any interest in the scheme. At last Watt found a patron in Dr. John Roebuck, who in 1759 had opened the first big Scottish iron works at Carron in Stirlingshire, where the famous guns called carronades were later produced. An engine was built at Carron, but at that time there were no tools accurate enough for such work. The result was disappointing, and as Roebuck was now suffering heavy losses in his own business, he could not afford further interest in Watt and his engine. Watt was in despair. He decided to give up engines, and take a job as surveyor of a new canal that was being made. His work brought him to Birmingham, where he met Matthew Boulton, the head of the prosperous Soho Engineering Works housed in a fine new building at Handsworth, which was later (1802) to be the first large building ever lit by gas. Boulton was a keen business man, and he agreed to take Watt into partnership. The engine, which had been first patented in 1769, was brought to the

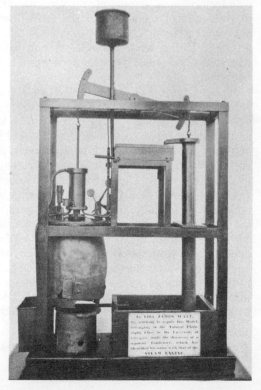

The model of Newcomen's engine which was given to James Watt for repair in 1764. It had recently been put in order by a London instrument-maker; Watt saw that, given the existing wasteful method of generating steam, the boiler was too small for the cylinder

Soho Works, where the workmen were more skilful than those at Carron, and it was soon functioning well.

The Boulton-Watt partnership, which began to operate in 1775, was indeed an event of great importance in the development of the steam engine. For behind the inventive genius of Watt it put the solid business ability and established position of Boulton. Matthew Boulton (1728–1809) was himself an outstanding man. He had succeeded to his father's business of silver-stamping, but he had gone on to build up a considerable engineering works with six hundred workmen, making metal articles of various kinds— perhaps the largest hardware business of the time. He was quick to realize the possibilities of development in Watt's early engine, for even in 1776, when the biographer Boswell visited the Soho works, Boulton declared: "I sell here, Sir, what all the world desires to have—Power." Later Boulton used steam power in coining, and produced coins for the East India Company and a copper coinage for Great Britain. He took interest in scientific and literary matters, and was a Fellow of the Royal Society. When Boulton and Watt retired, eventually, in 1800, they handed over the business to their sons, whom they had taken care to have well educated—and so the partnership went on in the names of Boulton and Watt.

Watt's engine was from the outset a great improvement on Newcomen's, because it had a separate condenser: when steam was generated in a cylinder which could be kept continuously hot and condensed in a condenser which could be kept continuously cool, the result was a machine of greater power and lower fuel costs. Late in 1775, the first Watt engine to be sold was at work in a colliery near Birmingham, and a second was on order for John Wilkinson's blast furnaces at Broseley in Staffordshire. Soon they were being sent to the Cornish tin-mines, where within ten years they had replaced all but one of the old wasteful Newcomen engines. But these engines were only an improved form of pump: in flat country they were sometimes used as part of a water-mill, pumping back the water that had turned the wheel. The next step was to make an engine with a rotary motion which could drive machinery for all purposes. With the help of his foreman, William Murdock, Watt solved this problem. Moreover, in the next year,

One of Watt's
first engines,
photographed
still in use in
1862

1782, he patented "a double-action expansive working engine",
in which the piston was worked up *and down* by steam, a great improvement on the earlier engines in which the piston fell by its own
weight.

The engine could now be adopted for general use in iron
works, for forge-engines and bellows in blast furnaces, and
for use in the sheet-iron rolling mills. In these mills, water-
power had been used, but steam proved a great advantage,
especially in severe winters, as a letter from Boulton to Watt
shows: "There is not a single water-mill at work in Staffordshire,"
he wrote, "they are all frozen up, and were it not for Wilkinson's
steam-mill, the poor nailers must have perished; but his mill goes
on rolling and splitting ten tons of iron a day, which is carried
away as fast as it can be bundled up; and thus the employment

and subsistence of these poor people are secured." The new engines were also adopted in some potteries, breweries, flour-mills, and—from 1785 onwards—in spinning factories. "The people of Manchester are steam-mill mad," wrote Boulton to Watt. Steam-power began to take the place of water-power, and mills and factories built on the banks of streams were deserted in favour of new premises in towns where coal was cheap.

But we must not be tempted to exaggerate. By 1800 Boulton and Watt's Soho works had produced more than fifty steam-engines and the steady growth of the coal and iron industries made it easy to provide the material to make and work more of them. Nevertheless, in 1830 the go-ahead cotton factories still used 30 per cent of water power, and all the industries of Birmingham, where steam-engines were first built, required only a dozen new ones a year—in 1826, for instance, thirteen, averaging $12\frac{1}{2}$ h.p. For the early steam-engine was a hand-made, individual machine: there were no standard spare parts to be had; and when it developed a fault (a fairly frequent occurrence), the men to repair it must be sent for from the original makers. These men who understood steam-engines—successors to the millwrights who used to mend the old water-driven corn-mills—were not numerous: not till the middle of the nineteenth century did they come to form a regular trade of skilled engineers. In the meantime the manufacture of standard steam-engines had gradually become possible with the development of machine tools.

The Earliest Steamboats

The next chapter in the story of the steam-engine was to make it useful on the water. Boats were rowed by oars; ships were moved by the power of the wind in their sails. Rowing was hard work; sails were useless if there was no wind, or if the wind was blowing in a completely contrary direction. In some parts of the world at certain seasons there was hardly a breath of wind, and ships might lie becalmed, unable to move for days, even weeks. When a steam-engine could be made to move a boat or a ship, that would be a great advantage.

The earliest experiments culminated in a paddle-wheel steamboat, which was used to tow barges on the Forth and Clyde Canal in 1801–2. This was seen by the American, Robert Fulton, who took one of Watt's engines home with him to America, and in 1807 was steaming up the Hudson River at nearly 5 m.p.h. The first successful British steamboat was the *Comet*,[1] which was built on the River Clyde in 1812, and made regular trips between Glasgow and Greenock. When the first steamboat appeared on the Thames many people disliked it—"It is strange to hear and see it hissing and roaring, foaming and spouting like an angry whale"—but they were already four in number by 1814. The early steamships were small and the coal took up too much space; they were preferred to sailing-ships chiefly in river navigation and ferry services, such as that maintained by the Dover-Calais steam packets, which began to run in 1821. As late as 1847 sailing-ships made up 96 per cent of the British mercantile marine, and iron was still a novelty in shipbuilding (as we shall see) long after it had set its stamp upon the whole life of the age.

[1] See illustration p. 95

12

THE NEW IRON AGE

It has been claimed that iron comes second only to the air we breathe and the water we drink in the list of substances essential to the life of modern men. Iron is so plentiful—about 1 cwt. of it, we are told, to every ton of the earth's crust—that we easily forget our dependence upon its use for nearly every kind of building and machinery, cutting-tool and magnet. But when we look back to early history, we readily divide the Ages of Stone and Bronze from the Iron Age when men first used implements and weapons of iron. It would be just as reasonable to make a further division at the time of the Industrial Revolution, when iron first became adaptable to its innumerable modern uses, and to say that after about 1800 civilized man was living in a New Iron Age.

The smelting of iron was carried on in Roman Britain, and throughout the Middle Ages. For smelting the iron ore, charcoal continued to be used till the middle of the eighteenth century. Smelting was a local industry to be found in various wooded districts, because it was easier to carry the ore to the forests than to carry timber to the iron-fields. The most important iron-smelting districts were the Wood or Weald of Kent and Sussex, the Forest of Dean, and the Wrekin district of Shropshire. As Kipling sings:

> Out of the Weald, the secret Weald,
> Men sent in ancient years
> The horse-shoes red at Flodden Field,
> The arrows of Poitiers.

During the Tudor period and afterwards, when timber was needed for shipbuilding, several Acts of Parliament were passed to check the cutting down of trees for iron-making and these Acts greatly reduced iron production. A cheap and effective substitute was now obviously needed for the use of charcoal in smelting the ore. In 1619 an ironmaster named Dud Dudley began experiments, but for various reasons he was not successful; his iron works were attacked and wrecked by jealous charcoal burners. The iron industry was in fact hampered by lack of cheap fuel until the middle of the eighteenth century. Abraham Darby of Coalbrookdale in Shropshire discovered about the year 1707 that, if the coal was first turned into coke, it could replace charcoal in the high-temperature furnace used for smelting. But for various reasons the secret did not get out into the trade until the days of the original Abraham Darby's grandson of the same name, about 1760. By that time the coking process could be worked under more favourable conditions, because engines, driven first by water-power and then by steam, were becoming available to produce a strong blast in the furnaces.

The production of iron and steel involves many processes. First, the metal must be extracted from the ore, which comprises other substances. This is done by smelting in a furnace; in order to obtain the great heat necessary, a blast of air is forced through coke, ore and limestone; hence the name "blast furnace". Iron ore smelted in a blast furnace with coke and limestone becomes pig iron, the raw material from which cast iron, wrought iron and steel are made. The use to which the iron is to be put determines its subsequent treatment. If cast iron is required, the "pigs" are re-melted in a foundry, and poured into moulds. To make malleable or wrought iron, the "pigs" must be heated and elaborately hammered in a forge. For steel, a still more elaborate process of reheating is needed to get rid of impurities and a proportion of carbon must be added, making true steel very costly. Cast iron is hard but brittle; wrought iron is soft but holds together; steel is strong and tough.

Abraham Darby's process applied only to the first stage of the iron industry, the smelting of the ore into pig iron. But there was greater demand for wrought iron, and this required refining—a process which used more charcoal than smelting had done until Henry Cort, a Lancashire man, discovered a cheaper method. In 1783 Cort planned a method of rolling out the iron by passing it between a series of rollers, instead of beating it with heavy hammers while still in a molten condition. The next year he perfected the use of the reverberatory furnace, invented twenty years earlier, in which the only contact between the fuel and the metal was the flame beating down on the pig iron, which was held in a basin-like container at the bottom of the furnace. Workmen used long poles to stir or "puddle" the molten iron to drive out impurities. The metal was then taken to the rolling mills in large balls weighing about eighty pounds each. The use of the reverberatory furnace at last enabled coal to be used instead of charcoal.

One of the difficulties of the eighteenth-century ironmasters was to obtain an effective blast to maintain the heat in the furnaces. At Coalbrookdale and other early iron works a water-wheel was used to strengthen the draught. Then Smeaton attempted to solve the problem with the help of blowing-cylinders, which were introduced at Carron about 1768. Next, Watt's steam-engine was employed by Wilkinson in 1776 for working the bellows in a blast furnace; this, as we have seen, was a few years before it was adapted for working forge-hammers and to provide power for the rolling and slitting mills. Finally, a Scot, a collier's engine-worker named James Neilson, suggested heating the blast before it entered the furnace. The "hot blast" (patented in 1828) proved a great success; it cut down the consumption of coal by one-quarter, thus further reducing the cost of production.

When the use of coal was possible for all processes of the iron industry, the ironworks ceased to be located in the woodlands, and were established on coal-fields, as in Yorkshire, South Wales, South Staffordshire, and the valley of the Clyde. The last charcoal smelting furnace was extinguished in 1827. The cost of manufacture was lessened, and Britain was able to produce all the iron needed for her own use and a surplus for export, instead of having to import pig iron from as far afield as the Urals, which had been her position earlier. Between 1788 and 1830 the total output of pig iron, the raw material of the iron manufactures, was multiplied tenfold.

New Uses of Iron

The use of iron for various purposes rapidly increased. Iron rails were laid down for the tramways at the collieries as early as 1767. By 1840 iron was even coming into use to build sea-going vessels. Iron was needed for the machinery in the new mills, and later for steam engines. The perfecting of cast-iron production enabled iron to be employed for domestic purposes; it was cheaper than copper, bronze, brass, or pewter; it was more easily handled than stone or wood. But these developments, and the kind of enterprise which made them possible, can perhaps be illustrated best from the career of the greatest of all the eighteenth-century ironmasters.

John Wilkinson, born in 1728, the son of a labourer in a Cumberland village, is said to have founded the family fortunes while still a boy by inventing a box-iron for laundry work, which his father patented. Next he developed the first accurate metal-cutting tool for large-scale work—a hollow, cylindrical boring bar, mounted on bearings. This was valuable for cannon and also to give precision to the steam-engines with which Watt was then experimenting. At Broseley in Staffordshire in 1776–80 he equipped himself for the large-scale manufacture of iron by introducing four of Boulton and Watt's engines to blow the bellows. This helped to make the fortunes of both firms, for Wilkinson became a regular supplier of cylinders for the engines of which Boulton and Watt became "designers and erectors". He also made 32-pounder cannon and howitzers for the government. In 1779 he built the first iron bridge, with a 100-foot span, across the Severn at Broseley—an elegant structure, well suited to figure in an engraving "by permission most respectfully inscribed" to King George III —and sent his munitions down the river in the first iron barge. He cast all the ironwork for the Paris waterworks and erected the first steam-engine in France; he built a Methodist chapel of iron. His nickname, "Iron-mad Wilkinson", is usually associated with his wish to be buried in an iron coffin; but a better illustration of his enthusiasm and single-mindedness (qualities which shaped the careers of many of his fellow-industrialists as well) is the tradition that Wilkinson never wrote a letter without a mention of iron.

The Cast Iron Bridge over the River Severn. Plate dedicated to
King George III by the Coalbrooke Dale Company, 1782

Steel

Fine steel, used mainly for weapons, cutting implements, and
small fittings, such as watch-springs, was not made in England
before the seventeenth century, when Sheffield began the manufacture of shear-steel, chiefly from very pure Swedish iron. The
first step towards the improvement of English steel production
was taken by Benjamin Huntsman in the middle of the eighteenth
century. Huntsman was a Sheffield clock-maker, who had difficulty in obtaining steel of a suitable quality for his work. In 1740
he succeeded in producing steel of a uniform quality by remelting
the shear-steel in clay pots, known as crucibles, subjecting it and
a small admixture of carbon to great heat, and so freeing it from
slag. The best steel is still made in crucibles, but the process was
too costly for general use, and a century passed before steel production was developed by further invention. The new iron age
was then succeeded by the age of cheap steel, in which we are still
living.

Engineering

With the revolution in textiles and the invention of machinery, with the development of the steam-engine and the growth of the iron industry, there went the development of engineering. It is rather difficult to say exactly what an engineer is. In America he is the driver of a train; in this country he may be anything from the man who repairs a motor car or wireless set to a highly trained scientist who has specialized in engineering. In the early days of machinery three trades supplied the men who undertook engineering jobs—clock-makers and instrument-makers; millwrights, who set up and repaired the machines in the textile factories and worked at first with wood and water power; military engineers, who understood cannon, siege works, and something of roads and canals.

Basic to the development of engineering was the machine-tool industry. The machine tool is a mechanically-driven tool which is employed to make the parts of other machines, and since these parts are machine-made they can be standardized. A skilled workman using a machine tool can make any number of parts of the same size. Except for the boring-machine mentioned above, Boulton and Watt had no such tools; they had to depend on hand tools, though they improved on some of these.

Joseph Bramah (1748–1814), working in London, devised some machine tools to use in making his patent locks, and he also invented an hydraulic press. He trained Henry Maudslay, who about 1800 perfected a self-acting lathe. Whereas previously a worker had had to hold the cutting or shaping tool against the work, now the tool was fixed in a rest and adjusted to the work. Maudslay also made a very accurate measuring machine, which led to yet finer work on the lathe. Such machine tools came into common use in the 1820's and enabled precise work to be done. Indeed, they were essential to the development of engines. "How", asked Nasmyth later, "how could we have good steam engines, if we had no means of boring a true cylinder or of turning a true piston-rod, or of planeing a valve face?"

James Nasmyth was trained by Maudslay, and set up for himself in Manchester in 1834. Five years later he invented his steam-hammer, which cheapened the production of wrought iron and made it possible to forge larger machine parts, such as the paddle-wheel shafts which were beginning to be required for steamships. His contemporary, Joseph Whitworth, also worked as a machine-tool maker in Manchester. He devised various standard sizes for machine parts, for example, for screws. Thus parts became interchangeable, and the supply of spare parts was made possible.

So it was that the making of tools became an industry in itself—the machine-tool industry. "Tools", it was said in 1841, "have introduced a revolution in machinery and tool-making has become a distinct branch of mechanics and a very important trade, although twenty years ago it was scarcely known." And with the machine tools, the machine makers were able to provide the machines and the engines required in ever-increasing numbers as the industrialization of the country went on. Machine-making also became more specialized. In the early days mill-owners had had to make their own textile machines before they could start to manufacture. But with the provision of machine tools, firms were established in the textile districts which specialized in making textile machinery.

Thus by about 1841 it was possible to distinguish three main types of engineers. There were the makers of heavy machinery, steam-engines, mill gearing, and hydraulic presses; the makers of the machine tools; and the makers of the textile machines. Engineers were employed by railway and steamship companies to construct the locomotives and the marine engines, and engineers of some kind worked also for contractors, and in the mills and mines to look after and repair machinery. In a country with growing industry engineering was a growing profession, and as industry developed in foreign countries there were also many opportunities for British engineers abroad.

13

CHANGES IN OTHER INDUSTRIES: POTTERY AND SHIPS

We have now seen the big changes which transformed the textile industries, transport, agriculture, and the manufactures based on coal and iron. But the same period witnessed similar, if less dramatic, changes in other branches of industry. Let us examine one or two of these before we pass on to consider, in the next section of our book, the new ways of living to which all these changes led.

The Potteries, that is the six North Staffordshire towns which have been united in recent times to form the city of Stoke-on-Trent, owe the rise of their speciality very largely to the coming of the canals to that part of the country, as already mentioned. For it was the clay industry of Cornwall which supplied the material for the potters. In old days, drinking-mugs and plates for ordinary use were made sometimes of horn, or of wood, or of pewter (the grey alloy of tin and lead) which has lately come back into fashion. Cups and saucers were not needed until coffee and tea first came to be drunk in England in Stuart times, and they were then imported from China by the East India Company. But coarse earthenware pots and jars were already being made in north Staffordshire, where there were supplies of black clay and terra-cotta which baked into a buff or reddish-brown colour. There was also plenty of brushwood there for fuel.

Like spinning and weaving, pottery was at first a cottage industry. Nearly every garden in the Potteries had its oven made of turf with a roof of boughs, and heated with charcoal, where they could bake such things as the large jars, in which at that time butter was sent from farms to shops in London and other cities. Packmen came round the Staffordshire villages each week to collect the jars and pots to be sold elsewhere.

At Bow and Chelsea there were potteries which tried to imitate the porcelain which came from China. The potters of Germany had already discovered that the secret of this fine ware lay in the material used for its manufacture: and in time they found deposits of the right kind of clay in Saxony. English potters at first used a mixture of pipe clay, sand from the Isle of Wight, and glass. But a great discovery was made about 1768 by William Cookworthy, a Plymouth druggist, when he decided that Cornish clay (kaolin) and china-stone were the materials the English potters needed to enable them to produce the fine kind of earthenware or "china" known as porcelain. Cookworthy took out a patent and set up a china factory, but it was not a great success, and in 1777 his porcelain rights were bought by a Staffordshire firm with works at Stoke-on-Trent.

The discovery of the china clay opened up a new industry for Cornwall, and in time the quarrying gave employment to many former tin-miners; but the absence of coal in Cornwall prevented the setting-up of Cornish potteries on a large scale. The clay was therefore sent by sea to Chester, and later to Liverpool, and then conveyed laboriously overland to Staffordshire. The quarrying and preparation of china clay is still one of the great industries of Cornwall. It is not only sent to Staffordshire, but is exported to America and elsewhere from Falmouth and other west-country ports. Cornish clay is now also used in some other manufactures besides pottery.

In Staffordshire, in the latter half of the eighteenth century, many changes took place. New methods of glazing were introduced. The white Cornish clay was used to make a thin layer over the local clay, so that the ware came out of the ovens smooth and white. The increase in the use of tea and coffee, and in the number of coffee-houses opened in London and elsewhere, had led to a great demand for cups and saucers, and Staffordshire potters began making these in quantity. More ovens were built, but the supply of brushwood was not sufficient. Fortunately there were coal seams close at hand, and the potters were able to fetch sacks of coal to feed their ovens. But as time went on, machinery and new methods made the old ways of working out-of-date, though the potter's wheel was still worked by hand—in fact, there is still some hand-decoration of the more expensive products, even in the twentieth century. Instead of working in their own little sheds, the men had now to work for a master-potter for a weekly wage. The industry kept the coal-miners busy, and attracted to north Staffordshire various craftsmen, who made crates, sieves, and other things needed in the potteries.

Transport was the most difficult problem the early master-potters had to face. The Cornish clay brought by sea to Chester or Liverpool had in the early days to be carried across country by pack-horses to Stoke-on-Trent and Burslem, and the finished goods were carried by pot-wagons along the roads to the River Trent or the River Severn and thence distributed to other parts of the country. But Brindley's Grand Trunk Canal, begun in 1762, joined the Cheshire town of Runcorn on the Mersey to the Trent, and thus solved the problem of transport. We can now see how it came about that the first sod was cut by Josiah Wedgwood, the greatest master-potter of the eighteenth century, as one of the main investors in the canal scheme.

Wedgwood

Josiah Wedgwood (1730–95), was the son of a Burslem potter and himself started work at ten. He became highly skilled at shaping pottery on the wheel, and it was he who perfected the fine art of English pottery. In the course of a most successful career, he built a large earthenware factory together with a village for the work people at a place near Burslem, which he named Etruria because of his special interest in the reproduction of classical designs recovered from graves in Italy. Wedgwood discovered and invented many improvements and machines for mixing clay, and for modelling and glazing of china. He engaged clever artists, such as the famous Flaxman, to decorate his fine wares; but he also insisted on careful work in the manufacture of ordinary domestic earthenware, so that the simplest articles were well shaped and finished. One of the improvements was to give a clean white finish instead of a dirty yellow. Wedgwood was not without rivals— Spode, for instance, who, like Wedgwood, became potter to King George III—and famous wares were established outside the

Potteries area at Derby and Worcester. But from his Etruria works came a vast variety of goods. As a result, the use of earthenware—"common Wedgwood"—became general in English homes, while large quantities were exported to European countries and to America.

Wedgwood's Etruria factory, opened on 13th June 1769 and sited so as to adjoin the projected Grand Trunk Canal. Typical pot kilns can be seen on the extreme right of the engraving.

Wedgwood himself was a real character. It was said that he used to stump around his works, and smash any article which did not satisfy him. On the bench alongside he would chalk: "This won't do for Josiah Wedgwood." He worked tirelessly to raise standards, both by experiment in new methods and by trying to turn workmen who were sometimes drunken and lazy into skilled hands. He was very active in promoting turnpike roads as well as canals, and by these means he helped to reduce costs of transport and also loss by breakage. He also tried to raise social standards by starting and encouraging schools and chapels, and took much interest in public affairs. He was a man of cultural and intellectual interests, and a Fellow of the Royal Society: members of his family have been well known in public life down to our own time. His name indeed became a household word, as his pottery and that of other English potters went all over the world. A traveller in the early nineteenth century reported that, all over Europe, "one is served at every inn upon English ware".

New Types of Ships

Shipbuilding was another of the industries for which inventive minds (such as "Iron-mad" Wilkinson's) suggested improvements, and it was another of the cases in which there was an obvious need for new development at this time. For under the Navigation Laws, which dated back to the time of Oliver Cromwell and partly even to the Middle Ages, it was in the main compulsory for British trade to be carried on by ships which were built, owned, and manned in British territory. There was also an expansion of the Royal Navy as a result of the wars against the French, especially the Revolutionary and Napoleonic Wars of 1793–1815, and the need for a special kind of ship in the growing trade with India— one that could carry the maximum of cargo on that long, expensive voyage and yet defend itself, if necessary, from attack in distant oceans.

By the end of the eighteenth century the oak-built ship had reached its greatest size. The ships of the East India Company, the finest merchant vessels afloat, were about 1,000 tons, while Nelson's flagship, the *Victory*, was just over 2,000 tons—one-fortieth of the size of the largest Atlantic liners to-day. About 1760 it had been found an advantage to fasten sheets of copper to the outside of the ships below the water-line to give the ships greater speed. The copper did not become fouled by crusts of seaweed and shell-fish, nor was it eaten by the Toredo worm as was the case with the wooden hulls of earlier ships; thus the vessels could move more easily through the water. Copper was expensive, but it did not need periodic scrapings. Moreover, the supply of timber for shipbuilding (like the wood for producing charcoal) was rapidly becoming used up, and shipbuilders began to experiment with the use of iron fittings to replace certain natural shapes of timber.

This was the beginning of a great change. The mixture of wood and metal was followed in due course by the all-iron hull which made it possible to build much larger ships. As early as 1787 iron boats were built in north Lancashire for use on canals, and a small iron ship was built near Glasgow in 1818. Many people thought iron ships would never be possible. How could iron be expected to float? Yet, strange as it may seem, an iron vessel did not weigh as much as a wooden one. Strong iron frames were only one-third the thickness of wooden ones—only four inches thick, while those of a wooden vessel had to be twelve inches thick. This gave the ship more room for stowing cargo and shipbuilders were therefore encouraged to use iron, though the Royal Navy (because of the deadly effects when iron plates were splintered in action) used only wood as late as the Crimean War.

Early in the nineteenth century, as we noticed in an earlier chapter, experiments were being made with steamships. But these first steamships were wide and clumsily shaped. They were driven by paddle-wheels, one on either side, but if the vessel rolled in rough weather, one wheel might be wasting energy by beating the air. In 1823 the General Steam Navigation Company was founded at Deptford, and other passenger lines followed; but steamship-building continued to be a small and uncertain business. For, while the early experiments in steam navigation were being made, shipbuilders were working on a newer and faster type of sailing ship, the clipper. Clippers, with fine lines almost like those of yachts, were first built in America, and when they appeared in British waters, notably the Thames and Mersey, British ship-owners were aroused to compete against these American rivals for the carrying trade. The first British tea-clipper was built in 1850, and until 1870 this remained the fastest type of vessel afloat. Sailing-ships of all kinds, making their voyages from London and the Clyde and Liverpool to every port in the world, were still the standard cargo vessels of the mid-nineteenth century.

The Shipyards

Shipbuilding on a small scale was carried on all round the coast in any convenient port or estuary, but the main centres in the eighteenth century were on the banks of the Thames and on

The steamship *Comet* (1812), which in favourable weather conveyed passengers between Glasgow and Greenock rather faster than the coach

Tyneside. On the Tyne, for instance, the work had originated in a very small way with the construction of shallow-draught boats, called "keels" (as in the famous song), which were used to carry coal down the river to sea-going vessels off the coast. Later, coastal colliers were built, and finally still larger and more ambitious types of vessel, the iron and steel of the modern shipyard being readily available there. Plymouth, Portsmouth, and Chatham were concerned only with the construction or repair of the ships of the Royal Navy.

For the first new developments we must turn to the Clyde, where the first British steamship, the *Comet*, was built by Bell in 1812. This was the start of an enterprise, based on the accessibility of coal and iron, which in time made shipbuilding rather than the cotton manufacture the premier industry of Glasgow; the manufacture of iron steamers was established there as early as 1841. Another new centre was Birkenhead, which made the first iron paddle-steamer ever seen in America, and in shipbuilding rapidly out-distanced Liverpool. As for London, it was not until 1835 that iron shipbuilding was started by William Fairbairn (1789–1874), a brilliant Scottish engineer who migrated from Manchester. His yard was at Millwall, in between the West and East India docks. But Fairbairn had to face much conservative opposition, and although he built about a hundred iron ships of different sizes, in the end he turned his attention to bridge- and boiler-making instead. Thus shipbuilding is an interesting example of an industry where the new inventions were applicable but, for a long time at least, were only slowly and fitfully applied.

In conclusion, we may notice two special features. Shipbuilding was a business which required much capital, to buy the raw material and pay for the long and elaborate processes of construction. It therefore had, almost from the first, big employers of labour, such as Sir John Laird (1805–74), who in the first half of the nineteenth century practically created modern Birkenhead. On the other hand, as soon as ships came to be of any considerable size, a large number of workers were necessarily employed together in the building, with the result that shipwrights, as they were called, were one of the first crafts to form strong trade unions. The clash between big employers and the trade unions, beginning in the shipyards as early as 1825, will be noticed in a later chapter.

Ports and Docks

The expansion of British shipping called for an expansion of port and dock facilities. The modern port systems, with their channels of approach, docks and landing quays, were a nineteenth-century creation.

London by 1800 badly needed docks. During the eighteenth century about three-quarters of imports into England passed through London, so that the Thames became congested with the fleets of merchant ships, and much of their cargo used to lie on the wharves out in the open. The first modern dock was the West India Dock, which was opened in 1802. Within five years this was followed by the opening of two more docks—the London and the East India—on the north bank of the Thames, and the Surrey Commercial Docks on the south bank. The last named occupied the site of the old Greenland Dock, used in earlier centuries by whalers. Further evidence of the pressure of trade demands is given by the fact that within two decades Telford was at work constructing St. Katherine's Docks, immediately below the modern Tower Bridge. The docks were built by joint stock com-panics, which charged dues for their use and for the use of the adjoining warehouses.

Each of the leading provincial ports developed a similar system. Hull built its first dock on the site of its ancient fortifications in 1774. Liverpool, as we might expect from what we already know of its rapid commercial growth in the eighteenth century, began early, its first dock being opened in 1715, a second in 1753. In the case of Bristol, on the other hand, where the Dock Company was incorporated in 1803, high dock charges are regarded as an important cause for its loss of trade to Liverpool.

Safety Measures

Danger has never been far away on the seas, and therefore measures were sought to safeguard both the cargoes and the lives of the crews. At the end of the seventeenth century London merchants had the habit of meeting at Lloyd's coffee-house. Here they developed methods of insuring ships and cargoes. At first informal, the meetings of merchants led to an association, which eventually became the world-famous insurance organization of to-day. By the end of the eighteenth century Lloyd's had a general form of insurance policy, and was issuing information on the movements of ships; about that time, or a little later, Lloyd's was keeping a classified register of shipping—a valuable indication to shippers of the seaworthiness of merchant vessels.

From an early date the need had been realized for lights to warn ships at night of danger spots. The exact origin of Trinity House is unknown, but a religious guild for mariners existed in the Middle Ages, and received a charter from Henry VIII; it was soon responsible for various maritime duties concerning lights and buoys. Later on, the Corporation of Trinity House gradually took over control of privately owned lighthouses and built some new ones. Between 1800 and 1830 it was busily engaged in setting up new lights round the English coast, in active competition with a newly established authority for Scotland, the poetically named Commissioners of the Northern Lights. In 1836 an Act of Parliament empowered it to purchase rights over coastal lights from the Crown and from private owners. The expense of building and working lighthouses the Corporation covered by the tolls levied on ships, but control over these dues was transferred in 1853 to the Board of Trade. The courageous efforts of lighthouse-builders is well illustrated by the story of the successive Eddystone light-houses, built on the Eddystone rocks fourteen miles from Plymouth. The first was built in 1698 and a few years later was destroyed in a storm, its builder being drowned; the second was built in 1709 but was destroyed by a fire; the third was built by Smeaton in 1759, but its foundations showed signs of weakening later on, in the nineteenth century. Trinity House decided on a new structure, and the present lighthouse was completed in 1882.

From time to time some fearful wreck on the coasts would arouse public feeling for seamen. Lieut.-Col. Sir William Hillary, who lived in the Isle of Man and had seen many a wreck on its shores, put forward a plan which resulted in the foundation in 1824 of the Royal National Lifeboat Institution. This has proved a grand example of a voluntary charitable organization. It soon began to place life-boats at danger spots on the coast, as did also some private individuals and other societies. Experiments were made with different types of life-boat, and a policy developed for rewarding the life-boatmen for their dangerous services and paying pensions to the families bereaved by accident. The R.N.L.I. has grown into a large organization, but is still maintained by voluntary contributions.

EARLY SOCIAL CHANGES

14

THE FACTORY TOWNS

In the next three chapters we shall look at some of the social changes at the end of the eighteenth and beginning of the nineteenth centuries. These were of course largely the result of the developments in industry and agriculture which have already been described. But in order properly to understand what happened it is important to bear in mind two other main facts governing this period.

One is that it was an age of great wars. In 1775–83 Britain had been fighting, first the American colonists, and then the big European alliance which was formed to help the rebels in America and to win back, if possible, what Britain had gained by her victories in the Seven Years War (1756–63). After the American war had ended in our defeat, there was an interval of barely ten years before the outbreak of the last and greatest of our struggles against France, which lasted with two short intervals for twenty-two years—up to the final overthrow of Napoleon. About the middle of this period it was officially estimated that more than 10 per cent of the male population of military age were under arms; probably one more war-worker would be required for every two fighting-men. Such a situation could not fail to impose a heavy strain both on family life and on industrial organization.

Moreover, the Duke of Wellington's victory at Waterloo marks, not only the climax to a series of great military exploits, but the end also of a great commercial struggle between Britain and France. Napoleon had called England "a nation of shop-keepers", which prompted Pitt's retort that it was also a nation which never lost its martial spirit. Napoleon realized that trade was the life-blood of his main enemy, and he did his best to ruin British commerce by a blockade of British ports. But even Napoleon could not manage without British goods, and British coats, caps and boots for the French army were smuggled into France by way of Hamburg. On the other hand, when the British harvest failed in 1810, and famine was near, Napoleon, anxious to obtain English gold, allowed the export of corn to Britain on payment of an export duty. Thanks to this action, famine was averted. And thanks to the courage and initiative of Nelson and to other British sailors and soldiers, Britain was able to hold her title of "Mistress of the Seas" and to keep her trade routes secure. As our industrial output rose, merchants were able to find markets for their products throughout the world, and although some of the war years had been years of deep depression in trade, others had seen our exports mount to greater heights than ever before in our history.

But a time of war is always a time of hardship for many people: in 1800–13 there were no fewer than five years in which the average price of wheat exceeded 100s. a quarter. This fact encouraged acceptance of the gloomy forecasts made by the Rev. Thomas Robert Malthus in his *Essay on Population*, first published in 1798. He taught that, apart from such special measures as deferment of the age of marriage, the growth of population always tends to outrun the growth of the food supply. Therefore permanent improvement in the standard of living of the masses, however desirable, was quite unfeasible.

This dismal conclusion, widely accepted by the classes to which it was not deemed to apply, connects with the second main fact which governs this period. Britain was fighting against the greatest of revolutionary movements, and this had the effect, from 1793 onwards, of making proposals for any kind of reform very unpopular because they could be denounced as unpatriotic, "the kind of thing we were fighting against". Accordingly, the policy of our government in this period was to refuse to listen to the grievances of the workers (or those who could find no work); to assume that the employer would manage his business best without government interference; and to concentrate on avoiding any possibility of a revolution in Britain by firm measures to check disorder.The panic outlived the war and the downfall of Napoleon. As late as December 1819 repression culminated in the Six Acts. One of these required public meetings to be sanctioned by magistrates; another extended the heavy Stamp Duties imposed on newspapers, so as to put any kind of political periodical out of the workers' reach.

The Factory System

We can now see how it was that the government welcomed the new factories, because they produced the wealth which helped us to beat the French, while it turned a deaf ear to complaints about the new conditions of work and life which factory employment brought with it. There had been attempts at introducing a factory system long before the Industrial Revolution. As early as the reign of Henry VIII, John Winchcombe—"Jack of Newbury"—is said to have employed six hundred workers, men, women and children, in various branches of the cloth manufacture; and other clothiers of that time also set up houses full of looms. But workmen complained bitterly of exploitation by wealthy clothiers; in most rural areas a special Weavers' Act (1555) forbade one man to own many looms; public opinion in general favoured the older system of work done at home. And so the development of the factory system was delayed until the eighteenth century, when conditions favoured important changes in the textile industry. A silk-throwing factory was set up at Derby in 1719, but it was the invention of the water-frame fifty years later which (as we have already seen) made factories essential to the rapid development of cotton spinning.

By 1769 our population, for reasons previously outlined, was almost certainly expanding more rapidly than at any earlier period in modern history. Britain had a growing market for textile goods in foreign and colonial markets overseas; prosperity had resulted in an increased demand at home also, and at the same time clothing was needed for our soldiers and sailors engaged in the recurrent wars in Europe and beyond. This increased demand was more readily met by a system of mass production, and this encouraged the building of mills or factories to house the new machines, and to collect under one roof a large number of workers employed by a single capitalist master or by a partnership or company of capitalists.

The growth of the factory system brought with it two important changes in the capitalist system as it had worked previously, in what is often called the "domestic" stage of industry. In the domestic stage, the capitalist provided the raw material, but not the spinning-wheels or, in most cases, the looms for weaving; he was concerned with the purchase of the raw material and the sale of the finished product rather than with the actual processes of manufacture, which were carried on mainly in the workers' homes. But under the factory system the capitalist employer owned the machines as well as the raw materials; the work was done on his premises; and it became part of his business to study and improve the processes of manufacture. This change clearly made the workers more dependent on the employer than they had been before, and one of the most hated features of factory life was its discipline—the need to start punctually, to work regular hours and to do the job systematically, things which people need not bother about when they worked in the privacy of their own homes.

But at the same time the mustering of so many workers under a factory roof gave opportunity for forming trade unions, and these unions enabled the workers in due course to bargain successfully for better wages and better conditions of employment. Other results of the coming of factories and of new capital into industry, and of increased production, were a cheapening of goods and in the long run a higher standard of living for all. But these advantages lay far in the future. The factory system first grew up, as we have seen, during a period when England was engaged in a series of wars. One consequence was fluctuations in trade and employment from year to year: another was financial crisis, resulting in the suspension of cash payments by the Bank of England (26 February 1797) and the first introduction of income tax. Yet a third was a panic measure, following upon a whole series of Acts of political repression aimed at "revolutionaries", by which the younger Pitt's government forbade the existence of trade unions. These Combination Acts of 1799 and 1800 will be considered later, as they were the starting-point of the history of the modern trade union movement.

The Village Poor

But the actions of the authorities to meet the emergency of the French wars were not all of them repressive. The Berkshire magistrates, when they met at Speenhamland, near Newbury, in 1795, intended at first to establish a minimum wage system for the county under the obsolete Elizabethan Statute of Apprentices. Even the alternative course which they adopted in deference to farming opinion—the "Speenhamland system"—was well intentioned. Berkshire, followed by most of the other counties in southern and eastern England, decided to make up the wages of "every poor and industrious man" to a total sum fixed by the size of his family and the varying cost of a loaf of bread. The dearer the bread, the higher the wage—that was reasonable; what was not reasonable was the undertaking to make up wages, which meant that farmers had no reason to pay a living wage since the smaller wage got a larger addition from the rates. The result was that the rates became a terrible burden on the country, while a great number of farm labourers, though kept from starving, were made to feel that they were a class of paupers, because they were unable to keep themselves and their families by the wages they actually earned. Some of the big farmers began at this time to employ regular gangs of women for hoeing and weeding. This tended to reduce the rates, since the women came from the labourers' families, at the expense of home life and probably of health. The practice was not abolished by law until 1867.

Moreover, the new farming robbed many villagers of the strips of land which had provided much of the family's food supply, and at the same time the money earned by the wife and children at wool-cleaning, carding, and spinning rapidly decreased. The handloom weavers, some of whom were also small-scale farmers, did not suffer appreciably by the competition of power-looms before 1815, but their weekly earnings then fell fast, until in the 1830's and 1840's a whole-time weaver did not earn as much as 10s. a week. Under these new conditions it was difficult to maintain a family, and many villagers drifted reluctantly and by slow stages (in days when there were no railways) to the new factories and mines. It was made easier for them to go because the Law of Settlement had been modified. After 1795 it was illegal to remove a new arrival from a parish until he actually asked for poor relief.

Movement of Population

One of the most striking features of the rise of the factory system was the shifting of population towards the factories of the north and the Midlands. The new industrial areas increased their inhabitants very fast. At the first census in 1801 Manchester was the only town in Great Britain (apart from London) with a population which exceeded 100,000. In the next twenty years Manchester reached 150,000, and four other towns—Glasgow, Edinburgh, Liverpool, Birmingham (in that order)—had risen above the 100,000 mark. Moreover, Edinburgh was the only one of these five which had been of any considerable importance a century before. The very first factories, because they were dependent on water-power, had often been placed at lonely spots in the upper valleys of Pennine streams where the current flowed fastest. But from 1785 onwards the steam-engine had been installed in many spinning-mills, replacing water-driven machinery, and by 1815 it was also beginning to be used for the new power looms. This led to a grouping of factories in large centres where coal was locally mined or otherwise obtainable. At the same time there was an increase in iron production to meet the demands for new machinery, which was now almost entirely of iron to stand the strain of steam power.

Isolated villages on the coal-fields or near the iron furnaces in the north and Midlands rapidly expanded into towns. These districts had been poor and thinly populated and now became rich and crowded, whereas towns in East Anglia and parts of the West

Scene on Thames-side between Lambeth and Vauxhall (*Pictorial Times*, October 1846): "The open sewers are one chief cause of the filth and disease of this locality."

of England—which had prospered under the old domestic system and were far from coal-fields—gradually declined and superfluous villagers moved from many districts. Few people moved long distances—many families went on foot and took their belongings with them. What usually happened was that they ventured to the nearest town or the next county, and it was the districts nearest to each of the industrial areas which contributed most largely to its new industrial population. The Irish travelled farthest but they travelled most easily, crossing the sea for as little as 4d. a head to fill the great ports like Liverpool and Glasgow, and bringing with them from their native land an appallingly low standard of life and aspiration. All too often the Irish made slums where they did not find them, and what they made they perpetuated.

The New Towns

This rapid movement of population led to acute overcrowding. New towns were built without proper supervision. There was in those days no planning of housing development to hinder this expansion: there were no building regulations, no sanitary inspectors, no government control, and indeed very few accepted standards even of decency, to prevent people from living where they chose or how they chose. A man who lost his job or his land in one place had no council house, no unemployment insurance or national assistance to enable him to go on living there. When he found a job in a new place he would welcome the enterprise of builders who ran up jerry-built cottages: for otherwise he would have had literally nowhere to live. And thus there soon arose a very grievous housing problem—as our reformers, of fifty years later, learned when they began to tidy up the towns which the early nineteenth-century had left for later generations.

Men who bought building sites put up as many houses as possible on those sites. The rows of houses were crowded close together; they were even built back to back, in which case through ventilation was impossible and half the rooms had no direct light. There was little attention to drainage, sanitation or water supplies. The building materials were usually of the cheapest quality, and there were special shortages which caused building-work to be scamped during the long war period. Lack of a good water supply was another of the evils of the new towns. Often water was sold: for example, at Hyde near Manchester, the poor people had to pay a shilling a week to water-carriers. "Many of the poor beg water, many steal it," said a witness to a Royal Commission on sanitary conditions in 1842. With this scarcity of water, even for drinking, impure water from stagnant ditches was used for cooking. It must be remembered that many houses—then as now again after two world wars—had to accommodate several families. And in those days of the early factory system, even undrained cellars were often let as separate dwellings.

Two other essentials to health—fresh air and light—were also lacking. The old window-tax, increased in 1784, amounted at one time during the Napoleonic Wars to 8s. for houses with six windows, or less; £1 for seven windows; £1 13s. for eight windows, and so on. To save expense, windows in older buildings were blocked up—as we can still see to-day in some old houses—and when new houses were built the number of windows was reduced as much as possible. Stairways were often without any windows, and were pitch dark at noon. Moreover, the windows in many houses did not open, and there was no inlet for fresh air. Factories, also, were built entirely to suit the work and not the workers. Until 1833 there was no State interference and no factory inspectorate.

The streets of many towns were badly drained and were full of holes. After rain the gutters were flooded with filthy water; and at other times were full of all kinds of decaying refuse. There were no regular scavenging services. Proper sewers did not exist: the drains from the best houses emptied into underground cesspools. It is little wonder that typhus, cholera and other fevers were prevalent, though the arrival of the first great cholera epidemic from Russia in 1831 caused the first local boards of health to be established by Parliament. But as soon as the scare was over they were allowed to lapse. To sum up, between 1815 and 1832 the death rate, which had been falling for about a century, was again on the increase.

How the workers lived was not then regarded as the business of the factory owner or capitalist; in the early years of the factory system, when all was experiment and change, he certainly had enough to do in organizing the output and sale of the factory's products. As the supreme head, he of course decided the hours of work and the rate of wages, though the larger factories had overseers for engaging and dismissing employees, and for keeping the factory hands at work. Again, the factory buildings and equipment were also the concern of the employer; but he normally regarded them from the standpoint of their cheapness and handiness without much consideration for health and safety.

However, while the conditions under which men, women and children of the labouring class worked and lived were in many cases worse than similar families had experienced before the Industrial Revolution, the value of the wages was not. Provided they were not among the unemployed or special groups like the hand-loom weavers, workers after the immediate post-war period, which may be said to have ended with a fall of prices in 1820–21, were on the average better off than the generations before 1793. As for the more limited group of workers employed in the new factories, a Government Commissioner declared in 1832 that their wages "were so large as to appear almost incredible to those accustomed to regard the scanty earnings of the agricultural labourers".

15

WOMEN AND CHILDREN; THE FACTORY ACTS

IN this chapter we are going to consider how women and children fared in this age of change, taking the children first, because the early Industrial Revolution brought some of them, the very poorest of the poor, into a prominence they had never had before. As we saw in the last chapter, the first factories were placed in the hills, where quick-flowing streams and rivers would turn the millwheel. But there were very few people living up in the hills of Derbyshire, Lancashire, and Yorkshire, so the difficulty of finding workers was solved by sending for children. One of the most terrible things about eighteenth-century life, as Captain Coram had shown, was the treatment of orphaned and deserted children, of whom London and the larger towns had great numbers for which to provide. The parish in which they were born used to apprentice them almost as soon as they could walk to any master who was willing to employ them and pay for their keep. Whether they really learnt a trade, as apprentices were supposed to do, or were just used as cheap labour and, when they came of age, turned loose on the world without any special skill, depended on the sort of master they happened to get. These pauper apprentices were sent off in large numbers to the factories, where buildings of a rough-and-ready kind were put up for the children to live in during the long period, seven or ten or more years, of their legal apprenticeship. They had few rights of any kind, and no right to leave their employer's service.

This was so hard on the children that in 1802 a law was passed to improve the conditions in which they lived when not at work and to forbid the factory owners from making them work for more than twelve hours a day; they were also forbidden to make them

Scene from *Michael Armstrong the Factory Boy* by Frances Trollope, published in 1840

work at night. From this we can imagine the sort of life these children had been leading. But this particular form of employment for children was already coming to an end by 1802, because the newer and larger factories were built near the coal-fields and towns quickly grew up round them. The people living in those towns sent their sons and daughters to work in the factories, not as apprentices but as wage-earners, just as naturally as in earlier days they would have found work for them to do at home. The children did not earn more than a few pence a week, but it paid for their keep. The employer, on the other hand, wanted the children not only as cheap labour but for two special reasons: their fingers were more sensitive than those of adults, so that they quickly learnt the work of "piecers", who join the broken ends of thread, and it was easier for small bodies to worm their way under or through the machinery for cleaning it. There was also, alas! the advantage of their comparative docility. Adults, as we have previously noticed, resented the regular hours and controlled activities of factory work and were less in awe of the foreman or manager. Children, on the other hand, as they had never worked under any other conditions, would accept factory rules without much audible protest, and if they broke them could easily be punished.

The work was not always exacting. *Michael Armstrong the Factory Boy* and his friends are not pictured in a scene of unending labour, and in real life we know how, in the Lanarkshire of the 1820's, young David Livingstone learnt his Latin grammar for college from a book propped up against the machines. But the hours were very long—often twelve hours a day and not infrequently more—and the conditions (heat, noise, dust, and unfenced machinery) often led to children becoming sickly and their bodies stunted. It is not a proud memory that the wealth of early nineteenth-century Britain was built on such a foundation; but before we condemn the factory-owners too sweepingly we should remember that child labour was nothing new—it was, for instance, a prominent feature of the woollen industry when Defoe was on his tour, long before the factories began. We ought also to take into account the sort of life which was led by other children in the time of the early factories.

Education

Only a minority of children attended school at all regularly, even if they were not otherwise employed. There was often a primitive Dame's School, to which the very small ones were sent at a trifling fee, to keep them quiet rather than to learn, and since 1782 Sunday Schools (popularized by Robert Raikes of Gloucester) had been available. These concentrated on teaching their pupils how to read the Bible and were supported by the Churches: having learnt to read the Bible, the ex-Sunday School scholar of course had the ability to read in general, but at the rate of one lesson a week progress was extremely slow. In some fortunate neighbourhoods there was a Charity School, probably dating from the reign of Queen Anne, or there might be one of the new National Schools attached to the parish church—the National Society had been founded in 1811 to promote education in Church principles —or a school belonging to the rival Nonconformist British and Foreign School Society, which dated from 1808. These schools would teach the three R's after a fashion, but attendance at them did not often lead on to the Grammar School, which commonly required the payment of fees and was in practice reserved for the sons of the middle and upper classes. For girls there were no grammar schools and very little education of any kind.

To complete our list, we must mention the half-dozen great Public Schools, like Eton, Westminster, and Harrow, though they were far out of reach of the ordinary people we are thinking of. But even there the life was hard, the teaching harsh, and the curriculum narrow—six hours of Latin and Greek six days a week, with the Greek Testament for a change on the seventh—from which we can judge what it was like at less favoured schools.

The latest method of teaching for the masses, thought to be a labour-saving device as valuable as the spinning inventions, was styled the "Monitorial System". Each lesson was to be taught by the master to a select group of older pupils; when they knew it by heart, the school was to be divided into classes, each of which would learn the same lesson from one of the older pupils or "Monitors"; in this way a single master, it was claimed, could teach a school of almost unlimited size. We can only guess at the means employed to keep order and secure results by this system!

Most children worked, as a matter of course, if their parents could hear of any work that they could do. Parents as a whole did not resist the employment of their children in factories, not only because they needed the additional earnings but because factory work was not necessarily the worst work. Apprentices in shops and handicrafts might have a kind master; on the other hand, they might be treated more inhumanly than by an overseer in a factory, whose activities were in public. Life on the farm, which often gave employment in bird-scaring to children who were only just old enough to walk, might be healthier but was often much lonelier than the bustle of the factory. Worst of all, perhaps, was the work in the galleries of the coal-mines, where the smallest children sat alone in the dark to open and shut the ventilation doors, while bigger ones dragged the trucks of coal with bent backs or even on all-fours along low passages.

Work Done by Women

Women also were employed to haul or carry coal between the face, where the miner worked with his pick, and the more or less distant pithead of the primitive collieries; they were employed in far greater numbers in the cotton-spinning mills. It was not a new thing, though a bad thing, for them to do heavy industrial work: we have referred before to the nail- and chain-making of the Black Country, in which women had for centuries been prominent. Indeed, it is a remarkable fact that in the case of the well-to-do merchant class the Industrial Revolution had the opposite effect. In the old days, when the master-craftsman or shopkeeper usually had his home above his place of business, his women-folk naturally took some part in the work that was going on; many a widow ran a business with success until her sons were old enough to take over. But with the growth of factories and factory towns, it became usual for the successful factory-owner to live in some select residential quarter remote from the factory, and it became a mark of his success that his wife and daughters lived in ignorance of his business or of any other business: their idleness advertised his wealth. The more energetic and adventurous women of this class

A child sweep of 1853, ringing the area bell for admittance to a town
house. Earlier in the year a proposal by Lord Shaftesbury to make 16
the minimum age for entering the trade had been successfully denounced by a fellow-peer as "a pitiful cant of pseudo-philanthropy".

looked with secret envy upon the comparative freedom of the mill-
lassie in shawl and clogs.

The Industrial Revolution gave two benefits to working women.
Firstly, by transferring the place of work from the home to the
factory it made it possible for the home to be kept tidier, healthier
and more private. How encumbered a cottage must have been in
the old days when it contained spinning-wheel, weaver's loom,
wool that was being prepared for use, unspun rovings, unwoven
yarn, raw material just arrived from the clothier, and parcels of
yarn or cloth due for return to him! Secondly, the regular if small
wage, earned in the factory and paid direct to the person who

earned it, gave women their first chance to be independent of father or husband. Of course, the wage of the unmarried daughter or the wife who kept on at the factory (the usual practice in the cotton towns) might all be needed to support the home, but what was earned was indisputably hers.

There might have been a third benefit. In theory, the factory system gave women workers the same chance as men now had of securing better wages and conditions by forming trade unions, when they had become legal again in 1824–5 after a quarter of a century of suppression. But women, it must be confessed, showed little readiness to give time or money or interest to organizing in their own defence, even where—as in the coal-mines—they were given degrading work to do, of a kind unsuitable to their sex.

Shaftesbury, the Children's Friend

However, it was not so much the efforts of the early trade unions as the devoted work of a great Tory nobleman and Evangelical religious leader, the 7th Earl of Shaftesbury (1801–85), which ended the gravest evils. As Lord Ashley he sat in the House of Commons for a quarter of a century (1826–51), and it was during this period chiefly that his campaigns on behalf of women and child workers established a higher standard than had existed before the Industrial Revolution. This last fact is clearly shown in his much longer struggle on behalf of the "climbing boys", exposed to death or injury inside the twisting chimneys of the big houses they were sent to clean, for this terrible practice dated from the earlier part of the eighteenth century. Not only did it arise before the worst evils of the new industrialism; it also outlasted them. Public sympathy was first claimed for these hapless children, who were employed as small and therefore as young as possible, by the eighteenth-century philanthropist, Hanway, and in William Blake's *Songs of Innocence*, published in 1789:

> *When my mother died I was very young,*
> *And my father sold me, while yet my tongue*
> *Could scarcely cry " 'Weep! 'Weep! 'Weep!"*
> *So your chimneys I sweep and in soot I sleep.*

Lord Shaftesbury: portrait by G. F. Watts, presented to the National Portrait Gallery by the artist

Yet the system went on almost unchecked until the time of Dickens—Oliver Twist, it will be remembered, narrowly escaped being bound apprentice to a sweep —and figures prominently in Charles Kingsley's *Water Babies* in 1863. Not until 1875 did Lord Shaftesbury finally triumph over custom and supposed convenience.

Nearly all the philanthropic works, which still cause Shaftesbury's portrait (here reproduced) to be among the select few that mean something to the average visitor when he sees it at the National Portrait Gallery, belong to a period a little later than that which we are now considering. But it seems appropriate to end this chapter with his great reforms; for the struggle for the Factory Acts marks the transition to the less inhumane Victorian era.

The Struggle for the Factory Acts

There was a long, painful struggle to bring about improved conditions in the factories, and the method was by getting Parliament to pass Acts which would prohibit the worst practices. To us to-day it seems obvious that such regulations should exist, but at the time people did not look at things in the same way. To begin with, very often the facts were not known, at least until government commissions were appointed to investigate and report. Many of the manufacturers held that Factory Acts would be an interference with private property and free enterprise. They argued also that they would increase their costs. And to increase costs would lead to a fall in sales and profits which would bring unemployment and so, instead of helping the workers, would do them harm. The manufacturers, without being deliberately cruel, wished to get their labour as cheaply as possible. At the same time, where self-interest is involved, people are easily led to ignore suffering and cruelty.

From time to time there was a demand for reform. In 1802 the Health and Morals of Apprentices Act was passed, following on some recommendations made by the better Manchester mill-owners, including the elder Sir Robert Peel. The Act, as has been noticed already, fixed the maximum working day for apprentices at twelve hours, and forbade their working at night. In addition, factories were to be properly ventilated and whitewashed. Apprentices were to have better clothes and sleeping accommodation, and were to be given a little elementary education. The J.P.s were to enforce the provisions of the Act, and to send visitors to the factories.

But the Act had little practical effect. The J.P.s were often friends of the local manufacturers, and did not enforce the law properly. It was possible also to evade the Act, which applied only to apprentices, by engaging unapprenticed paupers for a term of years—and other children were now readily available. Meanwhile one important factory-owner, Robert Owen, had shown in his New Lanark mills that it was possible to improve factory conditions and make the mills pay at the same time, and he tried to convince other mill-owners of this and to bring about State reform of the factory system. Another Act was passed in 1819, applying to cotton factories only, which forbade the employment of a child under nine. Once more, however, there was little result; there was still no adequate inspection, and the age of children employed might be unknown or concealed.

But the early 1830's were an age of reform of many kinds, and by this time factory reform in particular mustered a number of energetic supporters. Though Robert Owen had sold his factories and was engrossed in trade unionism, his place as leader was taken by Ashley (the future Lord Shaftesbury), and he acted in association with men who represented many different political, religious and social groupings. The best-remembered perhaps is John Fielden, Quaker and Radical M.P., whose spinning factories at Todmorden, Yorkshire, were among the largest works in the world. To him fell the honour of carrying the Ten Hours Bill in 1847, when Lord Ashley had temporarily vacated his seat in the Commons. Others were John Doherty, a trade union organizer; Richard Oastler, a Tory land agent, who stirred men's consciences by letters headed "Yorkshire Slavery", which he wrote to the *Leeds Mercury* in 1830; and Michael Sadler, an importer of Irish linen and Fellow of the Royal Society. There was strong agitation in favour of reform, inside Parliament and outside. Parliament set up a committee to make inquiries, and Ashley pressed for real reform. As a result the Factory Act of 1833 was passed, the first really effective Factory Act, often known as Althorp's Act from the name of the leader of the House of Commons who sponsored it in its final form. It applied to all textile factories—not only to cotton, like the Act of 1819. No child under nine was to work in a mill; children under thirteen were restricted to a nine-hour day; and young persons of thirteen to eighteen were restricted to a twelve-hour day. The most important feature of the Act was that it was to be enforced by the first salaried inspectors. These were men whose full-time job it was to see that the law was obeyed in the factories, and they largely succeeded. The Act also provided for two hours' schooling a day for each child-worker under thirteen— though what the sense of this was it is difficult to see. The children were at work while the schools were open, even if there were schools nearby; the factory-owners were not likely to be helpful in providing schools or teachers; and nine hours' work plus two hours' schooling made the children not much better off than before.

Further Factory Legislation

Nothing had been done so far to limit directly the hours of adult workers, and therefore the struggle had still to go on for a shorter working day and also for greater safety and better conditions in both factories and mines. Lord Ashley carried on his noble work of pressing for reform.

A Royal Commission brought to light some of the horrors of the mines, and in 1842 Parliament passed the Mines Act. This prohibited the employment underground of women and girls, and of boys under ten—Lord Ashley would have preferred to make it "under thirteen". Fifteen was at the same time made the minimum age for the highly responsible work of an engineman in charge of the winding apparatus on the surface. It required another Act in 1850 properly to establish inspectors of mines; they had been included in Ashley's Bill in 1842, but their powers were whittled away by the House of Lords.

The Factory Act of 1844 made an important step forward. Women were classed as "young persons" and so their working day was restricted to twelve hours. Children's hours were reduced to six and a half and more practical provision made for education. Very important, in this Act, was the provision for fencing machinery. Unfenced machinery, and also the practice of cleaning machinery while in motion, had caused many accidents. Women's hair and clothing were liable to catch in the machines, causing serious injury. The Act of 1844 made the fencing of machinery compulsory, and in this way it also protected adult men; in addition, the Act prohibited women, young persons or children from cleaning and shifting machinery while it was in motion.

Three years later the Factory Act of 1847 was passed. At last the provision of a ten-hour day for women and young persons became law. Ashley had long worked for this, and had hoped that it might also restrict the hours of men, because it was difficult to keep the factories working with the labour of men only. But some employers still found means, by working women and young persons in shorter shifts, to work the men for as long as fifteen hours a day, and two more laws were required, in 1850 and 1853, to establish the principle that factories might only be open to women and young persons for twelve hours daily (8 on Saturdays), within which they might work a 10½-hour day (7½ on Saturdays). The extra half-hour remained until 1874, but adult male workers were more interested in the fact that their own hours were now indirectly but effectively restricted—a change which marks the beginning of the transition away from the bleak age of the early nineteenth century and the heroic labours of Lord Shaftesbury.

16

BRITAIN AFTER WATERLOO – THE NEW SOCIETY

The growth and misgrowth of industrial towns and the hardships, slowly surmounted, of the industrial life of women and child workers are characteristic features of the first half of the nineteenth century in its entirety. But the period just after the close of the Napoleonic Wars in 1815 was also darkened for contemporaries by special problems, which we can now understand more easily in the light of two later post-war eras. War in this case had given an intermittent stimulus to industry—the "false and bloated prosperity", as the journalist William Cobbett called it; there had been heavy demand for arms, cloth and leather for the armies. Now slump followed. Factories and plants were now too big for peace-time needs; capital could not be used, profits fell, and employment fell also. Iron-workers, gunmakers, clothiers and food contractors all suffered. At the same time men came back from the Army and Navy; half a million men were looking for work in an economic system which was contracting.

War had helped British farmers. British agriculture had had a virtual monopoly, for war had shut out supplies of foreign corn. As population was increasing at the same time, there was a greatly increased demand for bread which led to high prices for wheat. As a result new land was ploughed, marsh and waste were reclaimed, enclosure was pressed on. When peace came, foreign corn was again available, and prices fell. Tenants could not pay their rents, poorer land went out of use, agricultural wages and employment were reduced. It was to give landlords and farmers a measure of protection that the Corn Law was passed in 1815. But this, by raising the price of bread, hit at the factory workers and the unemployed. Apart from a protective measure of this kind, govern-

MANCHESTER HEROES

A contemporary impression of the charge of the 15th Hussars at Peterloo, on which the Prime Minister (Lord Liverpool) commented that "the magistrates were substantially right" in giving the troops the order to "disperse the crowd".

ments at the time had little understanding of economics, and had no means of dealing with the economic problems facing the country. The general policy was to let things alone, a policy to which French economists had given the name of *Laissez-faire*.

Post-war Distress

Consequently, there was unrest and disturbance. We have already mentioned the machine-breaking activities of the Luddites in 1811–12; these were revived in 1815–16. Other rather similar outbursts of popular discontent occurred in places as widely separated as London (Spa Fields riot) and Scotland (the so-called Battle of Bonnymuir), though the most dramatic episode, the one

ed most stir at the time and is best remembered now,
Peterloo massacre" in August 1819 at Manchester. On
sion a squadron of Hussars, riding in to break up a huge
eful demonstration of workers, caused eleven deaths and
500 injuries to the panic-stricken crowd. These casualties,
which deeply impressed the public mind, were at least inflicted in
hot blood. When the farm labourers of southern England demon-
strated in the winter of 1830–31 against threshing machines and
starvation wages (between which they saw a connection), His
Majesty's judges sent three to the gallows and 420 to the penal
settlements in Australia.

The discontent had many causes—unemployment, low wages,
the high price of bread, unfair taxation, the need for parliamentary
reform—to which we might add the underlying resentment against
the whole nature of factory work and all the miseries of life in the
industrial town. Hand-loom weavers vainly struggling to compete
with machinery; workers who found themselves "stood off" by
some sudden slump in an export trade; and to a small extent
all the people who were trying to fit in to the new industries
and the life of the new towns were the victims of that change
from the old to the new. But we may pause here to remind ourselves by a brief survey that this was also an age of energy and
progress.

Agriculture and Industry

First, the methods of agriculture were greatly improved.
George III, "Farmer George", and the great landowners had been
united in their zeal for agriculture. The enthusiasm which animated
members of the Board of Agriculture and others was voiced
by Sir John Sinclair in 1803. "We have begun", he said,
"another campaign against a foreign country (France) . . . let us
not be satisfied with the liberation of Egypt, or the subjugation of
Malta, but let us subdue Finchley Common; let us conquer
Hounslow Heath; let us compel Epping Forest to submit to the
yoke of Improvement." In 1815 there were two centres of progress
in agriculture. First, there was "old England", the eastern counties—Essex, Suffolk and Norfolk, with Hertfordshire and Leices-

tershire. The second centre of successful farming was in the Lowlands of Scotland. The farms of East Lothian were among the best managed in Britain, and on them new methods of breeding and cultivation had been quickly adopted or in some cases invented.

In 1815 some people were already viewing with concern the growth in the number of persons employed in industry and commerce. Accurate measurement of change was now for the first time possible, as the first census taken in 1801 was to be repeated at ten-year intervals. In 1811, 6,129,000 persons depended upon agriculture and mining as against 7,071,000 engaged in commerce, navigation and manufacture. Agriculture and mining produced a revenue of £107,246,000; commerce, navigation and manufacture produced £183,908,000. Was it wise, men asked, to sacrifice agriculture to industry, for England to become like Tyre of old and Venice in the Middle Ages, a purely commercial and industrial state dependent on other countries for her bread and meat?

The coal-mines grew in importance year by year. Gas-lighting, for instance, started about the end of the war in London and other large towns, and by 1837 an ancient export trade in coal had risen to a million tons a year. On account of the demands of the Army and the Navy, the iron industry had been prosperous during the quarter of a century before 1815. The price of iron had been rising, and wages had also been increased. The restoration of peace in 1815 caused a sudden drop in demand, but soon iron exports, particularly to America, were rising more rapidly than any others. Many small masters shared in the profits during good times, for Sheffield and Birmingham were then towns of small workshops rather than large factories, Sheffield dealing in cutlery, Birmingham in machinery, hardware, and a great number of small articles. The largest factories in Birmingham represented a capital of £6,000 to £8,000, but the majority had a capital of less than £1,000.

In the textile industry, the woollen trade, which had long been the chief source of England's industrial wealth, now occupied second place, having been overtaken by cotton. In 1815 it was estimated that the profits from the cotton manufacture amounted to £23 million, while those of the woollen industry were only £18 million. Machinery driven by water power or steam was coming into general use in the cotton factories for spinning the yarn, and for finishing processes. All this pointed to future prosperity.

Hand-loom Weavers

But power-looms made slow progress; in 1823 the number of steam-looms in the whole country was apparently not much above 10,000. This was enough, however, to force down the earnings of the hand-loom weavers, who long continued to be one of the largest and poorest classes of the industrial population. They were about a million in number, including some who were reluctant to change from a job which had at one time given them good earnings and an independent way of life. But there were many more who could find no other job. It should be noted that these hand-weavers no longer included any large proportion of part-time farmers, for the loss of their "strips" had driven many of these to move to the industrial districts, where the women and children could find work in the mills while the men worked at home. The hand-weavers were to be found in the silk industry of Spitalfields and Macclesfield, and in all the woollen-weaving districts from Glasgow to Norfolk, and from the West Riding of Yorkshire to the south-western counties of Gloucester, Somerset, and Wiltshire. Their desperate struggle to stave off the introduction of the machine by cutting the price of handwork continued in out-of-the-way places until some time in the second half of the nineteenth century.

Improvements in Transport

By 1815 the means of transport had been improved. With better roads, there was great rivalry between various coach services. Newspapers viewed with concern the racing between drivers of stage coaches. In 1815 Edinburgh was only sixty hours' coach journey from London; in the middle of the eighteenth century, the journey had taken from ten to fourteen days.

Steam power had already been applied, as we know, to navigation in river estuaries and canals. The Calais packets began to ply in 1821, and in 1824 the holiday-steamers which made the fortunes of Margate and Ramsgate: regular Atlantic crossings by steamer date from the 'forties. A start had also been made with the application of steam power to the work of propelling a locomotive. The first "iron-horse" or steam carriage was made in 1801 by Richard Trevithick, a Cornishman; in 1804 his road locomotive ran adventurously through the London streets to Paddington and Islington. A number of steam coaches made a brief appearance on the roads during the next twenty or thirty years; but the future lay with George Stephenson, a colliery engine-man, who in 1814 had made an engine, named *Blücher* after the famous Prussian general who was shortly to fight at the side of the British against Napoleon. This engine drew coal trucks, not passengers—but the coming of the railway brings us to the Victorian Age.

Enough has been said to show that the era of Waterloo, marked by economic distress, is also marked by economic progress. Similarly, while this was a period in which appalling slums were being created, so that the horrors of Manchester, Liverpool, Birmingham, and Glasgow rivalled the horrors which had existed in East London for a century or more, it was also a period of important social advances.

Social Progress

London, for instance, was beautified by the great building schemes of the Prince Regent's architect, John Nash; he designed the processional way from his master's residence at Carlton House (where Carlton House Terrace stands now) up Regent Street and Portland Place to the great terraces at Regent's Park. This is also the period of the development of Belgravia as a sumptuous new aristocratic quarter for the world's wealthiest capital. The middle class in London and the provinces were housed in villas of little or no architectural merit, but it was a most important aspect of the change from old to new that they were increasing rapidly in numbers and influence. Merchants and bankers; the new factory-owners; the old profession of the law and the new profession of engineering—all these were beginning to have a new sense of their own importance, even in comparison with the landed magnates who had ruled Britain for five generations, unchallenged since 1688. After 1815 the men of influence in politics included Peel, the son of a successful cotton-spinner; Canning and Huskisson, men

of middle-class origins who represented commercial interests as successive Members of Parliament for Liverpool; and Brougham, a self-made Scottish lawyer with a special interest in the reform of education. In 1828 Brougham helped to found London University; the improvements which began about the same time at Oxford and Cambridge are another mark of the rise of the middle class.

As for the workers, it is impossible to generalize. It is not enough to say that the purchasing-power of their wages was on the whole greater than before the French Wars, though this fact is sufficiently important to bear repeating. For we cannot estimate with any accuracy what proportion of individuals or families gained less by the better wage rates than they lost through periods of unemployment. Nor is it satisfactory to point to the increased chances of self-improvement which the industrial towns offered, though it was obviously easier than before to change one's job for the better. By 1825 all the bigger towns had Mechanics' Institutes, with lectures and library, and in that year a Society for the Diffusion

Cumberland Terrace
Regent's Park, with it
seven huge portico:
built in 1827

of Useful Knowledge was set up to provide cheap books for the ambitious worker—all this by voluntary effort. But we have to admit that there may have been very many workers whose only ambition was to be allowed to return from the rush and din and ugliness of the new town to the simpler, slower life they had left behind for ever in the country.

The champion of this last type was William Cobbett (1762–1835), the self-educated son of a poor farm-labourer, who became soldier, farmer, politician, and journalist—but it is as a journalist that he is still remembered. In his *Rural Rides*, which were written in the 1820's as a series of diary items for his paper, the *Political Register*, Cobbett is never tired of praising country life in the good old days, before London became the "Great Wen" and the nation fell into the power of bankers, stock jobbers, and all the many new types which he heartily disliked and denounced.

Cobbett wrote so well that his opinions still colour our picture of the age. But perhaps we get a truer picture from the career of a man like Robert Owen (1771–1858), a penniless shop assistant from Newtown in far-off Montgomeryshire, who became one of the chief factory-owners of the day. Having made a fortune in a few years at his New Lanark mills (near Glasgow), he went on to be the pioneer, not only of improved conditions for his workpeople and their families, but of the co-operative movement, national trade unions, socialism, and other new ideas which grew out of the industrial changes. And, finally, Cobbett's outlook is certainly less representative than that of George Stephenson, the wholly uneducated son of a colliery fireman—he was seventeen before he learnt to read—to whom the Industrial Revolution gave the chance to develop the locomotive engine and plan the railways. The Stockton and Darlington railway, with which so much of our modern civilization begins, was being opened at the very time when Cobbett was riding through the country and saying that every change *he* saw was a change for the worse.[1]

[1] Cobbett's point of view had been largely shared by the poet Shelley, who died in the heyday of political repression under Lord Liverpool (See Appendix I, No. 3.)

THE GREAT VICTORIAN AGE

17

THE COMING OF THE RAILWAYS

QUEEN VICTORIA had been on the throne for rather more than a year when the first of the main line railways existing to-day was opened from London to Birmingham in September 1838. In the course of her reign, and chiefly in the first half of it, the network spread throughout Britain, so that the railway became the standard form of transport for passengers and goods alike—much quicker than the canal, much cheaper and easier and quicker than travel by road. Not only so, but the building of railways in foreign countries, in the Empire, and in India, became one of our most valuable export industries: the rails, the engines and carriages, and the skilled labour for making the permanent way—all these came from Britain and were an advertisement of our industrial leadership.

By the time of the great Queen's death in 1901, railways had spread to most civilized countries, but the British railway system was so complete, well built, and efficient that we still retained an advantage over our rivals in the ease with which raw materials, coal, foodstuffs, and finished goods could be moved about the country. Even to-day the railway viaducts and bridges and some of the big railway stations, like Euston with its classical entrance or the huge vault of St. Pancras, are regarded by many as the best type of architecture of all that we inherit from the Victorian age. So we may well make the railway the starting-point for our study of the period of Britain's greatest power and prosperity and self-satisfaction, which we call "Victorian".

Puffing Billy (still to be seen in the Science Museum, South Kensington) has two cylinders, rocking beams derived from Watt's engines and a cog wheel linking each pair of driving wheels: coupling rods were introduced on *Blücher*.

The railway resulted from a combination of two ideas—the mounting of a steam engine on a carriage so as to use its power to propel that and other attached carriages; and the propulsion of the carriages along a track made of parallel lines. We have already mentioned Trevithick's locomotive, which ran along the road in Cornwall and in London. Primitive railways, made at first of wooden planks, were then already a fairly common device for moving heavy material in mines or quarries, and on Tyneside and in South Wales iron railways often ran from the collieries down to the canal or river: the standard gauge of British Railways to-day reproduces what was found to be a convenient width for these early coal-trucks. It was in South Wales in 1804 that Trevithick's locomotive was put on to a railway, and in Northumberland in 1813 that William Hedley produced *Puffing Billy*. This engine, as we can see, is a very clumsy machine, but it is evidently intended to draw other wagons along an iron railway, though the smallness of the flange on the inner edge of the wheels suggests that its speed would be extremely slow. *Puffing Billy* attracted the attention of George Stephenson, the engine-wright at Killingworth, a neighbouring colliery, and in 1814 he built his *Blücher* on the same general plan; but it was so much better that it could draw no fewer than eight trucks containing thirty tons of coal along the level and even up slight slopes at a speed of about nine miles an hour.

The Stockton-Darlington Railway

Eight years later, a railway for goods traffic was being planned between the towns of Darlington and Stockton-on-Tees. It was first intended to use horse-drawn trucks, but Stephenson suggested that steam locomotives should be used, and he was appointed to carry out the work. He built another engine, the *Locomotion*, and this drew a train of trucks at a speed of twelve miles an hour when the railway was opened for goods traffic in 1825. At first many people thought it would be unsafe to travel in a train drawn by a steam engine—the engine might blow up, or the train catch fire. But before long, the merchants of Liverpool and Manchester decided to have a railway between their two towns, and Stephenson carried out the work. The directors' prize for the best locomotive was won by Stephenson's famous *Rocket*, which travelled at the rate of twenty-nine miles an hour.

The Liverpool and Manchester Railway, opened in 1830, ran passenger trains as well as goods trains. In 1831, over 256,000 people travelled by train in six months, although the total length of the railways was only sixty-nine miles. In 1836–37 there was a short-lived "boom" in railway construction, which provided more capital for two big schemes already under way for lines connecting London with Birmingham and Bristol, and the first of the big London stations was opened, Euston.

Of course, railway travel to begin with was by no means comfortable. There was much jolting and shaking. But in 1837, the diarist Charles Greville, when travelling from Birmingham to Liverpool in four and a half hours, found nothing disagreeable about it except the whiffs of stinking air. "Town after town, one park and country house after another, are left behind with the

Liverpool-Manchester Railway. Early train made up of four-wheeled
in 1831 for £800). Ten years later, however, George Stephenson advi
more comfort

rapid variety of a panorama. The most surprising feature of all,
apart from the speed, was the wonderful punctuality. It gave to
man something of the precision of a machine." Greville also notes
that "one engineer", on that journey in the first year of Victoria's
reign, reached the astonishing speed of forty-five miles an hour,
and that he was promptly dismissed by a prudent company
running no risks. In a leaflet, *Rules for Railway Travelling*, some
amusing advice is given: "If a second-class carriage, as sometimes
happens, has no door, passengers should take care not to put out
their legs." "Beware of yielding to the sudden impulse to spring
from the carriage to recover your hat which has blown off, or a
parcel that has been dropped."

At first some of the older and more select towns petitioned
Parliament to keep the "new fangled notion outside their boundaries". Other people asked what would become of coach-makers,
harness-makers, coach-masters and coachmen, inn-keepers, horse-
breeders, and horse-dealers if the railways were allowed to take
the place of travel by coach. Many landowners tried to prevent
railways being taken through their estates, and when they had to
sell the land to the railway company, they made them pay very
high prices. But the early fears of the new means of travel died
down, and the rapid development of passenger traffic proved even
more important than the carriage of goods.

Construction of Main Lines

Then came the great "railway mania", following nearly ten years
after the first boom and marked by great schemes for amalgama-

...and drawn by *Jupiter* (manufactured by Robert Stephenson and Co.
...of Trade that "Six-wheel engines and carriages are much safer and
...ers than four".

...tions as well as for new lines, with huge investments by the general
public, sensational profits, and sensational losses. The leading
spirit was George Hudson (1800–71), the "Railway King", a York
draper who organized the Midland Railway Company, with its
headquarters at Derby, and other shorter-lived combinations. In
1847 the bubble burst; Hudson and many other people were ruined;
and he was accused (but not convicted) of fraud.

But railways, like the habit of Stock Exchange speculation, had
come to stay, and between 1848 and 1870 the railway mileage in
Britain increased from 4,600 to 13,600 miles. The chief lines in this
country were constructed between 1833 and 1862, and most of
them were planned by George Stephenson (1781–1848) or his son
Robert Stephenson (1803–59). The latter was engineer for the
London to Birmingham line, which was built by 20,000 men in
five years. His other achievements included the high-level bridge
over the Tyne at Newcastle and the Britannia tubular bridge at
the Menai Straits. Another of the famous railway pioneers was
Isambard Kingdom Brunel (1806–59), the son of an exiled Frenchman. In 1838–41 he built the main line from London to Bristol,
with its tunnels and bridges. The long Box Tunnel between Chip-
penham and Bath set a particularly hard problem for him to solve,
as water gushed out freely through crevices in the rock. Brunel
was also prominent as the great advocate of the seven-foot 'broad
gauge', which the Great Western Railway did not finally abandon
until 1892. His last great railway undertaking was the Royal
Albert Bridge at Saltash, to carry the first lines into Cornwall.

The Brunels, father and son, were outstanding practical engineers and their careers illustrate how in those days able men

learnt their jobs by doing them, that is by practical experience rather than by specific training in a technical college. Their careers also show that jobs were less specialized than they are to-day and consequently a clever man might turn his hand to several different occupations in one lifetime. The father, Marc I. Brunel, served in the French navy but fled during the Revolution. He worked as an architect and civil engineer in New York. Then he came to England and was active as inventor and engineer. He invented certain machine tools, machinery for sawmills, and a stocking frame, and he drew plans for bridges in this country and abroad, and constructed the first tunnel under the Thames.

His son, after going to school in Paris, learnt his job as an engineer in his father's office and in working on the Thames tunnel. Apart from his achievements as a railway engineer, he designed at the age of twenty-five Clifton suspension bridge. Later he designed three famous ships. The *Great Western* was the first steamship built for the Atlantic crossing; the *Great Britain* was the first large ship with a screw-propeller; the *Great Eastern* held the world record for size—and, alas! uselessness—for nearly half a century. Brunel also designed a number of docks, piers and buildings. And he was a strong supporter of the Great Exhibition of 1851. Such men were the planners and pioneers of the railway age.

The work of the railway navvies, however, should also be remembered. It demanded great physical strength and powers of endurance. It was sometimes dangerous, especially when tunnels had to be blasted, often with insufficient safety devices. But it was comparatively well paid and attracted labourers from country places, especially districts where main lines were being constructed, of whom a large proportion eventually settled in the towns. A great many navvies came also from Ireland.

Although the express services between principal towns soon reached high speeds, comparable with some twentieth-century services, it took years of practice before local trains ran to time as often as they do now. Another problem for the early railway companies was the method of signalling. The electric telegraph, first patented in 1837, did more than any other device to ensure safety, railway companies being the first organizations to make practical use of this great invention: by 1848, 1,300 miles of telegraph wires had been set up along railway tracks. The telegraph could be used to send messages to advise station-masters of the approach of a train, to give notice of delays, and so on. But a better method of signalling to engine-drivers was needed. In due course the system of "distant" and "near" signals, operated by wires from a signal-box, was worked out, the intervening space being sufficient for the train to come to a halt at the second signal.

Further Development of Railways

In the second half of the nineteenth century more spectacular works were undertaken than had yet been known. Two of the greatest were the Severn Tunnel and the Forth Bridge, both of which took years to build. They were under construction at the same time. The Severn Tunnel, $4\frac{1}{2}$ miles in length, by taking the railway under the river greatly shortened travel between South Wales and the West of England. In 1886 the first train ran through the tunnel with a load of steam coal from Aberdare to Southampton. The Forth Bridge, with piers nearly as high as St. Paul's Cathedral, was formally opened in 1890. It provided a direct route for the railway from Edinburgh to Dundee, Perth, and Aberdeen, and thereby facilitated travel between London and the north of Scotland. Gladstone, when he visited the bridge, was strong in his admiration of the work. It did indeed mark a great advance in science, engineering and industry since his early days when, as he described it himself, he had "crossed the Forth in a little bit of an open boat, tumbling about".

At first the government had left the building of a railway to unrestricted private enterprise, once the railway company had received powers from Parliament to buy the land required and to make all the other complicated financial arrangements for the work. But it was soon found necessary to pass certain Acts regulating their management. The Railway Passengers Act of 1844 required every railway to run some trains carrying third-class passengers at the rate of a penny a mile. The companies found that the third-class "parliamentary" trains, as they were called, paid best of all, and third-class carriages were placed on all trains. An Act of 1871 required Companies to notify all accidents, and the

Board of Trade was to hold an inquiry when an accident occurred. About this time great improvements took place in the building of carriages; padded third-class seats, restaurant cars, and sleeping-cars for night travel began to be introduced; steel rails took the place of iron ones; and a better braking system made travel both safer and more comfortable.

Among the many small local companies which had built the railways by private enterprise a process of amalgamation went on. The Great Western Railway, for example, which had built the line from Paddington to Bristol, later took over four smaller companies which had laid down sections of line as far as Penzance. Similar amalgamations went on in other parts of the country, so that before the First World War the main railway companies were seven or eight in number. After that war, in 1921, the number of companies was reduced to four, the G.W.R., the L.M.S., the L.N.E.R., and the S.R. Since then the main event in the story of railway management has been the nationalization of the railways after the Second World War. Nationalization had long been a controversial political measure, and its good and bad features are still debated.

The Advantages of Railways

In the early days, of course, there had been considerable opposition to the railways, as there generally is to anything new. All those interested in coaches and road travel, and canals, and also country gentlemen who wished to preserve parks and country houses in peace and quiet, did what they could to oppose the coming of lines of track and steam monsters which disturbed cattle and frightened horses. Some people scoffed at the possibilities opening out; they argued that a speed greater than that of the old stage-coach would be too dangerous, and that the new tunnels and bridges would collapse. In spite of such fears the railways grew rapidly. Fears, however, were not altogether without foundation, for there were numerous accidents and some awful disasters.

Among the worst were the accident at Abergele in North Wales in 1868, when thirty-three people perished by fire, and the collapse of the Tay Bridge in 1879, when, in a great storm, the bridge and a train with all its passengers were destroyed. Accidents, though frequent, did not prevent the gradual establishment of public confidence. A prominent business man, who travelled much, declared: "I have proved that railway travelling is safer than walking, riding, driving, than going up and down stairs, than watching agricultural machinery, and even safer than eating, because it is a fact that more people choke themselves in England than are killed on all the railways of the United Kingdom."

The advantages of railways were indeed to become so obvious that they came to be accepted as a matter of course. The railways had effects, direct or indirect, on almost every sphere of life. Most important were the industrial and social effects.[1]

The industrial effects of the extension of railways were far-reaching. They enabled factories, wherever they were situated, to receive coal, machinery, and raw materials at cheaper rates, and to have their manufactured goods carried to all parts of the country as well as to the ports for shipment abroad. They brought standardized brick and slate to replace the use of local building materials, which were often more picturesque; but they also enabled farmers and others to improve upon local prices for their products by sending to the big industrial towns. Again, the speed and low rates of railway transport enabled fruit, vegetables, and milk to be sent safely, and there were special trains for bringing fish from the fishing ports to inland towns. The working classes benefited in many ways: in towns, food was cheaper and more plentiful; in the rural districts, increased production gave increased employment. There was also the speeding-up of the mails and—in the later part of the century—the institution of the newspaper train, which carried the London papers, for better or worse, far and wide into the provinces.

The social effects of the railways, their effects on the lives of the people, were also far-reaching. In the old days people had been tied by circumstances to their village; most were born, lived and worked, and died in the same place. The railways made it much easier to move. Men could leave the village and seek work elsewhere, and during the Industrial Revolution and the railway age new centres of population grew up, largely aided by travel on the

[1] See illustration p. 164.

railways. This mobility contributed much to our success as an industrial nation by enabling new manufactures to grow wherever development was easiest and most profitable.

In the new towns men escaped the old feudal influences of the countryside, the authority of the landlord and parson. The old class-structure was greatly weakened; in the towns men were largely free of the old influences, and new ideas were rife. Even to-day people in the towns are usually more open to new ideas in politics and economics than people in the country. Thus railways, with the freedom of travel, facilitated Victorian liberal and reforming ideas and contributed to the growth of democracy.

They also directly assisted the growth of active political life by enabling the leaders to speak at any centre of population—even from the train itself, as Gladstone did in 1879—and by carrying political material, in the form of newspapers, pamphlets, and books, to distant parts of the country.

The railways also made possible holidays by the sea or in the country. The railways opened up the Highlands of Scotland to walker and tourist, and the deer forests and moors to the wealthy and fashionable. A visit to "the seaside" became the summer holiday of millions; places like Blackpool, Bournemouth, and Weston-super-Mare were largely created by the railways. To all this excursion trains and cheap tickets contributed, and with them came the chance of pleasures and experiences for the masses which before had only been open to a few.

18

THE COMING OF FREE TRADE

IF the rapid spread of the railways was the physical change which was most typical of the Victorian age, there was an equally characteristic change in people's ideas which showed itself in the success of the Free Trade movement. This had its roots in Adam Smith's *Wealth of Nations* (1776) which said that the prosperity of a nation was helped by every increase in its external trade. But most countries had (and still have) an extensive tariff—a list of Customs duties which restrict the importation of foreign goods by making them more expensive. Adam Smith argued that, if there were no tariffs (except purely for revenue) every country would be able to sell abroad the things it produced most cheaply, and buy in return the things that it could not cheaply produce for itself.

What Adam Smith advocated was the kind of policy which his first great disciple, the younger William Pitt, adopted when he became prime minister in 1783. He tried to reduce any duty which was heavy enough to encourage smuggling: that on tea, for example, was brought down from 119 to 12½ per cent. He made a commercial treaty with France (1786), by which each country reduced the duties levied on the principal imports coming from the other one. He also proposed, and struggled unsuccessfully for, complete free trade between the United Kingdom and Ireland. Thus Pitt's policy was leading Britain in the direction of free trade, when the French wars of 1793–1815 intervened. These ended for the time being not only the treaty with France, but every project for the reduction of tariffs in the spirit of Adam Smith.

The attack on the tariff was renewed by William Huskisson as President of the Board of Trade in the 1820's. But it was not until the reign of Queen Victoria that Britain put free-trade principles systematically into practice, allowing unrestricted admission to almost all of the world's products, and relying on the skilful manufacture and cheapness of our own products to enable us to sell at least as much as we bought. The few duties which remained—on tea and tobacco, for instance—were not designed to restrict trade but as a convenient form of tax which nearly everybody would have to pay.

The great trial of strength in this matter concerned the importation into Britain of cheap corn. This would lower the price of home-grown corn, to the disadvantage of landowners and farmers, but it would make wages go further (cheap bread and more of it), to the advantage of town workers and farm labourers. It was a problem which had already arisen in the later eighteenth century, when Britain as the result of the growth of population and industry was ceasing to be in normal years an exporter rather than an importer of corn. There were already import duties in existence to protect the landowner and farmer against the possibility of very low prices for their crops. But they were lowered or suspended if prices rose to famine levels, as they did during the French Revolutionary and Napoleonic Wars. It was to meet the post-war situation, which we have already described, that a Parliament representing chiefly the landed interest passed the drastic Corn Law of 1815. This forbade the importation of foreign corn until British corn reached the price of 80s. a quarter, and thus the farmer was protected against foreign competition. But the law also had an adverse effect on the working population of the country. The price of the 4-lb. loaf now rose from 10d. to 14d., although the ordinary farm labourer earned only 10–12 shillings a week in cash. It is not surprising that there were riots and discontent.

But it was unreasonable to blame the Corn Law for all the troubles of the time. It now seems, looking back, as if the agitation against the Corn Laws was exaggerated and as a result their evil effects were overdrawn. The price of corn at that time still depended much more on the harvest at home than on the import of corn from abroad. In years of good harvest the price was relatively low and, in spite of protection, agriculture might be distressed. In 1821, for example, Huskisson presided over a committee of inquiry on the "depressed state of agriculture". Huskisson himself concluded that the law failed to help the farmers, though it hampered the course of our foreign trade. In bad times, however, the prohibition of imports did make it difficult to help the poor. And, as we shall see, repeal when it came did not lead to any immediate decisive fall in prices, such as its advocates had often confidently prophesied.

The Work of Huskisson

The teachings of Adam Smith, which had influenced the Younger Pitt to make a commercial treaty with France and generally to reduce the tariff, had rather been lost sight of in the stress of the great French wars of 1793–1815. But interest in them now revived, and not only the Corn Laws but also the old Navigation Laws were bitterly attacked. It was the advisers of King Richard II in the fourteenth century who had laid the foundations of our Mercantile policy by Navigation Acts that forbade English merchants to import or export goods except in English ships; but the most stringent Laws belong to the time of Cromwell and the Restoration. The various Navigation Acts still in force in the eighteenth and early nineteenth centuries required that goods imported from America, Asia and Africa into Great Britain, Ireland, or the Colonies be carried in British-owned ships, and that goods imported from Europe be carried in British ships or in ships of the country from which the goods came. These Acts had encouraged and "protected" British shipping, but aroused the jealousy of foreigners. During the French wars, however, British shipping had a practical monopoly. When peace came, other nations imposed or reimposed restrictions similar to our own.

The first easing of British restrictions on shipping took place in 1814 in favour of the United States of America; and in 1824–5 a number of other treaties were made to give ships of a foreign power as good access to our ports as that particular foreign power gave for our ships to theirs. But another twenty-five years were to pass before the Navigation Acts were finally repealed.

William Huskisson (1770–1830), the author of the treaties of 1824–5, although he had helped in Parliament to pass the Corn Law of 1815, had since then gradually changed his views in the direction of freer trade. He was a man of great knowledge and experience. As a youth he had worked at the British Embassy in

Paris, and this training was useful to him when he came to negotiate commercial treaties with foreign countries. He was a Member of Parliament from 1796 to 1830, and for the last seven years of that time he represented the commercial constituency of Liverpool. He was President of the Board of Trade from 1823 to 1827, and that was when his chief work was done. He was held in great respect by the business and financial sections of the country, but became more and more opposed to protection for agriculture. This disagreement with the strong agricultural interests in the government led him to resign in 1828; two years later he was fatally injured by a locomotive at the opening of the Liverpool and Manchester Railway.

Besides his revision and extensive easing of the Navigation Acts, Huskisson also strove hard after 1820 for reform of the Corn Laws—reform, for as yet there was no talk of total repeal. Huskisson aimed at a sliding scale of duties, so arranged that the duty on foreign corn would be gradually lowered as the price of corn grown in England rose. In 1828, after Huskisson had resigned, the government did make a law for a sliding scale, but it was not exactly what Huskisson wanted, and in practice aroused as much opposition as the original law of 1815.

In one respect, Huskisson followed a policy which would not have been approved by later free-traders. He maintained a policy of imperial preference. That is to say, he made the duties on colonial goods entering this country lower than those on foreign goods; and, since this country still dictated policy to the colonies, he fixed colonial tariffs in such a way as to give a preference to British as against foreign imports into the colonies.

During the years 1822–8, when trade was prosperous, the government under the influence of Huskisson and the Chancellor of the Exchequer (F. J. Robinson) followed a general policy of reducing tariffs and internal taxes. The Chancellor's optimistic budget speeches led people to speak of him as "Prosperity Robinson"; various taxes were abolished or reduced, including the ancient window-tax, which Robinson halved, although this was not finally abolished until 1851. This was the sphere of the Chancellor of the Exchequer, but Huskisson gave his attention to a thorough revision of the tariff system.

The revision lay mainly in the reduction of import duties on raw materials and semi-finished goods. Huskisson swept away prohibitions of import and prohibitive duties, and put in their place moderate duties, setting 30 per cent of the value of the goods imported as an upper limit. Goods on which import duties were greatly reduced included copper, zinc, tin, wool, silk, and cotton. Huskisson fixed the moderate level of 30 per cent as an upper limit, because he thought that duties above that level would encourage smuggling. Previously, smuggling of goods had caused considerable losses to the revenue. When, for example, in 1823 the duties on Irish and Scotch spirits were reduced it was soon found that the revenue was greater than before, because, with the lower duty, the profit to be made from smuggling was no longer worth the risk involved. A number of export prohibitions and bounties (i.e. sums paid by the government to encourage exports) were likewise abolished, thus freeing outward-bound trade as well.

Huskisson also repealed a law which forbade artisans to emigrate, and he would have permitted the free export of machinery, but this idea caused alarm in our manufacturing districts, so for the time being a licensing system was introduced. But in principle Huskisson made it possible for the foreigner to acquire both the machines and the skill for competing against British industry.

Huskisson was also responsible for a codification of the customs. Over a thousand separate Acts were repealed, and the remaining laws codified. By 1826 there was a consolidated tariff system for the United Kingdom (Great Britain and Ireland had previously had different customs duties). Free trade was coming about by stages. Huskisson was preparing the way for Peel, as Peel did for Gladstone.

Peel and the Tariff

Sir Robert Peel (1788–1850), was the son of a wealthy cotton manufacturer. The profits his father made gave him the best education of the time, at Harrow and Christ Church, Oxford, and he devoted his great intelligence and ability to public life. His main work, so far as free trade is concerned, was done while he was Prime Minister from 1841 to 1846.

Peel's principle was to carry on Huskisson's work of reducing the tariff. If trade expanded, sufficient revenue might still be obtainable from duties levied at much lower rates on a bigger turnover of goods, but as a temporary measure Peel revived a tax of the war period—which has grown and continued ever since. Thus in 1842 an income-tax at 7d. in the £ on all incomes over £150 was introduced, and Peel proceeded to the reduction of tariffs. He divided imports roughly into three classes: raw materials were to pay least, up to 5 per cent; partly manufactured goods were to pay more, up to 12 per cent; fully manufactured goods paid the highest rates, up to 20 per cent—although this compared well with Huskisson's 30 per cent. In 1843 the export of machinery was freed. In 1844 the remaining export and import duties on raw wool were abolished. In 1845 most raw materials were admitted free; in the next year this was virtually completed, and many semi-manufactured goods were also admitted free. The year 1846 also saw the reduction of duties on sugar, cheese and butter, and the abolition of those on live stock, meat and potatoes.

The Anti-Corn Law League

But the last stronghold of protection—the Corn Laws—remained, in spite of many proposals made to the government for their repeal. In 1839 the Anti-Corn Law League was founded in Manchester. The agitation against the Corn Laws was essentially a movement of the new manufacturing interest, which the Industrial Revolution had created, against the older agricultural interest striving to maintain its privileged position. Thus the League attacked the landlords as the one beneficiary from the Laws and maintained that they were standing in the way of industrial progress. It was argued that our export trade was hampered because we would not accept foreign corn in payment for our manufactured goods. It was also suggested that if foreign countries were not able to use their surplus corn in this way, they would take to manufacturing for their own needs, to the detriment of our factories. These arguments appealed strongly to the industrial employing class. To the wage earners it was pointed out that the Corn Laws were there for the purpose of raising the price of corn, and that their repeal would mean cheaper bread, and this argument attracted numerous working men from the ranks of the Chartists.

Richard Cobden and John Bright were the chief supporters of the League. Richard Cobden (1804–65), the son of a poor Sussex farmer, started his business life as a clerk; he later set up on his own account in Manchester as a calico merchant and manufacturer. He found time to remedy the weaknesses in his education, studied economics, and became an advocate of free trade. John Bright (1811–89) was a Rochdale cotton manufacturer and a wonderful orator. The League sent out numerous speakers, including Bright and Cobden, to address meetings in the chief towns. The new railways, spreading over the country, were a great boon to the organizers, carrying the lecturers on their tours. At the same time the reduction of the Stamp Duty on newspapers from fourpence to one penny made cheaper newspapers possible, and enabled the League to spread a strong Free Trade propaganda. "Honest Hodge", it has been said, found tracts in his village inn and learned to spell the big word "MONOPOLY". Not less important was the introduction of the Penny Post in 1840, which helped the League to shower anti-corn law literature on the towns and villages of England.

Cobden entered Parliament as member for Stockport in 1841, and set to work to form a party of Anti-Corn Law Leaguers among M.P.'s. Bright became M.P. for Durham three years later; he was a Quaker and he regarded his political activities as part of his religious duties. In spite of all this activity, however, a motion for free trade was defeated in Parliament.

Repeal

But in the autumn of 1845, an unexpected ally came to the aid of the Leaguers. After several good seasons, it was a year of exceptionally heavy rain. In England, the wheat crop was ruined; in Ireland, the potato crop, the peasants' chief food, failed, and the people there were faced with famine. "Famine, against which we have warred, joined us," said John Bright. "It was the rain," writes Lord Morley in his *Life of Cobden*, "that rained away the

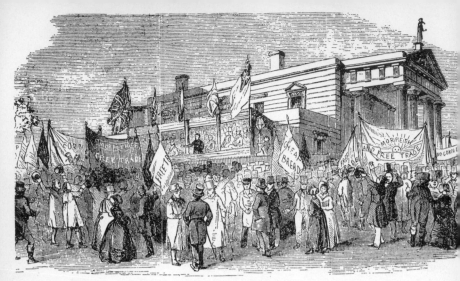

ELECTION FOR THE WEST RIDING OF YORKSHIRE.

Nomination of Lord Morpeth in front of the Sessions House, Wakefield, Wednesday, February 4. (from a sketch " expressed " by our own artist).

Scene at the Sessions House, Wakefield, when Lord Morpeth, a Whig Free Trader, was nominated as sole candidate for the West Riding. This by-election took place while the repeal of the Corn Laws was under discussion in the House of Commons: note banner depicting the rising sun of free trade (4th February 1846)

Corn Laws." It was impossible to refuse help to the starving Irish peasantry; England was also short of food; only an abundance of cheap corn from abroad could bring relief.

The Prime Minister, Sir Robert Peel, wished to open the ports to foreign corn, but his Cabinet was divided in opinion, so he resigned. Lord John Russell, the leader of the Whig opposition, failed to form a new government to take his place, and Peel came back to office. He was now completely converted to Free Trade by the potato famine in Ireland, the threat of famine in England, and the outcry of public opinion led by the Anti-Corn Law League. "It was the rotten potatoes that put Peel in his damned fright," said the Duke of Wellington. But when Peel was convinced as to the right step to take, he took it even though it practically ended his political career. In spite of bitter attacks, Peel succeeded, in June 1846, in passing the Bill to repeal the Corn Laws. All that was left was a maximum tariff of 10s. a quarter for the first three years (1846–9).

The effect of the repeal—of free trade in corn—was nowhere so disastrous as the landowners and farmers had predicted. The average price of corn in the following twenty years was 52s. a quarter, which had also been the average for the five years before repeal. The difference in the situation, a difference which did no harm to farmers, was that the industrial workers were now prospering and had more money, so they bought more. Imports from abroad increased: but it was not until the 1870's that the United States and Canada began to grow and export corn in large quantities at a price with which our farms at home could not compete. Then the result came which Peel's opponents had prophesied—the fall of rents and profits, the ruin of farmers, and the depopulation of the countryside. As we shall see, it took two world wars to set British farming on its feet again.

On the very day on which the repeal of the Corn Laws was finally accepted by the House of Commons, Peel was outvoted on another matter, and his government came to an end. In his resignation speech, he said: "It may be that I shall leave a name sometimes remembered with expressions of good will in the abodes of those whose lot it is to labour and earn their daily bread by the sweat of their brow, when they shall recruit their strength with abundant and untaxed food—the sweeter because it is no longer leavened by a sense of injustice."

Triumph of Free Trade

In 1849, three years after the repeal of the corn laws, the Navigation Acts were also abolished after a long and bitter struggle in Parliament, and at last all our foreign trade was thrown open to the ships of all the world. The ship-owners declared this would be the ruin of British shipping; but the quarter of a century following the repeal of the Navigation Acts was one of the greatest periods of expansion in the history of British shipping. As freight charges were now necessarily competitive, this is another case where the withdrawal of protection proved to be an all-round advantage. Thus the Great Exhibition of 1851 was meant to demonstrate the merits of our free trade system, as well as of our other freedoms, to the outside world. The scene at the opening ceremony is worth looking at. It gives something of the atmosphere

Queen Victoria in the "great transept", receiving the Commissioners for the Exhibition at its opening on May Day, 1851

of an aristocratic society long past; there is the group composed of the Queen, a regal figure in pink and gold brocade, her young children, and ladies of the Court; we see the marvel of the Hyde Park trees growing inside the crystal palace and providing the reason for its imposing height; but above all, this famous scene marks the moment when Victorian Britain emerged triumphantly from the difficulties of the long post-war period.

Peel had died from an accident in 1850, but the most brilliant of his followers, W. E. Gladstone (1809–98) took up his work, and as Chancellor of the Exchequer in a series of great budgets used all his skill to reduce import duties to the absolute minimum, that is, to what was needed for revenue. When Peel opened his attack on customs duties in 1842 some 1,052 articles had been subject to duty; in 1853 Gladstone still found 466 taxed articles, and by his budget of that year reduced the number; in 1860 he found 419 and reduced them to 48. Only 15 of these were of importance, including the duties on spirits, sugar, tea, tobacco, coffee, wine and timber. Gladstone abolished the timber duty in 1866, and took the first steps with regard to sugar, that duty being abolished by his successor in 1874. When in 1860 Cobden had negotiated a commercial treaty with France, so that both countries made certain tariff reductions to the advantage of the other, it began to look as if Adam Smith's views might prevail and all Europe, or even the whole world, exchange its goods freely on free trade principles. The immediate effect of the treaty was to double the export of British manufactures to France, though the French silks which came in return hurt the trade of our silk-weavers. Every system of trade probably injures the interests of some groups: but it is safe to say that to the average British worker free trade at that time spelt cheap food, more employment, and the absence of any serious grievance about taxation.

The customs duties which Gladstone made use of were used for revenue purposes only, that is to say, they were not protective of British producers by keeping foreign goods out but were used only to raise revenue. In levying duties for revenue he concentrated on a few great articles in general consumption. Hence the duties on tea, sugar, beer, spirits and tobacco. He avoided taxing raw materials and foodstuffs—hence he abolished the tax on timber as soon as the revenue could afford it, and moved towards the abolition of the sugar duties, for sugar, besides being a food, was also a raw material in the making of jam, sweets and confectionery. He aimed in all respects to free industry, and to help the wage earner by reducing the prices he had to pay and by giving him employment. These principles were the principles of free trade.

Free trade had come. The basic fact was that, before Huskisson, Peel and Gladstone, the country had suffered under an incredibly complicated and muddled system of taxes, both customs duties and internal excise duties, which had for the most part originated in an earlier age and under different conditions. A great army of collectors had been required and, so complicated were the laws, even the officials had difficulty in understanding and applying them. Now, after the Industrial Revolution, British industry and commerce no longer needed protection. Britain was ahead of other nations, and our trade was expanding. What paid us best was not protection and restriction, but the vast expansion of trade all over the world—the export of more and more British goods, which could only be achieved if we were prepared to take foreign imports in return for our exports.

Many free traders believed also that free trade would make for international peace. Free exchange of goods would bring prosperity not only to this country but to other countries as well. And in exchanging their goods countries would become dependent upon one another. It would be foolish to make war on one's customers, and war would dislocate the intricate machinery of transport, exchange, and banking. Hence it was thought that the more international trade developed, the more secure would be the peace of the world. This belief contributed to the feeling of security and comfort in Victorian England.[1]

[1] The contrasted insecurity and discomfort of the preceding period, for which Free Traders later invented the name of the Hungry 'Forties, were movingly portrayed by Tom Hood. (See Appendix I, No. 4)

19

THE COMING OF TRADE UNIONS AND
CO-OPERATIVE SOCIETIES

THE prosperity which came to Victorian Britain with the building
of the railways and the establishment of free trade was shared by
the workers in the form of higher wages, shorter hours, and more
regular employment—but only to an extent which would nowadays
seem very small and unfair. Their share in this prosperity would
have been even smaller than it was if the workers had not made
tremendous efforts to form special organizations to protect their
interests, both against employers, who naturally wished to keep
down the wages they had to pay, and also against unscrupulous
shopkeepers, who often overcharged and swindled the poorer
classes.

Trade unions came into existence early in the eighteenth century,
particularly in the woollen industry, to keep up the level of wages,
either by striking for more money or by trying to exclude any
worker who had not served a full seven-year apprenticeship: for
the smaller the supply of workers in a trade, the easier it was for
them to get their way about wages and other conditions. In some
trades unions were forbidden by special statutes, and they could
also be proceeded against at common law, for "conspiracy in
restraint of trade". But it was not until the great French wars
that their activities, in the eyes of the law, came abruptly to
an end, when Pitt in 1799 and 1800 passed the Combination
Acts, which banned trade unions as a revolutionary danger to
the safety of the realm. We say "in the eyes of the law", for
some unions continued an underground existence throughout
the period when they were illegal. Either they held their meetings
in secret or, like the Greenock Coopers' Society in June 1811, went
on issuing their regular membership cards and, if questioned,

could doubtless pretend that they were merely a club or friendly society. They might admit they were all interested in making the barrels for the salted herrings but not that they ever combined to help each other over wage rates.

Repeal of the Combination Laws; the G.N.C.T.U.

The hero of the first period of trade unionism was Francis Place, a tailor, who had worked his way through hard times, from an apprentice to a master. He owned a very successful shop in Charing Cross, and his parlour there became a meeting-place for

A Trade Union Membership Card of 1811

reformers. In this and other ways he gave publicity to the cause he had in hand—the repeal of the Combination Acts. His friend, Joseph Hume, a Radical M.P., with Huskisson's help secured the appointment of a parliamentary committee. As a result of its enquiries, in 1824 all laws against trade unions were repealed. The immediate result, as might have been expected, was an outburst of strikes, culminating in one by the shipwrights which reduced the entire port of London to idleness. Employers were angry and alarmed, and another committee was appointed amid great excitement. But petitions from Manchester, Sheffield and other industrial towns poured in to Members of Parliament, and workmen even made their way to the House of Commons, demanding that their case should be heard. This determination on the part of the workers defeated attempts to reimpose the Combination Acts, but severe limits were set to the powers of the unions. They must confine their activities strictly to "consulting upon and determining the rate of wages and prices"; special penalties were fixed for any "molestation" or "obstruction".

Another man who influenced the early Trade Union movement was the Welshman, Robert Owen, whose experience in improving the conditions of labour in his own cotton-mills at New Lanark led him to try to extend his ideas of industrial organization over the rest of the country through the now legalized trade unions. He realized that the isolated strikes of small local unions would not avail. There must be co-ordinated, national action. He founded a Builders' Union, which he hoped would be strong enough to take over the whole of the building work in the country and run it without any employers. This was followed in 1834 by a Grand National Consolidated Trades Union, which was joined by half a million people.

There were at this time far-reaching, though often vague, plans in the minds of the union leaders. One plan was for a general strike or "national holiday" (the Chartists later spoke of a "Sacred Month"). This would be a means of breaking the capitalists' hold over industry, and giving the workers power. There were two ideas of how this would happen—either through a violent revolution or by a peaceful change-over from capitalism to socialism. "The men may remain at leisure," it was said, "no law can compel them to work against their will. They may walk the streets with the arms folded. . . . What happens in consequence? . . . Government falls into confusion, and every link in the chain which binds society together is broken in a moment by the inert conspiracy of the poor against the rich." Thus, some of the workers thought, might come the social revolution which would give them power and redress their ills. The leaders of the G.N.C.T.U. seem also to have pictured as the final development a scheme of workers' control over the whole industrial system—a kind of syndicalist organization of society, with local lodges as the base of a pyramid which might have at its apex a kind of trades parliament. Such ideas were to appear again—much later. In the meantime nothing came of them, but the movement for the G.N.C.T.U. gave rise to one of the most famous episodes in trade union history.

The Tolpuddle Martyrs

While workers in mines and the textile and other industries were forming unions, farm labourers had been doing the same. In 1830 starvation conditions existed in many rural districts of southern England, and there were demands for higher wages. Bands of farm labourers marched from village to village, appealing sometimes to the squire, sometimes to the local magistrates, sometimes to the farmers themselves. We have already mentioned the severe repression which followed this episode, sometimes known as the Last Labourers' Revolt. Another of its consequences was a brief flare-up of trade union activity in the countryside.

Owen's Grand National Union formed a special sub-division, the Friendly Society of Agricultural Labourers, and wages tended to rise. When the labourers in the Dorset village of Tolpuddle were threatened with a reduction, they wrote to the Grand National Union for advice. As a result two brothers, named Loveless, and four other men formed a branch of the Friendly Society of Agricultural Labourers, and many labourers joined it; the authorities became alarmed. Although farm and other workers could no longer be tried for "combining" to obtain higher wages, it was known that members joining the Union went through a quaint ritual with masks and other curious things; so it was decided to charge them under another of Pitt's repression laws made during the French wars—the Unlawful Oaths Act of 1797. The Loveless brothers and four other men were arrested, tried at Dorchester in 1834, and sentenced to seven years' transportation. It was a savage sentence to pass upon men of good character who had done no violence, and George Loveless was a Wesleyan local preacher.

This fierce vengeance on the Tolpuddle Martyrs, as the men were sympathetically called, aroused great indignation. Nevertheless they were shipped off to Tasmania to work in chains; it took four years to get the remainder of the sentence remitted, and it was another two years before they returned to England. As for Owen's Grand National Union, it was wrecked by internal strife, and fell to pieces about the end of 1834. The Builders' Union also perished.

Trade Unions in the 'Forties and 'Fifties

The Tolpuddle trial alarmed other Unions. For fifteen years or so we hear less of their activities. The energies of the workers were devoted instead to the agitation for the People's Charter, a six-point political programme drafted by Francis Place, of which the main object was to demand the parliamentary vote for every man. If this movement had had any success, then no doubt Parliament would have been used to help the trade unions. But up to the time of the final failure of the Chartists in 1848, the chief benefit the trade unions brought to their members was through their eventually successful organization of support for the Ten Hours movement, which had been begun in the factory districts as early as 1831. The bitterness of the hostility shown towards any interference with the power and authority of the employer, such as a trade union must necessarily seek to practise, may be judged from *The Economist's* description of the Ten Hours Bill of 1847 as "The Lords leagued with the Commons to prohibit Industry".

In the middle of the century, however, there was a revival of trade unionism, based on new aims and a better organization for the new Unions of better-paid workers. There was more thought of conciliation and of the closely related material interests of employer and workers. In many cases the strike was no longer regarded as the best weapon. In addition to such practical advantages as insurance of tools, the Unions offered Friendly Society benefits of payment in times of sickness or unemployment, and assistance to the family on the death of a member. They also helped members to emigrate, to reduce competition for jobs, though this device was exploited by rogues who made the round voyage. But the important fact is that, when men paid a high weekly subscription in expectation of substantial benefits, they were not so willing to risk the Unions' funds in long disputes with employers. They settled disputes by arbitration rather than by strikes. In 1851, a number of Unions connected with the engineering trade united to form the Amalgamated Society of Engineers. It had a full-time paid secretary, and headquarters in London, and its organization was established on such sound principles as to become a "New Model" for others to imitate. In course of time the Carpenters and Joiners and other trade unions, each composed of skilled artisans who were able to pay a fair-sized regular subscription, followed the same policy. Such unions were respected by employers because they had money in the bank and prudence as their first principle.

Growing Power of the Unions

But some of the smaller unions were less respectable: in 1866 at Sheffield, for instance, they put gunpowder in the grinding-trough of a cutlery worker if he did not conform with their requirements, or dropped a keg of gunpowder down his chimney. Sometimes injury or death resulted. Many employers became alarmed at the growth of trade unionism, and some of them hoped that the Combination Acts would again be brought into force. In 1868 the Unions began to meet together in an annual Trades Union Congress (T.U.C.) to discuss matters of general welfare. Parliament, having in 1867 given the vote to working-class householders in towns, who included many trade unionists, decided that it would be wiser to give the unions more power rather than less, and this was done by the Trade Union Act of 1871. This measure for the first time provided full legal protection for their funds, and gave them the status of Friendly Societies. The Unions, however, were not satisfied with the Liberal Government which passed the Act, for it did not allow picketing during a strike. They therefore looked in 1874 to the new Conservative Government. Disraeli, who was anxious to win their support, gave the Unions what they wanted. His Act of 1875 legalized peaceful picketing during strikes and also made it impossible to prosecute strikers under the common law of conspiracy.

At the 1874 election two working men had taken their seats in the House of Commons; they were the first working-class M.P.s. They were both miners: Thomas Burt, M.P. for Morpeth; and Alexander Macdonald, who was returned for Stafford. A dozen years later an Oxfordshire stonemason, named Broadhurst, who had been a trade-union leader, became an under-secretary in Gladstone's third Ministry.

THE GROWTH OF THE TRADE UNION MOVEMENT
IN GREAT BRITAIN (1872-1951)

Year	Membership (in thousands)	Percentage of Population
1872	270*	
1882	404*	
1892	1,501	4·5
1902	1,966	5·3
1912	3,416	8·3
1922	5,614	13·1
1932	4,444	9·9
1942	7,810	17
1951	9,235	18·8

Note. The figures marked * include only those unions affiliated to the T.U.C.: the total membership would probably be 50 per cent larger.

A wave of trade unionism that swept the country in the early 1870's aroused farm workers to form the Agricultural Labourers' Union, led by Joseph Arch, a Warwickshire farm-hand and lay preacher. But in the later '70's, when agriculture suffered an acute depression owing to the importation of American wheat and there was widespread unemployment on the land, membership of this Union decreased. By 1894 it had ceased to exist, and the present National Union of Farm Workers was not formed until after the First World War. Trade Unionism also experienced great difficulty among railway workers, for the employing companies said that, to be safe and efficient, a railway ought to have the same sort of discipline as an army. The Amalgamated Society of Railway Servants was formed in 1872, but it was too weak to organize a strike. In 1890, however, the first serious stoppage resulted in some Government help over dangerously long hours. But down to 1914 the Companies, all except the L.N.E.R., refused to recognize the unions.

The members of the earlier trade unions were in the main skilled workers. The first of the great Unions of unskilled workers was that of the London Dockers, dating from 1886. At first few believed that such a tough body of men as the dockers could be controlled by a Union, but in 1889 under the leadership of John Burns they won a strike in London for the "Dockers' Tanner" (6d. an hour) and a minimum of four hours' employment. The gas workers were another unskilled and underpaid body of workers who achieved the same kind of success at this time. By 1920 (to look ahead) a score of these struggling groups had been united into a single Transport and General Workers' Union, which the late Ernest Bevin (a farm boy who rose to be Foreign Secretary) built up into the most powerful organization of its kind in the world.

The Co-operative Shops

Robert Owen was the pioneer of co-operation as well as of nation-wide trade unions. He had a non-profit-making store for the benefit of his employees at New Lanark, and later on gave much of his energies to schemes for co-operative production, that is, forming groups of craftsmen who would join together to sell the things they made, thus getting rid of the capitalist employer. Too many slackers flocked to the co-operative workshops, as they were called, for them to achieve any lasting success, but it was as a result of Owen's teaching that in 1844, during a trade depression, twenty-eight flannel weavers joined together to establish the first modern consumers' co-operative. The modest-looking shop which they opened in Toad Lane—Lancashire for "the old lane"—Rochdale, was the home of one of the weavers, used to keep the stock which they bought with their original capital of £1 a head.

The system was as simple as the place where it was first practised.

Copyright of the Co-operative Union Ltd.

The premises at Toad Lane, Rochdale, where the Society of Equitable Pioneers opened shop on 21 December, 1844. The upper floors were occupied by a nonconformist congregation until 1849.

They bought at wholesale prices and sold at retail prices. The profit, after allowing for the cost of running the shop, was shared out among themselves in proportion to the amount of the purchases each of them had made. This profit was the Co-operative Dividend. Membership grew; the capital also grew, for each new member had to pay for a small share (on which he would get interest); and there was no limit to the number of similar societies which could be started anywhere. The idea spread fast—in Lancashire and Yorkshire, then into Scotland and the Midlands, last of all to London and the southern counties, where conservative prejudices were strongest.

In 1863 the first Co-operative Wholesale Society started business, in Manchester: this meant that the retail shops were now large and numerous enough to join together to form their own organization to make wholesale purchases on their behalf. This enabled them to buy more cheaply, as large concerns can usually do; and although the C.W.S. made a slow start—after twenty years their annual profits were only about £20,000—they grew to have their own factories, bakeries, etc., and nowadays are among the largest trading organizations in the United Kingdom.

But what did all this do for the people, comparable to the steady pressure of the trade unions for higher wages, shorter hours, and better working conditions? The answer is threefold. First and foremost, the "Co-op" helped people to a higher standard of living by giving good value for money, since the dividend was really a reduction in prices. It also played a part in the struggle against adulteration of food, and helped the trade unions to get rid of the last "truck" shops. The second main virtue, however, was that the movement encouraged thrift, because it was always made easy to leave the dividend to accumulate at a good rate of interest.

Third, the "Co-op" was a real contribution towards the growth of democracy. Each store was managed by a committee elected by members and composed of members, working under the eyes of critics who had a direct interest in checking each mistake or extravagance. This makes it all the more creditable that the stores have also kept up the tradition, derived from Owen's teaching of a century ago, of devoting some part of their profits to educational and cultural objects. This mixture of hard-headed business with a genuine desire for self-improvement was one of the strongest features of the great Victorian age.[1]

[1] Compare Tennyson's description of a Mechanics' Institute outing (Appendix I, No. 5)

20

THE WORKSHOP OF THE WORLD

THIS proud title was in a sense held by Britain throughout the nineteenth century, but its third quarter is the time when our industries had become big enough to supply all demands. It was likewise the epoch when the rest of the world had reached the stage of making big demands for the goods we could supply but had not yet gone on to the next stage, of supplying the goods for themselves. At the 1851 census our population was shown to be one-half urban, one-half rural—perhaps the ideal mixture, but in any case one which indicates the great growth in our manufacturing towns since 1815. About the same time the nations of Europe and the United States of America, which might have begun to overtake our industrial lead, entered upon a period of conflict and upheaval—the struggle for national unity in Germany and Italy, the rise and fall of the Second Empire in France, in America the slavery dispute and the war between the States—which in varying degrees distracted their attention in the next two decades from the peaceful development of manufactures.

British businessmen saw their chance and took it. Between 1850 and 1872 the value of our exports rose from £71 million to £256 million. In the same period the total quantities of coal, pig-iron, and cotton cloth—three staple commodities in which we already dealt largely—produced in Britain were approximately doubled. The tonnage of shipping cleared from British ports multiplied itself two and a half times in just over twenty years (1854–75), and in 1870 the volume of our external trade (i.e. goods coming into, and going out of, the country) was more than that of France, Germany and Italy put together and was between three and four times that of the United States of America. Gold discoveries in California and Australia helped to make this a period of rising prices, and in such periods profit-making is comparatively easy;

what is more remarkable, wage-levels rose sufficiently for their purchasing power to go up a little, year by year. It was a period of tremendous optimism, in which Dr. Samuel Smiles, the author of *Self-Help* (1859), *Thrift*, *The Lives of the Engineers*, etc., used the careers of the earlier industrial pioneers to point an attractive road to fortune to English and Scottish youth.

Science and Self-Help

This worship of self-help perhaps does a little to explain one most extraordinary deficiency in the equipment of the Workshop of the World, namely the poor provision made for scientific and technical education. Several foreign countries outstripped us in this respect, although we were the wealthiest country and owed our wealth largely to scientific progress. An adequate training in science could only be obtained in a rather haphazard way, by private study and experiment, or by apprenticeship to industry or to some private researcher. Improved provision for medical training had been made early in the century; but it was not until its last decades that organized courses of study in chemistry, physics, engineering, and so on, began to be established in universities and technical colleges and, in the case of chemistry and physics, in schools.

Thus the great Victorian scientists, the men who laid the foundations of modern science and opened the way to so many practical applications of the principles they discovered, usually "picked up" their knowledge and training by following various paths very different from the broad highway now offered in the science courses of grammar schools, universities and technical colleges. The scientists of those days, like the businessmen, were self-made men. Sir Humphry Davy, for example, who was responsible for "discovering" Faraday, the central figure in the scientific advances of this period, had himself begun life as apprentice to a surgeon and apothecary. He studied chemistry on his own, and then assisted Dr. Beddoes, who had set up at Clifton, Bristol, a Pneumatic Institution for treating disease by breathing. Davy, by his own researches in chemistry, became known; he was appointed a lecturer at the Royal Institution, which had been set up privately for scientific research and lectures and granted a royal charter in 1800. Gaining knowledge and training in these ways, Davy went on to his own great researches in chemistry, which make him one of the pioneers of that subject. And, as we know, he invented the safety-lamp for miners.

Michael Faraday (1791–1867), another self-educated scientist, was a blacksmith's son. At twelve Faraday was an errand boy, and then he was apprenticed to a bookbinder and stationer. He read much and went to lectures. He went to hear Davy at the Royal Institution. Afterwards he bound a set of notes and sent them to the great man. Davy was so impressed that he took on Faraday as his assistant and thereby opened a scientific career to him. Faraday indeed went on to a lifetime of research. He made basic advances in chemistry, but is to-day best remembered for his work as a pioneer in physics and electricity. It is hardly too much to say that the whole development of electrical engineering, on which twentieth-century life is so dependent, can be traced back to Faraday's discovery of electro-magnetic induction in 1831.

Lord Kelvin (1824–1907), another great pioneer worker in the field of electricity and physics, had what seems to-day a rather more conventional scientific education. For his father happened to be a mathematics professor at Glasgow University, and Scotland was in many matters of education ahead of England. As a Glasgow student the young William Thomson, as he then was, was able to get a little laboratory training from the professor of astronomy. He proceeded to Cambridge, distinguished himself as a mathematician there, and almost at once became professor of natural philosophy (science) at Glasgow, where he was the dominant scientific figure for over fifty years. Besides his achievements in pure science, Lord Kelvin was concerned with the laying of the Atlantic cables and the improvement of the mariner's compass. He also set up the first physics laboratory for students in Great Britain.

Yet, as late as the 'seventies and 'eighties, our most important inventors had no proper scientific training. Swan, whose incandescent electric lamp shone out in 1878—a year before Edison's—was a manufacturing chemist, who had left school at twelve and been an apprentice in a chemist's shop. Sidney Gilchrist Thomas, the inventor of the modern method of basic steel-smelting, had a

Paddington Station in 1862, shortly before the replacement of iron by cheap st
his figures (including the two detectives) were drawn from life, gives a won
Wo

classical education and a clerical post, though he studied metal-
lurgy as a spare-time occupation at the Birkbeck Institute.

Cheap Steel

The outstanding invention of the mid-nineteenth century was
cheap steel, the use of which brought to an end the age of universal
iron associated with the name of Wilkinson. Hitherto, even after
Neilson's hot blast had enabled a great new iron-making centre to
develop on Clydeside, ousting cotton, the amount of iron pro-
cessed into steel had remained small—in the early 'fifties the ratio
of pig-iron to steel was more than $7 : 1$. Then came the Crimean
War, the need for efficient cannon, the consideration that they
would be more efficient if they could be made of steel, and Henry
Bessemer's discovery (in 1856) that steel could be produced
cheaply by applying a powerful hot blast to molten pig-iron in a

g stock, and even station roofs. But the painter, Frith, who guaranteed that all
of the youthful vigour, enterprise, and opulence of Victorian England, the
orld

"converter", carbon being added after the impurities had been
expelled. The adoption of this method (which was further improved
by the German Siemens, who used a new kind of furnace instead
of the converter) now provided cheap steel, with only one restriction—the iron ore used must not contain phosphorus. Such ore
was to be found in Cumberland and could be imported from
Sweden or Spain: the result was to encourage the growth of the
iron and steel industry (as we must now call it) at Barrow-in-
Furness and still more in the Middlesbrough area and South
Wales, to which ore could be cheaply shipped. Our steel trade
therefore flourished on the restriction to one kind of ore. But it
lost its advantage when in 1879 S. Gilchrist Thomas, a clerk in a
London police court, found the method of making steel from
phosphoric iron-ore: for Germany then began to develop her huge
rival industry from the phosphoric ores of Lorraine.

By the 'seventies, therefore, cheap steel was replacing iron in most of its manufacturing uses, with the result that every kind of structure became more durable: railway lines, for instance, lasted three or four times as long as before. It helped also in the final triumph of the steamship, for steel plates were thinner than iron though equally strong, so the steel-built ship was lighter and rose higher out of the water. This enabled it to stow more cargo before being weighed down to the Plimsoll safety-line; and this was very important because the great drawback to the steamship had been the difficulty of carrying cargo *and* coal in sufficient quantity.

The Age of Steamships

This problem was already being tackled from the other end by making the propulsion of the steamship more efficient and thus economizing in fuel. The screw had replaced the paddle-wheels of the earliest steamboats, and in 1854 John Elder of Glasgow invented the compound engine; this was followed by the triple and quadruple expansion engines, which reduced fuel consumption by 50 per cent in ten years. Even so, such beautifully designed sailing-craft as the tea clippers of the China trade, built latterly of wood on an iron frame, might still have held their own in some cases against the iron steamer; but the opening of the Suez Canal in 1869, the year when the *Cutty Sark* was launched, provided a handicap on the route to the East which no sailing-ship could surmount.

Thus all through the second half of the nineteenth century the British iron and steel industry was building the most up-to-date vessels for our own mercantile marine, still easily supreme, and for many of our competitors. The shipbuilding industry flourished at Glasgow—where the Clyde, once fordable at low tide, had to be dredged to nineteen feet to serve the shipyards stretching along its banks for twenty miles. It was also well established on Tyneside and elsewhere on the north-east coast of England and on the west at Birkenhead; and was even carried across the Irish Sea to Belfast, where Harland and Wolff (a German immigrant) developed after 1860 shipyards which grew to be the largest in the world. It was not until about 1900 that ships were equipped with the steam turbine engine, which had been invented by Sir Charles Parsons in 1884, with the different purpose of generating electricity. But long before this Britain was deriving full benefit from all the changes. We built the ships; being faster and more efficient than before, they carried more goods at lower cost; every voyage in British service meant a profitable exchange of our cotton and other manufactures and coal for foreign raw materials and food; or else other profits were made by us from selling the ships to foreigners or from hiring them out in the carrying trade of foreign countries.

The construction of shipbuilding yards and of merchant ships was accompanied by the building or extension of docks. The work of the earlier part of the century was continued. New docks were added to the London system, including Tilbury (1882-6) some twenty miles down the river. Liverpool docks were extended and Manchester built its Ship Canal, opened by Queen Victoria in 1894, to the Mersey. Southampton, with its magnificent estuaries, revived after 1850; it became the headquarters of the P. and O. Line to the East, though the famous Ocean Dock which can take several of the world's largest liners at the same time was not constructed until 1912. During the second half of the nineteenth century, some ports, thanks to railway communication, sprang up almost out of nothing, like Barrow-in-Furness and Grimsby. Cardiff, which had fewer than 2,000 inhabitants at the first census, and built its first dock in 1839, built further docks and came to pass Newcastle as the world's greatest coal exporter. Bristol, the second port in the kingdom in the Middle Ages, likewise enjoyed a great revival of trade and prosperity after 1884, when the corporation bought up the recently built docks at Avonmouth. These accommodate the larger vessels, which cannot be brought up the river into the heart of the ancient city.

As steamships gradually took the place of sailing-ships, steamships did on the ocean what railways did on the land. Just as the railways linked one part of a country or continent with another, so steamships linked up distant parts of the world and all its different continents by regular ocean lines, until it was no more expensive to bring many tons of corn from Canada than it had been to bring a few hundred quarters from Norfolk to London in the seventeenth century. There was also the effect on trade of the opening of the Suez Canal, already mentioned. This was the work of the French engineer, Ferdinand de Lesseps, and by linking the Mediterranean with the Red Sea, it provided a shorter route for ships bound for the East—India, China, Australia, New Zealand —and saved them making the long voyage round the Cape of Good Hope. The East India Company had for many years tried to trade with China, though the Chinese disliked foreign "barbarians" (as they called foreigners) on the soil of the Celestial Empire. But after our Chinese War of 1840–2, China was opened to British and other European trade, and our exports to China increased from £936,000 in 1850 to £6,138,000 in 1870. Trade was also opened up with Japan, the Malay Peninsula, and even Siam.

Opening-up of New Lands

During the nineteenth century, great developments were taking place in lands overseas. The great prairies of mid-western America were being settled, and as the American trunk railways were extended from the Atlantic coast, corn could be sent to Britain to supplement and replace home supplies for our growing urban population. British trade with Canada and the United States increased yearly. In return for wheat and flour, Britain supplied manufactured goods. In South America, Britain found a new customer, the Argentine, which after long years of strife, settled down to corn-growing and cattle-rearing. In 1889 the first shipload of cattle from the Argentine was landed in England, and already our merchants were sending British goods there, establishing offices in Buenos Aires, and investing capital in railways and factories. By the beginning of the twentieth century the Argentine chilled-beef industry began to rival the Australian trade.

In the southern hemisphere, Australia developed sheep-farming until it became the chief source of our raw wool, and by 1914 Australia normally had about 90 million sheep—one-sixth of all the sheep in the world—and an annual export approaching 800 million lb. of wool. Australia also became a wheat-growing country, with its harvest reaped during our winter, and so the grain reached Britain when the stocks from northern harvests were becoming exhausted. It was in the Australian grain trade that the long-distance ocean sailing-ships rendered their last service, steering adventurously east-about round Cape Horn. New Zealand sheep farmers also became prosperous when a means was discovered of sending meat to England by refrigerator ships.

With the rapid growth of new towns, Britain offered a big market for all qualities of meat. In America surplus beef was cooked and packed in tins for export. In Australia also a tinning industry was set up, and as early as the Great Exhibition of 1851 there was an exhibition of tinned mutton, though this does not seem to have become popular. A freezing machine was invented to assist in keeping the meat in good condition on the long voyage from the southern hemisphere to Britain. At last, in 1880, the first satisfactory cargo of frozen meat—beef, mutton and lamb—reached England from Australia, and in 1883 from New Zealand. Later improvements in chilling and freezing made it possible for them to send butter to Britain, and specially constructed fruit ships brought us the harvest of South African orchards and West Indian plantations. Thus an important advance had been made in our trade with the Empire overseas.

Zenith and Decline of British Agriculture

But this lavish importation of food from abroad, while it greatly benefited the workers in the "workshop of the world", had the opposite effect on our farmers and farm labourers. To understand this we must go back a little.

The repeal of the corn laws in 1846 did not ruin agriculture as many people foretold. Indeed, the decade 1853–62 proved to be the golden age of English agriculture, and "high farming" with plentiful capital expenditure continued to show good profits up to the 'seventies. The foundation of the Royal Agricultural Society in 1838 and of the Rothamsted Experimental Station in 1842 had prepared the way for an era of scientific progress.

Better methods of land drainage were now introduced. It was at a Royal Society Show in 1843 that a drainage engineer, Josiah Parkes, first saw some little clay pipes made by a gardener for heating his master's forcing frames. Parkes at once realized that such pipes could be used instead of ditches for draining fields.

"My lord," he said to Earl Spencer, "with this pipe I will drain the whole of England." In order to encourage farmers to spend money on scientific drainage, Sir Robert Peel introduced the first Public Drainage Act, by which the government set aside £2 million for making loans to farmers for that purpose. The study of agricultural chemistry became more than guesswork, and fertilizers, such as guano, bone meal, and phosphates, were applied to the soil with good results. Swedes, mangel-wurzels, and other novel root crops were grown. Russian linseed and North American meals were imported for feeding cattle, and the improvement in the breeding of stock continued. Again, the railways played an important part by providing wider markets for the staple farm products, corn and cattle, while also making it easier and cheaper for the farmer to acquire such things as machinery, fertilizers and high-quality seed corn. These changes enabled high profits to be combined with economy in the use of labour. For agriculture, which had employed nearly 2,000,000 in 1851—it was then much the largest industry in Great Britain—employed less than 1,500,000 persons in 1871. Yet at the latter date the cultivated area had reached record size—nearly twice as much land under wheat, and more than twice as much bearing root crops, as at the present day.

But the position of the farm labourers of the 'fifties and 'sixties, who were not driven from the country though they might be attracted by the higher wage rates of the towns or better prospects overseas, was fortunate indeed in comparison with the lot of their fellows—and of the farmers who employed them—when the prosperity of the country-side came suddenly to an end.

Between 1875 and 1884 cold springs and wet summers resulted in poor harvests; the harvest of 1879 is said to have been the worst in the century. About the same time, the home market was suddenly flooded with the cheap corn from the great new cornfields of America, which were large enough to derive full benefit from machinery such as the McCormick combine harvester, then practically unknown in Britain. Their new railways enabled the corn to be brought eastward for shipping, and steamships brought it to Britain where it could be sold at a lower price than our own—and there were now no Corn Laws to protect the British farmer. The price of corn dropped. In 1876, wheat had fetched 44s. a quarter, in 1877 it rose to 50s., but by 1885 it had dropped to 32s. A second wave of agricultural depression followed in 1891–9: in 1894 the average price of wheat fell below 23s., a figure to which the records of three hundred years afford no parallel. Many British farmers were faced with ruin, and there was great distress among labourers.

Farmers now turned much of their land into pasture for rearing cattle, which was fairly well worth while in spite of imported frozen meat. Stock farmers, if able to invest money in their farms, found the breeding of pedigree herds very profitable. The increasing population in towns demanded more milk, butter and eggs, so dairy farming became prosperous. Fruit-growing and market-gardening and, in some districts, potato-growing—all of which served town populations—increased. But all this amounted to very little in comparison with the good profits and plentiful, if ill-paid, employment—a man to every twenty acres, or thereabouts—which the great corn-farming districts had formerly provided. Many of the younger men had to leave the countryside and look for work in the towns, which was not easy to find because during the 1880's there was a trade depression in the towns as well. Britain had over-produced during the good years, and both America and Germany were beginning to compete seriously with our manufactures in the world markets. The export trades recovered again, but at the end of the century (and right up to 1914) our agriculture struggled on without much success, being undersold all the time by cheap imports from distant continents.

However, the steamers which, as we have seen, made it possible for free trade in corn to bring about the ruin of British farmers, also provided a means of relief: for this was one of the great ages of emigration. Altogether about 19 million people emigrated from Britain in the hundred years after Waterloo. They left from town and country alike, inspired to move in good times by the hope of bettering themselves and making a good use of their savings, and in bad times by the belief that any change must be beneficial to them. But of all the emigrants those who were the best adapted to settle overseas were probably the dispossessed farmers and farm labourers and their stout-hearted wives, who went to till the

Emigrant ship embarking passengers at Waterloo Dock, Liverpool, in 1870

wheat-lands of the American Middle West and the prairie provinces of Canada.

The uprooting of thousands of families was nevertheless in any case a very painful business:

> *From the lone shieling of the misty island*
> *Mountains divide us, and the waste of seas—*
> *Yet still the blood is strong, the heart is Highland,*
> *And we in dreams behold the Hebrides!*

The Scots were perhaps readier to express their emotions than the exiled English, but all who went left much behind, though they gained much in the new homes they created. This was the cost of empire-building. It tells us something of the tremendous vigour of our country that industrialization and emigration went on side by side—we had the people to man the ever-increasing machines of our towns and also the people to found new Britains overseas. It was no idle boast but a fair summary of Queen Victoria's great reign, when her successor inscribed his coinage with a new royal style—*Britanniarum Omnium Rex*, King of All the Britains. But we have no space within the limits of this little book to tell the proud story of the growth of Canada, Australia, New Zealand and British South Africa. Instead we must now turn aside from the social and economic development of the British people within these islands, which is our main theme, to look in a different direction—to see how the shape and activities of government were changing to meet the needs of the industrial age.[1]

[1] See Appendix I, No. 6, for a poet laureate's appreciation of Victorian economic achievement at its zenith.

21

NEW TRENDS IN GOVERNMENT

THE reign of Queen Victoria (1837–1901) had begun soon after a series of reforms, passed by Parliament in the years 1832–5, which greatly affected the lives of all the Queen's subjects. These included the Factory Act of 1833, already described; a new poor law, designed chiefly to do away with the wasteful Speenhamland system; and a law which started the modern Town Councils. But the first and most important of all was the Parliamentary Reform Act, passed in June 1832, for this brought to Parliament the sort of M.P.'s who were interested in passing other reforms; it also enabled people to argue that, since Parliament itself had been reformed once, it could be reformed again—until after a hundred years of change we arrived at the present democratic rules for choosing members.

The great Reform Act, as it is often called, did two things, both of which are connected with the industrial changes which had been taking place. A number of small towns and villages which had returned Members to Parliament in earlier centuries lost their special representatives, and most of these seats, totalling 143, were redistributed to the big towns, like Manchester, Birmingham, and Leeds, which had expanded enormously through the Industrial Revolution. Others were allocated to the most populous counties, as an addition to the two M.P.'s which each county had returned since the Middle Ages, or to the newer outlying districts of London. In the second place, the Act recognized the fact that the middle class—small capitalists, tradesmen, shopkeepers, minor professional men, even clerks—had been made more important by the growth of industry. In towns the old and complicated system of voting, which often enabled one or two rich men to control the entire result, was swept away and the right to vote was given to every householder (male and over twenty-one) who owned or rented premises worth £10 a year.

An Era of Middle-Class Rule

For a generation, accordingly, the middle class, in so far as its members chose to study political questions and used their right to vote, decided the result of every General Election. But by 1867 the skilled artisan or other working man in regular employment had come so near to the middle class in respectability and knowledge of affairs that Parliament, with much less fuss than in 1832, extended the vote to all householders in towns, however small the value of the property, and to occupants of lodgings worth £10 a year unfurnished. In 1884 this system was applied also to the county seats, so that farm labourers and coal-miners (who often lived in villages straggling over the coal-field) might have the vote. In 1872 the Ballot Act had established secret voting, and in 1885 the Redistribution Act made single-member constituencies almost universal, so that each vote cast might be equally independent and equally important.

The franchise laws of 1867, 1884, and 1885 were not further altered until the end of the first world war;[1] it is often said that they established democracy in Britain. They certainly were important steps in that direction, but there was still a considerable way to go. Women were left out altogether. Of the men, the proportion who still had no right to vote, either because they were not householders or £10 lodgers, or because they did not remain in one place for a minimum period of twelve months, or because they received poor relief, was at least one in every three. Moreover, as M.P.'s were not (until 1911) paid for their services, candidates for Parliament came from the families of the aristocracy and landed gentry, or—to an increasing extent as time went on—from the middle classes: a working-class representative, for whom a trade union or other organization would have to find money, was still a rarity in Parliament right up to the death of Queen Victoria. Of course, there were many M.P.'s who sympathized with the workers and helped to pass reforms for their benefit, but it was not the same as if they had been free to elect men who understood their needs from their own experience.

[1] See Table, p. 185

Chartism and the New Poor Law

The history of the Chartist movement (1838–48) is really an illustration of this. It is usual to point out that, when payment of M.P.'s was authorized in 1911, all the six political points of the Charter had been in principle conceded, except the not very sensible proposal for general elections to be held annually. But William Lovett and Feargus O'Connor, the two principal leaders —both of whom were sent to prison during the period of agitation —and the bulk of their followers wanted something more than manhood suffrage, vote by ballot, and other changes in electoral procedure. They aimed at getting a different kind of M.P., the sort of Member who had first-hand experience of the sufferings of the poor. The result would be the enactment of a policy of social reform. So far from being completed in 1911, the Chartist demands in this sense only began to be considered about 1906, the year in which (as we shall see in due course) Members of Parliament of a new social type first appeared in significant numbers.

The social reforms which the Chartists advocated were often vaguely described as impracticable or inconsistent with each other. But they were certainly united in their outcry against the new poor relief system of 1834. Joseph Naylor Stephens, a Wesleyan minister turned Chartist agitator, called it "this damnable law, which violates all the laws of God". Yet the law which bore most hardly upon the lives of the workers was left unaltered throughout the Queen's reign.

The new poor law of 1834 stopped the Speenhamland system of rates in aid of wages by trying to abolish outdoor relief. If the poor needed help, let them come to the workhouse for it. If they came to the workhouse, let them find that the help they got—food and shelter for themselves and their families—was administered in such a strict, mean, and humiliating fashion that people would rather die than become paupers. If they would not become paupers, then they must either find a job, however hard and poorly paid, or emigrate, or die. In spite of Dickens's *Oliver Twist* and in spite of the Chartist agitation, the grim new workhouses remained the typical public buildings of Victorian England.

Outdoor relief was never wholly abolished, especially in the case of the aged, and after about 1870 the principle of abolition survived chiefly in rural areas. Some relieving officers and workhouse masters administered the law in a kindlier spirit than others,

Marylebone Workhouse in the West End of London: new ward to accommodate the "houseless poor", designed in 1867

and the workhouse infirmary, where the sick lay, gradually took on more the character of a hospital than a place of punishment. But the fear of the workhouse remained one of the biggest factors in creating and maintaining the habits of hard work, thrift, and adaptability—whole families would move about the country, on foot if necessary, in search of employment—which made what the books call our "Labour Force" (i.e. the workers) so efficient an instrument for creating wealth.

The supervision of the Poor Law, at first entrusted to commissioners, was the main task of a new government department set up in 1871. This was the Local Government Board, having as its other work the control of the town councils, which had been reformed and put on an entirely new basis in 1835. Local government was a second point at which the law affected the life of the workers, especially in the new industrial towns, for the law intervened to restrict within narrow limits the improvements which a council could provide for the town it served.

Local Government

As with the central government, so also with local government there was a need for reform. The corporate towns were in a deplorable state, and the reforming Parliament in 1833 set itself to this task also. First a commission of inquiry was appointed, and in its report it revealed how corrupt were the conditions prevailing. The town government or corporation was, in many cases, elected by only a handful of residents, those who claimed an ancient right to be "freemen", and the majority of residents were excluded thereby from any share in control. When elected, the corporations were often neglectful of their duties. Funds, which had been placed in their hands for charitable purposes, were not properly used, or were even used for private purposes. Charities for schools, when in the hands of the corporation, were often abused; salaries would be paid to masters where there were perhaps only one or two pupils. To put an end to these abuses, the Municipal Corporations Act was passed in 1835 and it applied to about two hundred corporate towns. In all cases, the town council was to be elected by all the male ratepayers. The councillors in turn were to elect their mayor, who held office for one year, and a number of aldermen, who are additional members of the council, for six years (the councillors themselves serve for three years at a time). At regular intervals there was to be an audit of the town's accounts. This important Act, which marks the beginning of democratic government in local affairs, should be remembered along with the great Reform Act of 1832 in the history of Parliament.

Further important local government legislation was passed late in Queen Victoria's reign. The Local Government Act of 1888 created new local government authorities—the county councils, whose members were to be elected by popular vote—and these took the place of the older administration of county affairs by the J.P.'s. London was made a separate county. The larger boroughs, with a population of over 50,000, were given a position of equal importance with the counties; they were made County Boroughs. These new authorities, the County and County Borough Councils, became the most important local government authorities. They were given by Parliament powers to look after bridges and roads, public health and housing, and by subsequent Acts (e.g. the Education Act of 1902 and the Local Government Act of 1929) powers over other matters, including education and the maintenance of the poor.

In 1894 another Act was passed setting up a number of lesser elective authorities—Urban District Councils, Rural District Councils, Parish Councils, and, for the smallest parishes, a Parish Meeting.

These various local government laws prescribed in detail how the ratepayers were to elect councillors, how aldermen, mayors, chairmen, etc., were to be appointed, and what salaried officials (town clerk, borough treasurer, etc.) were to be provided. These laws also indicated certain jobs for each council to do—preservation of good order, street lighting and cleansing, and so forth—to which other laws from time to time made additions. But in Britain, unlike many other countries in Europe, a local council, however enthusiastically it may be supported by local opinion, had (and has) no power to engage in any activity, however praiseworthy, which the law has not declared to be a proper activity for local councils. It was the business of the Local Government Board to watch for, and check, any attempt to expand. When Birmingham, for example, wanted to collect the savings of its citizens and have its own municipal bank, it required a special Act of Parliament, secured by the influence of Joseph Chamberlain; less influential towns have asked to follow Birmingham's example, but their requests have always been refused.

Growth of Municipal Services

If we ask what local councils did with the rates they collected for the benefit of the ratepayers they were collected from, the answer is that until well on into the second half of the century they did very little but keep up the streets—and keep down the rates. The Improvement Commissioners, remaining from an earlier epoch in about half the boroughs, were only one of the many vested interests which fought against a forward policy. One advance, however, was in the work of police. A force had been established for London under the control of the Home Secretary in 1829, and each borough was required by the Act of 1835 to appoint a special watch committee for organizing a salaried body of police. The counties were allowed in 1839, and in 1856 compelled, to do the same; but until county councils were set up these police were placed under the county magistrates, who in 1888 combined with the new county councils to share control by means of a Standing Joint Committee—the method still employed to-day. The respectable poor no doubt profited from the institution of the police, though the richer classes gained most.

The faint beginnings of what we may call a more generous type of service may be dated from a clause in the Public Health Act of 1848, permitting the establishment of municipal parks, and the Libraries Act of 1850, which allowed the use of a rate of $\frac{1}{2}$d. in the £ for library purposes, provided the money was not used for the actual purchase of the books! But it was Joseph Chamberlain's mayoralty in Birmingham in 1873–6 that set the example of municipal enterprise, which our towns have imitated and improved upon ever since.[1] To acquire ownership of the town's water supply was often the first step towards a careful study of public health. A municipal gas company paved the way for municipal control of the use of later innovations—trams, electricity, buses, etc. Parks —or at least a recreation ground—and a public library were now to be found in many towns, but Birmingham led the way with a

[1] See illustration p. 188

municipal School of Art. To all this, Chamberlain added a famous housing scheme, which cleared more than forty acres and developed the main shopping street of Birmingham, Corporation Street, on a system of short-term leases from which the Corporation (and hence the ratepayers) derive great benefit as owners of the sites.

Such schemes, requiring the sanction of Parliament either through general Acts, such as Disraeli's Artisans' Dwellings Act of 1875, or through the private Acts by which a particular town gets special powers for its own development, were numerous from the 'seventies onwards, and they acquired additional impetus from the Local Government Acts of 1888 and 1894. The new county councils gave rural England, broadly speaking, the services of which they had enviously watched the growth in the towns. The new county borough councils helped matters on by providing the larger towns with more powers and greater dignity than heretofore. The lesser councils also organized certain services in their smaller spheres, especially the Urban District Councils, which tried to meet the needs of town life in large suburban areas and the straggling streets of the coal-fields. Rural districts and parishes, on the other hand, being sub-divisions of rural parts of counties, were kept more closely under the financial supervision of the county councils.

Growth of Government Departments

The needs of the age likewise produced some growth in the central government and its scale of activities. In 1900 the Civil Service was still, in comparison with to-day, numerically small and very sparing in its expenditure. Its modern development really only begins with the decision taken by Gladstone's government in 1870, which caused higher officials, forming the administrative grade—the level at which the most responsible work is done—to be recruited exclusively by a competitive entrance examination from highly qualified university graduates. But the number of departments was slowly growing. Those which had most dealings with the public were the Home Office for police and prisons, the factory inspection system, and the maintenance of good order generally; the Board of Trade; and the newer Local Government

Board. In 1889 a Board of Agriculture was set up to deal with the pressing problems of the great depression; in 1885 a separate Scottish Office for the affairs of the Northern Kingdom. The Board of Education, created out of a committee of the Privy Council, was newer still (1899) and shared with such minor departments as the Office of Works (controlling Crown property) and the Post Office the unenviable position that the Minister in charge of the Department was not necessarily a member of the Cabinet.

The Post Office

The multifarious activities at the post-office counter of to-day—pensions alongside parcels, licences jostling letters, and a special queue for the Savings Bank—are a natural development from the fact that in Victorian times the Post Office was the only centrally administered government service with which people in every class of society had any regular dealings. When Queen Victoria came to the throne in 1837 the public post had already been in existence for two hundred years, but was about to be transformed as regards both speed and scope and cost.

Until the end of the eighteenth century, mails were carried by post-boys on horseback. Then a certain John Palmer, who had charge of the mails at Bath, suggested to the Prime Minister, William Pitt, a scheme for running fast mail coaches which could carry letters cheaply because the passengers paid well for extra speed. The first of these coaches started from Bristol for London on 2nd August, 1784, and services soon multiplied throughout the country. Each coach was accompanied by an armed guard in case of attack by highwaymen. At the end of the eighteenth century, most large towns had a daily delivery of letters, and small ones two or three a week. By 1829, the date of the opening of the General Post Office at St. Martin's-le-Grand, on the north side of St. Paul's Cathedral, the mail coaches had long been the standard means of fast travel between London and the provinces. But the railways, even in their earliest days, transformed the speed at which letters were conveyed. The first travelling post office began to ply between Birmingham and Liverpool in 1838, and soon the wayside stations on all main lines were being serviced by special sorting wagons and contrivances for picking up and setting down mailbags at speed.

The early steamships, too, though lacking space for bulkier cargo, were well suited to speeding-up the overseas mail. When in 1840 the British Admiralty invited tenders for carrying American and other mails, Samuel Cunard, a Canadian shipowner, obtained a contract and a subsidy for carrying the mails from Liverpool to Halifax, Nova Scotia, and Boston, Massachusetts. He was a pioneer in the use of steamships for long journeys, and his example was followed by the Peninsular and Oriental Line, which undertook mail services to India, Ceylon and China. By 1874, when the Universal Postal Union was founded to regulate charges and conditions for postage between countries, it was possible to send a letter almost anywhere in the civilized world at a cheap uniform rate, prepaid by an adhesive stamp.

It was the distinctive achievement of the British Post Office that it led the way in bringing the postal service within the reach of the masses. In January, 1840, a penny post for the whole of Britain was introduced by Rowland Hill (1795–1879) in place of the old system of charges which varied according to distance and weight and were paid by the recipient—a very complicated business. Hill, who had been a schoolmaster, had long advocated postal reforms. He was specially attached to the Treasury in order to carry them out. Postage stamps came into use in May of the same year, being defined by Hill as "a bit of paper just large enough to bear the stamp, and covered at the back with a glutinous wash which, by applying a little moisture, might be attached to the back of the letter". A few years later, in 1855, the first street letter-boxes were set up in London to save people going to the Post Office with their stamped letters. The penny post led to a great increase in the number of letters—the quantity had already multiplied ten times by 1870.

Post cards (an Austrian invention) came into use in Britain in 1870. But it was not until 1883 that the Post Office undertook to carry parcels, though it is evidence of Victorian earnestness that the book post had been instituted in 1848. One other landmark in postal history was the extension of penny postage to all correspondence within the British Empire. This principle—of enormous value to imperial good feeling—was first brought into limited practice on Christmas Day, 1898.

New Functions; The Savings Bank

Besides organizing the transmission of letters and parcels, the Post Office acquired the telegraph and telephone systems. The first experiments in electric telegraphy were made in 1837. But it was not till 1868 that the government decided to take over all the private telegraph companies, excepting the systems used by the railways for their own business. The transfer took place in 1870; the government paid a total of £11 million to the companies, and from that time telegrams had to be sent through the Post Office. Submarine cables enabled the telegraphic system to be extended to other countries. In 1851, the first successful cable was laid between Dover and Calais, and from that time business men in the Stock Exchanges of London and Paris could keep each other informed as to prices of stocks and shares during the day's work. In 1866, the first regular telegraphic service between Britain and America was established, and there was soon a network of cables, the joint property of British and foreign governments, which gave direct and instant communication with most parts of the world.

The telephone, which was invented in 1876, was also taken over by the Post Office for development in 1896. But it was not until the twentieth century that the habit of telephoning made letter-writing in some circles appear old-fashioned. It is more important for us to refer now to one completely non-postal activity which dates back to 1861 and is very characteristic of the Victorian age about which we are thinking, namely the Post Office Savings Bank.

Gladstone, who as Chancellor of the Exchequer was responsible for its foundation, regarded it as one of the greatest achievements of his career. On the opening day there were 435 deposits of an average amount of £2; these had grown by December 1951, to 22,450,000 accounts, averaging about £85 each—a remarkable growth, even when we make full allowance for the fall in the value of money. But the great thing about the Savings Bank was the idea that it stood for—to encourage the saving of small sums by enabling the depositor of a shilling or two to earn interest on his money and to feel that his deposit, being guaranteed by the State, was at least as secure as the investments of the richest man in the land.

Gladstone and other chancellors of his period kept taxes low by rigid economy and a stern refusal of social services. National expenditure per head of population remained stationary for thirty years (1857–87). The money was left, as Gladstone once said, "to fructify in the pocket of the tax-payer". A system of government which kept things cheap (including for example the cost of postage) and did all it could to encourage the habit of thrift was, in his view, helping the people in the best possible way by enabling them to help themselves. If they failed to struggle upwards, then in the Victorian view the poor might have a claim to private charity but not to any generous assistance from the State.

THE EXTENSION OF THE FRANCHISE IN RELATION TO
THE GROWTH OF POPULATION IN GREAT BRITAIN

Year	Number of Voters	Percentage of (Male) Population	
1831	439,970	5·6	
(Act of 1832)			
1833	717,254	8·8	
1866	1,162,153	9·8	
(Act of 1867)			
1868	2,230,795	18·3	
1883	2,920,894	19·9	
(Act of 1884)			
1885	4,931,371	32·7	
1913	7,356,405	36·9	
(Act of 1918)			
1919	19,456,000	58·0 (male)	35·4 (female)
1927	21,117,000	59·5 ,,	37·1 ,,
(Act of 1928)			
1929	28,080,000	62·7 ,,	64·1 ,,

Note. In comparing the percentages of population enfranchised at different periods, it is important to bear in mind that the proportion which is too young to vote has decreased greatly since 1900; also, that this proportion is higher among men than among women, who are longer-lived.

22

TOWN LIFE AND HEALTH

ONE of the problems which the Victorians were very slow to tackle, and which to some extent is still a problem for us to-day, was the effect on people's health when more and more of them were packed together to live and die in the streets of ever-growing towns. The health conditions of London and other ancient urban centres had been very bad, though mitigated towards the end of the eighteenth century by the work done under the Improvement Acts. The quality of the new industrial towns was worse, with a great mass of 'shoddy building (dating often from a period of maximum growth in the 'twenties) which deteriorated as it grew older. Meanwhile the population was still increasing fast: the Queen's subjects in the United Kingdom numbered 26 million at the beginning of her reign, 42 million at the end of it. If we exclude Ireland, where the population after the famine of 1846 had declined at every census, the increase is still more remarkable: England, Wales, and Scotland—in spite of the millions who emigrated—had two inhabitants in 1901 for every one they had had in 1837. In 1851 the division between town and country was almost exactly even, but by the end of the century three-quarters of the people lived in the towns and the total of country-dwellers had actually declined by 5 per cent.

It was therefore a very important fact that the conditions of town life, which up to the 'sixties were getting worse rather than better, did at last begin to improve, so that the 'seventies brought a decisive fall in the death-rate. The horrors of the earlier years had been eloquently described, not only in several of the widely-read novels of Dickens, but by Disraeli in a story called *Sybil or The Two Nations* (the widely-separated nations of the rich and the poor) and by an earnest German named Engels, the friend and associate of Karl Marx, the founder of Communism. His account of *The Condition of the Working Class in England in 1844* gives an unforgettable picture of Manchester—grim factories overshadowing dark streets and lanes, the undrained, uncared-for rows of poorly built cottages, the clouds of black smoke, the malodorous River Irwell swirling underneath the narrow bridges. Twice there had been a big scare, in 1832 and 1848, when epidemics of cholera in London and the provinces ravaged the homes of rich as well as poor, with the result that Boards of Health were set up by Parliament to see to matters of water supply, drainage, etc. But each time, when the epidemic subsided, health measures were allowed to fall into neglect, even though they were championed by one of the first great civil servants in our history. This was a social reformer as determined as Lord Shaftesbury, but, unfortunately, greatly inferior to the "Children's Friend" in social influence, sympathy, and tact.

Edwin Chadwick

Edwin Chadwick (1800–90) was a native of Manchester, who had much to do with the making of the Poor Law in 1834 and became Secretary to the Poor Law Commission established to carry out the new system. In that connection he visited the worst slums to see for himself how the poor lived. His experiences led him to press for a government inquiry on Public Health and Housing; a rise in the number of deaths from typhus made an examination of conditions in London urgent, and the Bishop (Blomfield) suggested that it should cover the whole country. So in 1842, Chadwick published his famous *Report on the Sanitary Conditions of the Labouring Population*, which revealed the startling fact that owing to insanitary conditions the number of deaths in one year from typhus fever alone was double that of the lives lost by the Allies in the battle of Waterloo.

Besides the lack of sanitation there was the evil of overcrowding. In 1840 there were 15,000 persons in Manchester living in cellars. In Liverpool the number was twice as great. To find a parallel Chadwick harked back to gaol conditions in the eighteenth century before they were reformed by John Howard, declaring that "more filth, worse physical suffering and moral disorder than

displaced 21,000 persons from unwholesome houses, and have erected within the municipal boundaries healthy dwellings for about 150,000 persons. In 1875 an Act entitled the "Artisans and Labourers' Dwellings' Improvement Act" received the assent of Parliament. This Act confers on the sanitary authorities of all towns of more than 25,000 inhabitants very extensive powers of dealing with unwholesome and dilapidated houses, especially as regards compulsory power to buy land or other property, as formerly any owner who chose to be cantankerous or greedy could paralyse any contemplated municipal improvement which touched his property.

Mr. Cross's Act has recently been taken up in good earnest by the authorities of Birmingham—a town which, though exceptionally salubrious among great cities as far as advantages of site are concerned, yet has, in its central districts, a miserable region of damp, dilapidation and decay; where the deaths are twice as numerous as in the suburb of Edgbaston—young children die especially fast, as one of the tenants pithily put it, "There's more bugs than babies"—where perfect health is unknown and decent habits almost impossible. Those who have read Mr. Councillor White's graphic description of the condition of St. Mary's Ward will not deem the above expressions a whit too strong. A plan of improvement drawn up in accordance with the representations of the Medical Officer of Health has been brought forward by Mr. White and carried before the Council, and it is gratifying to add that it was unanimously accepted, although a few aldermen and councillors abstained from voting owing to motives of delicacy, because they owned property on the line of intended demolition. It will be perceived, on reference to our map, that the proposed scheme is one of an extensive character; it is intended to combine the advantage of new and improved dwellings for the poorer classes with convenient thoroughfares. Those who know Birmingham are aware how much a route for vehicular traffic is needed between New Street and Bull Street. By the proposed improvement a new thoroughfare will commence in New Street, opposite the Exchange, and will be carried right through, across Legge Street and Bagot Street, into the Aston Road. New subsidiary side streets will also be made, and it

"A miserable region of damp, dilapidation, and decay"—an area in central Birmingham as depicted by *The Graphic* before reconstruction under the Act of 1875.

Howard described as affecting the prisoners, are to be found among the cellar population of the working people of Liverpool, Manchester or Leeds". Nevertheless, the Board of Health scheme which he succeeded in establishing in 1848 did not include London in its sphere of action; in other towns it could recommend but not, usually, compel the appointment of a local Health Board; and for want of support it came entirely to an end in 1854. Chadwick then turned his attention to more hopeful projects—omnibuses, post-office telegraphs, and London University all benefited by his many-sided activities.

The reasons for the long delay in tackling the needs of the towns are many and various. We may put first the strength of *laissez-faire* opinion, that is, the widespread belief (to which the economic writers of the day contributed) in leaving things alone. Any government measure was bound to interfere with people's liberty of doing what they liked with their own property, and would probably result in a muddle; whereas if there was no measure taken, the situation might get better of its own accord or through some private and voluntary work of benevolence. This view was very popular among the well-to-do classes: *Punch*, for example, saw fit to caricature the public health movement in the guise of a severe nurse trying to scrub a reluctant Master John Bull, with whose reluctance the reader is clearly expected to sympathize. There were powerful vested interests—jerry-builders; landlords of old, deteriorated, but profitable property; water companies whose affairs (and water) would not bear looking into, and so forth—which made it difficult for town councils and even for M.P.'s to inquire into the housing conditions of the poor.

There was also much genuine ignorance, for the expansion of the towns had been accompanied by the removal of the better-class homes into "eligible residential areas", situated usually in the outskirts and distant from the homes of the workers. As late as the 1880's, it was a great novelty when the first university settlements brought even a handful of university graduates to reside in the poor quarters of London and other large towns. To find out how the workers lived therefore required an effort and a deliberate venturing into strange and disagreeable scenes, for which the hard-worked head of a business or professional man had no time, while for his women-folk it would be thought unladylike and unsuitable. Many people genuinely believed accounts of slum conditions to be hopelessly exaggerated or, alternatively, accepted them with resignation as originating in the drunkenness, laziness, and folly of the poor. There were many besides his own horse that seemed to agree with Tennyson's *Northern Farmer*, when he said: "Take my word for it, Sammy! The poor in a loomp is bad."

But the biggest difficulty of all lay in the physical facts of the situation. In days when surgeons used to operate in dirty overalls, it is obvious that the connection between dirt and infection was understood but dimly if at all; and without the modern microscope the influence of a tainted water supply was easily ignored. Mass-produced drainpipes, water-closets, and hot-water systems were eventually among the greatest gifts of the Industrial Revolution to man, but these objects and others like them were still neither cheap nor plentiful in Early Victorian England. In 1832 a bath with a hot-water supply was the latest novelty at the London Mansion House, and we may surely suppose the City Fathers to have budgeted a little more lavishly for the honour of the Lord Mayoralty than for their personal requirements. Therefore, as the crowds poured into the towns it seemed sufficient to subdivide old houses and build new ones, at top speed, without considering that there was any need to improve on the standards of accommodation which had been found adequate by the immigrants before they left their original home, no doubt small and overcrowded, or perhaps a mere hovel on the edge of an Irish peat-bog. A typical village had had no drainage system or artificial water-supply: it took time for men to face up to the fact that, when the equivalent of fifty villages were laid side by side to form some raw new town, a new problem of building and planning had been created, for which our new industrial methods must somehow find a solution.

Reforms of the 1870's

Health of towns, fortunately, was not made a party issue. A Royal Commission, the report of which laid down a list of requirements "necessary for civilized social life", was appointed by Disraeli, completed its work under Gladstone, and had its recom-

mendations carried partly by the Liberals, chiefly by the Conservatives. The requirements included: good water, proper
drainage, removal of nuisances (such as excessive noise, smells,
and smoke caused by industrial processes), healthy streets and
houses, measures to prevent the spread of disease. The first step,
taken in 1871, was to establish the Local Government Board to
supervise all "local government". The novelty of its work is shown
by the fact that the phrase itself had only been coined a dozen
years before. Then in 1875 a Public Health Act laid down rules
for sanitation which all owners of houses had to obey. Every local
council had to appoint a medical officer of health, a surveyor,
and a sanitary inspector, and it might provide a water-supply for
its area unless this was already provided efficiently by a private
company. Sewers must be maintained in good condition; the
making, paving, cleaning and lighting of the streets must be
attended to and scavengers must be employed to collect refuse regularly. Other duties of the sanitary authorities included the supervision of markets and slaughter-houses; and their inspectors
had the right to seize and destroy unsound food. They might, if
necessary, provide public baths and wash-houses. The medical
officers must take proper measures to prevent the spread of infectious diseases. Later, the inspectors were also empowered to
examine the sanitary conditions of workshops.

Some cities had already taken the initiative in these matters.
Liverpool had appointed a medical officer as early as 1847. London
got its first medical officer in 1848; Manchester came next in 1869;
Birmingham also had its first medical officer already at work in
1875. But the whole basis of the law was the past experience that
the areas which were most reluctant to adopt health measures
were often those where they were most needed.

In the same year as the Health Act, the Artisans' Dwellings Act
gave local authorities power to condemn, clear, and redevelop
slum areas. Mention has already been made of the great work
undertaken at this time in Birmingham, though this required the
help of a special Act of Parliament. But Birmingham did not
stand alone. Manchester had a similar big clearance scheme in
Deansgate under another private Act of 1869. Liverpool in the
'eighties was prominent in getting rid of cellar residences; Leeds,

rather later, tackled the back-to-back houses for which it was specially notorious. In London the Metropolitan Board of Works, soon to be superseded by the London County Council, in eight years secured the rehousing of 28,352 persons—less than 1 per cent of population, but a beginning. Established in 1855, this now long-forgotten local authority had already provided London with its main drainage system and the Victoria Embankment, under which one of the principal sewers lies gracefully concealed.

A third law of 1875 was the Sale of Food and Drugs Act. This tackled the problem, not peculiar to towns, of articles prepared from injurious and falsely described ingredients; the law made arrangements for inspection and analysis of samples and was not greatly altered until 1928. In this connection it must not be for-gotten that the Education Act of 1870[1] played a part by making people less ignorant and on the whole less gullible. Universal elementary education also stimulated the activities of the town councils: people could understand more readily what was being done for their benefit and therefore co-operate—they could also understand what was *not* being done, and therefore agitate. The provision of parks and recreation grounds, for instance, the so-called "lungs of the great cities", now went ahead without much prompting by Parliament, and the growth of education certainly encouraged the growth of municipal art galleries, museums, and libraries, and—in some enlightened neighbourhoods—the use of local government powers to make towns less ugly. Not all the new town halls, for example, were hideous; the erection of municipal buildings on the grand scale often marked the moment when a town began to take a new pride in its appearance.[2]

Medicine

Although the provision of a complete public health service in the modern sense was utterly beyond the imaginations of the con-temporaries of Gladstone and Disraeli, the "shilling doctor" of the poorer quarters of the town, no less than the up-to-date physician visiting the rich in his brougham, had an important

[1] See page 253.
[2] See also Chapter 29 for the growth of outdoor games and activities.

cumulative effect on public health. It has already been mentioned that medical training provides an exception to the general rule of indifference to the need for scientific education. Between 1818 and 1831 medical schools were established in Bristol, Manchester, Sheffield and Leeds, and interest in the subject also revived at Oxford and Cambridge. By the end of the century every industrial area had its quota of qualified medical practitioners; the type is described for us from first-hand knowledge in the novels of Francis Brett Young and A. J. Cronin.

Meanwhile surgeons were faced still with two old but formidable problems. One was the pain caused to the patient who was operated on without anaesthetic, the other was the blood-poisoning which so often set in after operation, wound or accident. Various experiments in the use of gases to limit pain had been made, including some by Davy and Faraday. Eventually Professor J. Y. Simpson of Edinburgh himself inhaled a number of vapours, and in 1847 he found that chloroform was the most useful. It soon came into general use as the first anaesthetic.

The other problem was made worse by the crowding of patients into hospital wards, especially when the hospitals were old and dirty. The connection between dirt and disease was scarcely suspected, and so infection spread easily on the hands of doctors and nurses and from patient to patient. Blood-poisoning, or hospital gangrene as it was called, was so deadly that it was safer to be treated at home than to go to hospital. In the 1840's Semmelweiss in Austria and Oliver Wendell Holmes (doctor as well as writer) in America practised and advocated the use of antiseptic materials in hospitals. But they were opposed by conservative medical men, and made no impression at the time. Later the French scientist Pasteur (1822–95), working on fermentation and decomposition in connection with brewing and wine-making, discovered that these processes were caused by living organisms or germs, and that these germs came from the air. Joseph Lister (1827–1912), who was professor of surgery at Glasgow and Edinburgh, realized in 1865 that such germs must also be the cause of blood-poisoning. By using antiseptics to destroy germs—by sterilizing hospital equipment and treating wounds—he revolutionized surgery and, though his methods are now outmoded, he first made it comparatively safe. His great work was recognized when he was made Lord Lister in 1897.

Every improvement in hospital practice was powerfully assisted by the long-maintained influence of Florence Nightingale (1820–1910). By her work during the Crimean War and afterwards in England, she made a revolution in hospital administration and in nursing. She raised the standard of cleanliness in hospitals and she did much to make nursing a regular and respected profession, with training standards of its own.

From 1880 onwards a number of the germs, or bacteria, causing diseases were isolated and studied, and means of counteracting them discovered. The use of soap and water to secure household and personal cleanliness, new methods of avoiding contamination of food, and the process of pasteurization of milk to destroy bacteria, have all furthered improvement in health. To attack bacteria directly in the human body is, however, difficult by means of antiseptics: they destroy the bacteria but may also destroy or harm the patient. But the old method of inoculation was further developed by Pasteur, who treated hydrophobia by inoculation with a weakened form of the rabies virus. Another method is to inject a blood-serum from an infected animal, and not the living organism of the disease. Thus in 1890 a German doctor discovered a serum which could be injected against tetanus, and in 1892 a serum or anti-toxin was prepared for immunization against diphtheria. As a result tetanus was very greatly reduced in war wounds and diphtheria, once the scourge of childhood, in the long run almost disappeared. In 1954 for the first time the County of London recorded not a single death from this cause.

Below the Poverty-Line

Improvements in medicine and higher standards of sanitation, hygiene, and building practice combined to produce a fall in the death rate, which was approximately halved in fifty years. The decline was slower in the first half of the period (1875–1900), but even then it was commonly believed that reasonably healthy conditions of town life were at last assured. That this, alas! was not so was shown, to the general surprise, by a remarkable book on *The Life and Labour of the People of London*, of which the first volume was published in 1889. The author, Charles Booth, a retired Liverpool shipowner, collected full details, by door-to-door inquiry in carefully chosen "sample" areas, of how people lived—wages, rent, size of family, regularity of employment, etc. What he discovered was that no less than 30 per cent of the population of the world's richest city lived below the poverty-line: that is to say, the food, clothing, and shelter which they could buy with their earnings were not sufficient to keep them in proper physical condition. Clearly, for those 1,200,000 souls the metropolis must be a place of ill-health and misery or dumb despair; the legislation for the betterment of town life completely passed them by. It was thought and hoped that these dreadful statistics applied to London alone, but a dozen years later a similar inquiry at York, a city which was neither particularly large nor particularly poor, gave a corresponding figure of 28 per cent—and this was believed to have been calculated more exactly than Booth's. This established the fact that all our industrial towns must contain, chiefly in the families of the unskilled workers, a mass of people who never had a chance to live even physically satisfactory lives. The problem was perhaps at its worst in the large ports, crowded with Irish immigrants and destitute foreigners, such as the Jews fleeing from persecution in Russian Poland. But another class of people who were conspicuously poor in material goods at least were the farm labourers. Their pay was about half that of a factory hand; their hours of work were unlimited; and their whole life was passed under the often tyrannical eye of the farmer by whom they were employed.

The efforts of Parliament and local authorities had largely got rid of the squalor and disease, if not of the drabness and boredom, which had made the early Victorian town a wretched place even for the craftsman and factory worker in steady employment. Rising wages had helped them on, so that in the 'nineties this class was sure that progress had been made: for them Victorian comfort was no illusion. But it was left for the twentieth century to begin the task of pulling up the "submerged tenth", now found to be nearer three-tenths, for which the Victorian world planned no benefits—except casual employment, some casual charity, the Poor Law, and the police.

Voluntary Action

Meanwhile, however, something was also being done by voluntary action. A strong point in the progress of English society has always been the part played by individuals and societies. People have not been content to wait for the State to do things for them; they have agitated, worked, and organized to help themselves and others. Thus while economists and social theorists might argue for *laissez-faire* and individualists feared that State action would be destructive of liberty, there were always some people to whom evil social and spiritual conditions called urgently for redress, and such people worked out their own ways of bettering those conditions. Charity was often privately organized, collections made of money and goods, and aid distributed to the sick and aged. Two notable examples of private initiative which developed organization on a national scale are to be found in Dr. Barnardo's Homes and the Salvation Army.

Dr. Barnardo (1845–1905) was born in Dublin, though his father was Spanish and his mother English. He studied medicine in London, Paris and Edinburgh, and his practice in London showed him how many destitute children there were in England's capital. He began to devote himself to their care. The first Dr. Barnardo's Home was opened in 1867 in Stepney Causeway, London, where the headquarters of the organization are still to be found. The movement greatly expanded during the founder's lifetime and there were 112 district homes by 1905. It also brought into being imitators, such as the National Children's Home, which was founded in 1869 and grew with equal rapidity and to an approximately equal size. Dr. Barnardo's organization devoted itself to finding, feeding, clothing, housing and educating homeless children. Industrial training, training for the Navy and Mercantile Marine, and an emigration scheme to Canada have all played an important part, and religious teaching was made a foundation of the work. Between 1867 and 1905 about 60,000 children had been brought up, trained and given a start in life. The principle still adhered to is that no destitute child is refused admission.

The creation of the Salvation Army was the work of William Booth (1829–1912). Booth was born in Nottingham. For a time he was a Methodist minister, and he showed from the first his passion for open-air meetings and forceful evangelism. Later he worked at a mission in the East End of London, and what he saw there convinced him of the need for some organized, disciplined effort to improve the spiritual state of the people. He therefore formed the Salvation Army in 1878. He directed it himself as "General" and built it up into a large organization on semi-military lines. His book *In Darkest England, and the Way Out* (1890) told something of its story. From its small beginnings in the East End of London, the Salvation Army has become a vast international organization. Its religious teaching is at one with that of other Protestant faiths, but it believes in realistic and popular methods. A large place is given to music and song—the brass band and street-corner meeting mark the Salvation Army everywhere. The Salvation Army is also active in social work—night shelters, homes for the destitute, and training and emigration schemes. Its work has been most valuable socially and spiritually in helping the poor and distressed. Thus the history of the Salvation Army shows how, amid the general indifference to squalor and poverty in the great Victorian age, individual consciences nevertheless were roused, with results from which we are still benefiting to-day.[1]

[1] See Appendix I, No. 7, for a description of London as seen through the eyes of a down-and-out who was also a poet.

23

VICTORIAN ASPIRATIONS

IN Victorian times the view held was that, if you worked hard enough, you deserved to get on and very probably would get on, and that, if you got on in the world, you would be able to buy everything you or your family needed in order to lead a happy and healthy life. Good food and good shoes, good schools and good holidays—money would buy them all, without any difficulties of scarcity or overcrowding, so the great Victorian motto was Self-Help.

Victorian Interior

For all who could follow this motto there was a standard of comfort to be attained, which centred upon the home. A parlour, overcrowded with furniture and knick-knacks, was a thing which the middle class had always had. Now the thrifty artisan in regular employment was also getting one, as the long rows of respectable brick houses spread to right and left of the tramway lines, which, from the 'seventies onwards, made residence in the congested central area of the town avoidable. Outside amusements were few: hence the frequency with which the piano figured in the home. Furniture was solid and heavy, designed to last a lifetime, during which perhaps the only visible changes would be the accumulation of family photographs, from the 'seventies onwards, as the camera and its products became cheaper and more efficient. In an upper middle-class home the *objets d'art*, displayed on stands significantly known as what-nots, would be more expensive but not necessarily less crowded or more artistic than those on view elsewhere. But the drawing-room in which they stood would look more lived in than the parlour of the less leisured classes, used chiefly on Sundays or to impress an unfamiliar visitor.

The quality and still more the quantity of the food was a distinguishing feature of the way of life to which Self-help might lead —otherwise there was the unskilled labourer's unwholesome and unvaried diet of white bread, margarine, cheap jam, tea, and potatoes. The skilled artisan and the shopkeeper ate meat (including breakfast bacon) to an extent which astonished the thrifty foreigner; they favoured rich, often indigestible puddings and cakes; and "something tasty" would commonly be cooked for supper. On Sundays and other festive occasions hospitality was often the excuse for what we should nowadays regard as gluttony, all the more so if the household had been caught up in the growing teetotal movement, so that there was no additional expenditure to be allowed for on bottled beer or something stronger. The price of food fell rapidly in the last quarter of the nineteenth century, so wages went further, and the imports from overseas which (as we have seen) spelt ruin to the farmer, spelt the cheap loaf, Empire meat, tinned salmon and tinned fruit for the tables of many wage-earning families.

Then, as now, the standard of life depended a good deal upon the number of members of the family or household actually at work. This often tended to put the middle and working classes more nearly on a level, so far as money was concerned, than either side would have supposed. For workers' children usually left school as soon as possible—at some point between the eleventh and thirteenth birthday; those who had reached the top standard were allowed to leave early, and the factories could take on any child as a half-timer at eleven (up to 1893, at ten). They therefore contributed something to the family budget at an age when the perhaps more fortunate children of the middle class were only about half-way through their education and training.

The Position of Women

The same thing was true of the women-folk of the family. Working-class girls were employed in large numbers in the mills of Lancashire and Yorkshire and, indeed, in the lighter jobs throughout industry. They also provided the vanished Victorian army of domestic servants, well over a million strong, which cleaned and cooked and looked after the children in the three- and even four-storied houses of the suburbs. The daughters of the middle class might become shop assistants in the better trades; if they had acquired a reasonable education (rather a big "if") they might aspire to the rank of governess in wealthier homes. But the typewriter, and consequently the typist, was still a novelty, and the City office, until very near the end of the Victorian era, had usually an all-male staff. In the well-to-do Victorian family woman's place was emphatically the home, with Mrs. Beeton's *Household Management* (1861) as an appropriate guide to duties as well as menus.

Nevertheless, it would be wrong to ignore the efforts which were being made to alter the position of women, for there was perhaps no social movement of the time which had in the long run such important consequences. Florence Nightingale and her band of nurses in the horrors of the Crimean winter of 1854–5 gave the first impetus to the demand that women of the upper classes should be allowed to play a part in the world outside the home. The advance was on three fronts. By a series of laws beginning in 1870 an end was slowly made of the monstrous legal position, by which the property of a married woman—land, a share in a business, or money in the bank—used to become the property of her husband to do as he liked with. Then there were educational developments, especially the foundation of women's colleges at Cambridge and Oxford, which made it possible for pioneers to enter the professions.

The first modern girls' schools, such as Queen's College, Harley Street, and Cheltenham Ladies' College, dating from 1848 and 1850, had great difficulty in recruiting suitable staff. Now it was possible for the whole standard of the education of girls at school to be gradually raised. But the old practice of employing an untrained governess for the daughters of the family died hard, because it was firmly rooted not only in a Victorian parent's notions of feminine modesty but often also in the desire to make up for the heavy public-school fees expended on the sons. There was even an unreasonable prejudice against the entry of women into the profession where they were most obviously needed, that of medicine. The pioneer, Elizabeth Garrett Anderson, was obliged to take her own medical degree in Paris; but she secured the opening of London medical degrees to her sex in 1877. The modern hospital in the Euston Road, which is called by her name and was the first to be staffed exclusively by women, has grown out of the dispensary for women started by her in the same poor neighbourhood in 1866.

Lastly, women began to be allowed to figure in public affairs—a natural development, we might suppose, of the great Queen's reign, though she herself did nothing to help it on. In 1867 a proposal was made that they should have the parliamentary vote—eighty Members of the House of Commons were in favour, though nothing came of that until half a century later on. But women ratepayers were allowed the vote in municipal elections in 1869, and in county council elections from the start in 1888; and when the century closed women could also serve on (not merely vote for) district councils and the boards which managed poor relief and schools. A late-Victorian cartoonist, however, could still make an uproarious cartoon on what he took to be the utterly ludicrous idea that some day there might be women police.

Interests and Amusements

Another factor which made the old saying "An Englishman's home is his castle" less true was the appearance in the 'nineties of a new style of newspaper. Hitherto the papers had been serious, informative, and largely local in their circulation: *The Times* and *Telegraph* might reach the north of England, but local organs of opinion—not merely the *Manchester Guardian*, *Liverpool Post*, and *Yorkshire Post*, but papers published independently in every one of the larger towns—were more usually read in their particular areas. When the Victorian age began there were heavy duties, which their opponents called "Taxes on Knowledge", to keep the price of newspapers high: but even when these were all repealed and 1d. became the standard price (except for *The Times*), the regular readers belonged mainly to the middle class. Parliamentary debates, reported in great detail, filled the unattractive columns of small print; there were no big headlines, no photographs to catch the eye; no "stunt" articles to disturb the home.

The *Daily Mail*, first published in 1896, changed all this. Within three years it had a circulation of more than half a million, far greater than that of any other newspaper: they were therefore forced to adapt themselves to the new pattern of journalism.[1] A paper was now expected to be entertaining, exciting, full of new ideas (both good and bad), and always giving people something to talk about. For the first time it became usual for a working-class home to take a daily paper, and it was no longer possible for strict fathers to pull up the drawbridge of the home, as it were, against new thoughts of which they disapproved.

Not all Victorian homes were strict, of course. They might even be divided into types, according to their outside interests. There were those whose members found society and entertainment, as well as deeper things, in the affairs of church or chapel—the Bethels, for instance, which filled the Welsh mining valleys with song. And there was also the society of the private bar and the music hall—the East End of Albert Chevalier's Cockney songs. The former was probably the more representative type, since respectability of appearance, habit, and behaviour commonly

[1] See illustration p. 266

distinguished the skilled from the unskilled worker; and drunkenness, against which the temperance movement, inspired by the churches, was leading a slowly victorious campaign, was thought of as the great cause—though it was equally often the consequence —of failure in the struggle for livelihood. Saturday-night drunkards sprawling in the gutter, Sunday-morning families marching primly through the streets to church—we must admit that both belong to the true picture of Victorian Britain.

Indeed the Victorian age was an age of contrasts. We still hear of Victorian piety, prudery, even of hypocrisy and ugliness, but we know that there was Victorian energy and optimism, and Victorian achievement. To many people the word "Victorian" carries the feeling of stuffiness—of over-filled and decorated rooms with the curtains shutting out the view and the windows tight-closed, of people in dark, sombre and formal clothes, men with high, uncomfortable and stiff collars and women in clothes of great length and complexity. The solid domestic comfort, the large meals and the large families were maintained by domestic servants, sometimes household drudges, who slaved in the basement kitchens, who carried endless trays, coal and hot water upstairs, in the tall Victorian houses, and who carried the slops down. But at the same time the solid material progress of the age had been unsurpassed in any previous period in history, and the standard of life in Victorian England was almost certainly higher than anywhere else in Europe or the America of those days and, of course, far in advance of the countries of the East.

The Religious Background

The progress and prosperity of Victorian days had a religious basis. As one leading English historian[1] has said: "No one will ever understand Victorian England who does not appreciate that among highly civilized, in contradistinction to more primitive, countries it was one of the most religious that the world has known. Moreover, its particular type of Christianity laid a peculiarly direct emphasis upon conduct. . . . If one asks how nineteenth-century English merchants earned the reputation of being the most

[1] Sir R. C. K. Ensor, *England, 1870–1914*, pp. 137–8.

honest in the world (a very real factor in the nineteenth-century primacy of English trade), the answer is: because hell and heaven seemed as certain to them as to-morrow's sunrise, and the Last Judgment as real as the week's balance-sheet. . . . Evangelicalism made other-worldliness an everyday conviction and, as we say, a business proposition; and thus induced a highly civilized people to put pleasure in the background, and what it conceived to be duty in the foreground, to a quite exceptional degree." The Victorians put duty before pleasure—that means they worked hard, and, as England's position was at that time highly favourable, they worked to good effect; they therefore made money and prospered. And as they avoided spending their money on pleasure and did not waste it, they saved. A part of those savings passed by gift or by bequest to the churches and chapels which were springing up in their thousands and to the great charitable organizations of the day. But most of it went back into industry and made more money. Thrift, like honesty, was manifestly the best policy.

The outstanding popular heroes—heroes whose great qualities are still admired—were religious men and men of serious purpose in life. Such were Shaftesbury, Bright, and Gladstone; David Livingstone, the missionary and explorer of darkest Africa; and General Gordon, the devout soldier who fell facing the spears of the heathen dervishes in lonely splendour at Khartoum. It is true that this was also the age of Charles Darwin, whose *Origin of Species* in 1859 first confronted the educated public with a picture of a world of slowly evolving creatures in marked contrast to the traditional notion of a single act by the Divine Creator. A highly simplified idea of evolution as meaning "man descended from a monkey" then produced a vigorous controversy between some scientists and the Churches. A few free-thinkers and agnostics became conspicuous in high places, and there was a more numerous class of those who kept silence about their religious doubts. But the general tone of the national life was scarcely affected. Up to the last years of the reign the English—still more the Scots and the Welsh—continued to be a sabbath-keeping, God-fearing race, who christened their children "Gordon" and flocked to Hawarden Church to hear Gladstone, "the People's William", read the lessons for the day.

Holidays

Let us end this brief survey on a lighter note. The coming of the machine meant the spread of the holiday habit. Both the Saturday half-holiday—still known on the Continent as "the English week-end"—and the Bank holidays, the first of which was celebrated in August 1871, were innovations characteristic of the new industrial Britain. Indeed, by the 'seventies so many people had the leisure and means to seek recreation in the country that the great enclosure movement, which had been slowly eating up what was still left of the commons, came at last to an end. The saving of Epping Forest for the Londoners (it was opened by Queen Victoria in 1882) was only the most spectacular of the triumphs of the Commons Preservation Society, an early precursor of the National Trust.

The Lancashire Wakes weeks, which took the cotton worker in his (and her) thousands to pack the sea-front at Blackpool (the first mere holiday resort to reach borough status, in 1876), are a reminder that "going away" for something more than a day or half-day trip out of town was an activity in which a considerable part of the masses could now afford to share. These were not "holidays with pay", but holidays for which families saved up, in order to enjoy once in the year the benefits of living on an island. The pier and the front at Brighton spelt London by the sea to the millions of the great city: Bath in its great days had had no such meaning. As for the middle-class family, the fortnight or so in seaside lodgings was so inevitable a part of the yearly round that a host of fishing villages grew into resorts as fast as the railway could reach them.

Brighton, as depicted for the readers of *The Graphic* on a fine winter afternoon in 1879, has a more fashionable public than in summer, though nigger minstrels are still to be seen on the promenade. The dresses of the women would obviously prevent any athletic activity except riding, for which the side-saddle provides a rather dangerous facility. The girls' school crocodile reminds us of some of the other restraints of Victorian education. The variety of conveyance—from bath-chair and goat-carriage to victoria and landau—lends interest to the scene and reminds us of the depen-

Victorian Street Scene—The

dence upon servants : notice how many of the carriages have two
men on the box. But if one should ask, how this particular scene
would be changed, say twenty years later, the answer will remind
us that Victorian society, which we have been trying to picture,
was the creation of the new machinery. For the newest social

Brighton, in December 1879

influence—cheapening travel, emancipating women, loosening home ties, adding enormously to the enjoyment of life, and providing Britain with yet another export trade—was the coming of the bicycle.

24

A NEW ERA IN POLITICS

WHEN Queen Victoria died at Osborne on 22nd January 1901, she had reigned so long that most people felt it to be the passing of an era in English life. They were quickly proved right. Even before the outbreak of the First World War in 1914 the Tariff Reform agitation (1903–5) had shown how trade rivalry, such as we had not experienced for well over a century, was creating new problems for Britain. About the same time the appearance of the first motor omnibuses in the streets and of electric light for everyday use drew attention to new scientific discoveries leading to something like a second Industrial Revolution—a revolution that is still in progress. There was also a third change, which showed itself at the general election of January 1906. The record Liberal majority and the election for the first time of a substantial number of Labour members both pointed to the same thing—the voters were now determined to use their votes to redress what may be broadly described as the economic and social grievances of the poor.

There had been nothing like this since the final collapse of Chartism in 1848. Chartism had failed; the new movement of the people succeeded. Up to 1914, however, its success lay in the series of social reforms introduced by the Liberal Governments of Campbell-Bannerman (December 1905–April 1908) and Asquith (April 1908–May 1915). We shall therefore outline them first, and in the rest of this chapter trace the growth of the Socialist and Labour movement from its small beginnings far back in the nineteenth century up to the outbreak of the Second World War.

At the end of that war the Labour Party secured at the 1945 election a big majority for more sweeping reforms. Thus the Welfare State of to-day has grown out of the two things we are now going to examine—the pioneer social reforms of the Liberals, with some additions made by the mainly Conservative governments of the 1920's and 1930's; and the long, slow growth of the Labour movement.

The Liberal Social Reforms 1906–14

The reader of this book need not have experienced more than one general election in his life to be aware that the issues involved and the reasons for the result obtained are never simple. So it was in January 1906. A long period of mainly Conservative government—the party had held office for sixteen and a half of the preceding twenty years—had come to an end, a month before the election, for a variety of reasons, of which unpopularity on account of the lack of social reforms was only one. Nor would it be true to say that they had refrained entirely from making such reforms. Balfour's Education Act of 1902, which will be described in a later chapter, is an important exception. Another was the Workmen's Compensation Act, introduced by Joseph Chamberlain in 1897. As a Birmingham manufacturer Chamberlain was well aware of the frequency of accidents at work and of the very limited extent to which employers had accepted liability. His Act threw the cost of compensation for loss of life and limb upon the employer in a large number of dangerous trades. The main social reform made by the Liberals in the first year of office extended this principle to 6,000,000 more workers, ranging from seamen and fishermen to postmen and domestic servants. The last-named group, which was the biggest, was included at the personal insistence of the Prime Minister, Sir Henry Campbell-Bannerman.

But in 1908 the Liberals showed clearly that they regarded themselves as having been elected with a special mission to help the very poor, who had shared so little in the tide of Victorian prosperity. For it was the very poor—persons with a total income of less than 10s. a week—who benefited by the Old Age Pensions Act, under which the State gave 5s. a week (reduced to 7s. 6d. for a married couple) to support them after the age of seventy. In favourable circumstances, such as a married daughter having a room to spare, this was enough to banish the fear of ending one's days in the workhouse, which had haunted the lives of so many.

Younger people of the same distressed class were the chief gainers from two new institutions of the following year—trade boards and labour exchanges. The trade boards, composed of representatives of employers and employees, together with a neutral chairman, had power to fix minimum wage rates in "sweated industries". These were occupations such as cheap tailoring, the refuge of the unskilled, the unfortunate, and the newly arrived foreign immigrant, where the crowd in search of a job—any job—kept wages at starvation level. It was no new evil. Thomas Hood's picture of the "sweated" sempstress:

> With fingers weary and worn,
> With eyelids heavy and red,
> A woman sat in unwomanly rags,
> Plying her needle and thread—
> Stitch! Stitch! Stitch!
> In poverty, hunger, and dirt

had appeared in *Punch* at Christmas 1843. What was new was the attempt to remedy the evil otherwise than by casual charity. Labour Exchanges had a parallel object—to reduce the amount of casual employment, too often followed by casual unemployment, by providing centres at which accurate information of jobs available in all parts of the country should be freely available to any inquirer.

The special achievement of Lloyd George, who followed Asquith as Chancellor of the Exchequer when the latter became Prime Minister in 1908, was the introduction of compulsory, State-aided insurance. Part I of his big Insurance Act (1911) insured the whole of the wage-earning population against sickness, by means of a fund to which the employee contributed on a stamped card 4d. a week, the employer 3d., and the State the equivalent of a further 2d. This provided the sick with doctoring, medicine, and maintenance. Though a direct imitation of what had been done in Germany since 1883, the scheme caused a loud but ineffectual outcry from some employers. The Insurance Act, Part II, was experimental in character. It created a fund in much the same way as the health fund to insure against unemployment, but the benefits (and of course contributions) were restricted to a small number of trades—building, engineering, shipbuilding, and ironfounding—where employment was known to fluctuate violently. This benefit was also restricted in time, to a maximum of fifteen weeks in any one year.

In other respects, too, the Liberals set the nation's feet upon a path which it has not ceased to tread since. Children benefited by the introduction of school medical inspection, free school meals for the necessitous, and humane juvenile courts for the iniquitous. The whole administration of the criminal law was softened by the introduction of probation of offenders and the Borstal institutions. Trade-union pressure secured an eight-hour day for miners, but shop assistants, who have never been a well-organized body, were also given their legal weekly half-holiday. The list might be further prolonged, but it is more important to notice two big limitations.

One was the failure to reorganize the Poor Law. A Royal Commission had begun to inquire into this subject in 1905, just before the Conservatives left office. The majority of the Commissioners wanted to transfer the work of the boards of guardians to the local councils: but John Burns, who as President of the Local Government Board turned into a complete reactionary, refused to agree. This obvious reform waited in fact until 1929, and other, more thorough-going changes, proposed by a minority of the Commissioners under the powerful influence of Beatrice Webb, were in some cases delayed until after the Second World War.

The other self-imposed limit upon the Liberal social reforms was their hesitation in using taxation, as it is used nowadays, as a means of redressing inequality of income. The House of Lords provoked a constitutional crisis, which resulted after a mighty struggle in the restriction of their veto through the Parliament Act, on account of the increase of taxes proposed by Lloyd George in his "People's Budget" of 1909. The most revolutionary of his proposals was to levy a super-tax on incomes over £5,000, additional to the regular income tax (then 1s. 2d. in the £); and to exact a charge of 20 per cent of the unearned increment (i.e. value not created by the landowner) when landed estate changed hands. It is a sufficient comment to point out that, three years after this Budget was forced through the House of Lords, the British working man was still making a larger contribution to the revenue, chiefly through the indirect taxes on beer and tobacco, than the amount paid from that revenue to benefit him in social services. The Socialists had long intended, and were ultimately destined, to change all that.

Origins of Socialism

Socialism was a direct result of the Industrial Revolution. Wherever industry grew up—first in Britain, but later in France, Germany and elsewhere—Socialism showed itself. The new machines produced great wealth and created a new, well-to-do class of factory owners, managers, and others who benefited by the changes. Economists taught that the efforts of private business men and competition among them were essential to the smooth working of the economic system. *Laissez-faire*—leaving well alone—would then produce what was best for everybody. But it was soon apparent that the industrial system also brought with it many abuses—the ruthless exploitation of the labour of women and children, overcrowding in slums, poverty and unemployment for many. The Socialists were those who argued that industry should be taken out of the hands of private owners and business men, and that land and capital should be brought under State control, so that the whole industrial system could be organized and run for the common good.

Robert Owen, in the early nineteenth century, has often been called "the father of English Socialism". Owen was one of the self-made men, a successful mill-owner and capitalist. But he could also see the evils of the system. Accordingly he said: "All individual competition is to cease; all manufactures are to be carried on by National Companies." Here was the essential idea of public control. He was also interested and active, as we know, in working for factory laws and trade unions. His social principle is expressed by the motto, used at the time by working-class movements, "Each for All and All for Each". But the national movement of trade unions he supported, the Grand National Consolidated Trades Union, broke up in 1834, and for the time being Owen's socialist ideas came to nothing.

Marx and other Influences

Later on a German Jew, Karl Marx, who spent much of his life writing in London, worked hard to formulate a scientific theory of Socialism or Communism, as it was sometimes called. Marx published his *Communist Manifesto* in 1848, and his long and long-winded *Das Kapital* (Volume I) in 1867. These works have immense importance in the history of socialism abroad; their teachings were taken up by Lenin and were behind the Russian Revolution in 1917. Marx argued that capitalism was marked by a class war: the rich got richer and the poor poorer, and thus there was a lasting struggle between them. The capitalists, driven on by greed for expansion and profit, would concentrate capital into fewer and fewer hands. Small businesses would disappear and great monopolies develop. In this process, the fate of the workers would be increasing misery. Capitalism, he maintained, could only be overthrown by a violent revolution of the workers; they would overthrow the capitalists, seize control of their monopolies, and work the capital for themselves.

Marx dismissed Owen and other early English socialists as mere Utopians: but his own theory of violence never really had much effect in this country. For one thing, laws passed in 1855 and 1862 opened wide the privilege of working a business with limited liability. The shareholder was now liable, in the event of failure, only to the extent of the loss of his share and not to that of his whole resources, as had been the case earlier. This encouraged the growth of a large number of small shareholders—thus there were more capitalists than ever, not fewer as Marx had supposed. And already, when he was working in London, many improvements in the workers' lot were gradually coming about. Some of the workers' leaders, like William Lovett, the hero of Chartism, came to see that in spite of all its disadvantages private enterprise had produced great wealth and had led to improvements all round, so that disturbances which would frighten capital and lower production would most likely do more harm than good.

In 1881, however, a group of intellectuals, influenced by what was going on in Germany, where the socialists were Marxist, formed the Social Democratic Federation. This organization, of which H. M. Hyndman and William Morris, artist, craftsman, poet, were leaders, adopted a programme on Marxian lines; the leaders split among themselves and little was achieved. But its meetings, in Trafalgar Square and elsewhere, did something to spread socialist ideas.

Much more influential and much less Marxian was the Fabian Society, founded in 1884. It was perhaps the least Marxian of socialist bodies, and its members believed in a "policy of permeation". They therefore concentrated their efforts on educating public opinion by means of the *Fabian Tracts*, which proved the need for social reforms, and on getting their ideas carried out almost unnoticed in the field of local government. The 500 members of the Fabian Society included a number of influential people, like the economists Sidney and Beatrice Webb and the dramatist Bernard Shaw. With his many popular plays in the coming years, most of them dealing with topical social issues, Shaw did much to awaken in all classes criticism of the existing order and to stimulate ideas of socialist reform.

Other influences on socialist thought came from Henry George and Robert Blatchford. Henry George was an American who published in 1879 *Progress and Poverty*. He proposed a Single Tax, on land values, and stimulated a demand for nationalization of the land. Robert Blatchford, not an intellectual but an ex-soldier, was nevertheless master of a vigorous and expressive style. In 1891 he started a socialist weekly, called *Clarion*. He showed great sympathy for the under-dog; he was not a Marxist but more like the earlier Utopian socialists. His books, *Merrie England* and *Britain for the British*, like the *Clarion*, aroused much popular interest.

Beginnings of the Labour Party

Two miners had been elected to Parliament in 1874. The total of working-class candidates elected became 3 in 1880, 11 in 1885, and 10 in 1886. But all of these sat with the Liberals; they were sometimes known by the term "Lib-Lab".

In 1893, however, an important step was taken when the Independent Labour Party was founded under the chairmanship of Keir Hardie. Hardie was a fervent Scotsman of humble birth, a coal-miner at the age of ten, who made himself a devoted exponent of the working-class cause: when elected to the House of Commons in 1892, he arrived in a cap and workman's suit. He was determined to build up a separate parliamentary Independent Labour Party. At the next election, in 1895, the I.L.P. had twenty-eight candidates, but all of them—even Hardie—were defeated. The I.L.P. was a beginning, but something more was needed. It was the support of the Trade Unions, and Hardie set out to win this support.

Keir Hardie

So it was that in 1900 a meeting was held in London, to which came representatives of the I.L.P., the S.D.F., the Fabians, and the Trade Unions. They set up what was known as the Labour Representation Committee. Two of their candidates, including Hardie, were elected to Parliament in that year. In 1906 the L.R.C. became simply the Labour Party. At the general election of that year twenty-nine members were elected to Parliament, including Ramsay MacDonald and Philip Snowden, who were destined to be the first Labour Prime Minister and Chancellor of the Exchequer. The new Labour Party also had the general support (in 1906) of twenty-four other M.P.'s, including fourteen representatives from coal-mining districts who had been elected through the influence of the miners' unions. These finally adhered to the Labour Party in 1909.

Influence of Trade Unions

Trade Unionism was, in fact, having an important influence on the whole growth of the Labour Party. Two challenges to the power of the Trade Unions had in the outcome effects favourable to them, and led at the same time to a strengthening of the Labour Party. The first challenge came in the Taff Vale case. The Taff Vale Railway Co. in South Wales had suffered loss by a strike, and in 1901 sued the union, the Amalgamated Society of Railway Servants. The court decided that the union must pay large damages. The result was an outcry from trade unions in general, for it appeared that, in spite of the Acts of 1871 and 1875 which had seemed to protect them, trade-union funds were in danger. Their funds might melt away altogether if, after strikes, the employers brought a number of successful actions. The unions were determined to overthrow the Taff Vale decision. They gave increasing support to the L.R.C., and assisted it in the victories of 1906. The Labour Party in Parliament pressed the new Liberal Government to help it, and the result was the Trades Disputes Act of 1906. It gave the unions a powerful position : they could not be sued at law for losses caused in trades disputes, and the right to picket in strikes —about which there had been a separate law case, *Quinn v. Leathem*, also in 1901—was more clearly recognized than before. The result also gave enhanced prestige to the Labour Party and increased its numbers, as more of the unions became affiliated to the party.

The second challenge came in the Osborne case. The unions were contributing out of their funds to the Labour Party. Was this legal—or should their activities be confined to trade union and benefit purposes? It was an awkward point. And some of the trade unionists, who were themselves Liberals or Conservatives, objected to the money they paid for membership of the unions being used to finance the Labour Party. In 1908 W. V. Osborne, a branch secretary of a railway union, went to the courts to seek to stop his union using its funds for that purpose. He lost, but appealed and in 1909 the House of Lords decided in his favour. This was a blow to the unions and to the finances of the Labour Party—16 M.P.'s were deprived of a salary.

Once more, however, the Liberals helped the struggling Labour members out of their difficulties. In 1911 the Liberal Government introduced payment of M.P.'s—a great boon to the working-class member. In 1913, responding to Labour pressure, the government passed the Trade Union Act. This allowed trade unions to take part in political activities and to finance them, provided that the members expressed their approval by ballot, and provided that any member who did not wish to contribute to the political activities could contract out. This was really quite satisfactory for the Labour Party—for many trade-union members would shirk the trouble of signing a special form to contract out and some might also hesitate to draw attention to their belonging to another party.

Other events in these years illustrated the increasing power of the trade unions. They grew in size, and they organized more and more as great unions to cover the whole of a particular industry rather than as small unions covering a single craft. Thus they aimed at one union for railwaymen—not separate unions for engine-drivers, porters, clerks, etc. There was already the Miners' Federation, founded in 1888. In 1910 Tom Mann and Ben Tillett formed the National Transport Workers' Federation (all transport workers, except railwaymen). In 1913 several railway unions amalgamated to form the National Union of Railwaymen. Next year there was a triple alliance, of miners, railwaymen, and transport workers. New ideas of government were discussed by trade unionists and socialists—Syndicalism, Industrial Unionism, Guild Socialism. Syndicalism came from France and favoured local action, Industrial Unionism from America, where the programme envisaged action by "One Big Union". But both stood for direct revolutionary action by the workers in each industry, and their devotees hoped that this might lead on to control of the whole country. The Guild Socialists were not so violent, but hoped for guilds of producers to run each industry. Syndicalism had much to do with a series of big strikes—by railwaymen, seamen and ship's firemen, dockers, and coal-miners—which filled the public mind in 1910–12. They were in each case the largest the particular industry had experienced: nearly a million miners were out early in 1912. They were also marked by unusual acts of violence, especially in Liverpool and South Wales. Tonypandy in Glamorganshire earned a certain fame, both as the scene of a riot, to which the Hussars had to be dispatched from Salisbury Plain, and as the place of publication of the most notorious syndicalist pamphlet, entitled *The Miners' Next Step*.

These industrial stuggles had somewhat diverted Labour energies from the political movement. But by 1914 the Labour Party was firmly established. It had over forty supporters in the House of Commons, and it had its own newspaper, the *Daily Herald*. Backed by the powerful trade unions and profiting by its parliamentary experience, the Labour movement was now considerable. Nevertheless, in Parliament the Labour Party was still small when compared with either of the old parties.

The Labour Party after the First World War

An outstanding event was the rise of the Labour Party to the position of second party, and the decline of the once-powerful Liberal Party. The war brought a new social atmosphere—the idea of reconstruction; the determination to build a better world on the basis of the common sacrifices made during the war years by all classes; a new and more drastic attack on slums, poverty, and unemployment. New voters were enfranchised by the Representation of the People Act of 1918—all men at twenty-one, and women at thirty. The Labour Party put forward its policy of Socialism—"the nationalization of the means of production, distribution, and exchange", to be brought about not by violent revolution, as in Russia, but by parliamentary means. In 1917 the Co-operative movement had formed its own small party: this worked in close alliance with Labour. The Labour Party grew rapidly in strength, as the results of successive elections show:

Year	Seats contested	Votes received	Members elected
1910	56	370,802	42
1914–18	First World War		
1918	361	2,244,000	57
1922	414	4,236,000	142
1923	427	4,348,000	191

As a result of the election of 1923 the first Labour Government took office early in the following year—with Liberal support. It was an uneasy arrangement, which lasted for less than ten months, and was followed by a strong Conservative reaction. There was another Labour Government in 1929–31, but it broke down during a financial crisis, which will be discussed later in connection with the gold standard. The Prime Minister (MacDonald) changed sides, and continued as head of a new government, which was formed by a coalition between the Conservatives and a section of the Liberals and a tiny fragment of the Labour Party. This lasted, under three successive leaders, until the first great crisis of the war (May 1940). Churchill, on becoming Prime Minister, then formed a genuine all-party ministry with full Labour support.

During the period of the two Labour Governments there had been no radical Socialist measures passed—partly, no doubt, because Labour had not a clear majority. But the Labour Party had clearly established its place as one of two main parties in the state; in 1940 its future prospects might be judged by the fact that it provided two out of Churchill's four colleagues in the inner War Cabinet. But we must now consider the inter-war period from a different angle.

The General Strike, 1926

Ever since the end of the First World War there had been industrial trouble. The world economic system had been dislocated by the war, and Britain found it more difficult than ever to secure buyers for her exports. Coal was particularly affected. Britain was losing her markets for a number of reasons—new sources of supply had been developed during the war in Germany and Poland, then came a general decline in world trade, and there was increasing use in ships of oil fuel instead of coal. There was a growing demand for nationalization of major industries, especially coal-mining, for which it had been recommended in the majority interim Report of the official Sankey Commission in 1920. It was hoped by workers in these industries that in this way the threat of lower wages and longer hours might be escaped. Meanwhile, unemployment grew and unrest continued. There was a railway strike—a virtually complete stoppage—late in 1919; a long miners' strike in 1921. Unemployment, at the end of 1921, was nearly 2,000,000, and it remained above the million mark throughout the decade.

The troubles of the coal industry persisted, despite two commissions of inquiry. Both miners and owners resisted compromise over wages and hours in 1926, and the miners' strike—or lock-out as they regarded it—began. This time they had been promised support, and the Trades Union Congress called a General Strike. It lasted nine days. It was a direct threat to the government—and was declared to be illegal. Voluntary workers responded to appeals to keep essential services running, but the life of the people as a whole was endangered. The trade-union leaders, who had planned for a sympathetic strike and not for class war, called the strike off, though the miners struggled on for some months.

It was a real moment of national crisis. Fortunately the country as a whole remained calm, there was little or no violence, and the trade-union leaders showed moderation and wisdom in bringing the use of this too-dangerous weapon to an end. In particular, it should be noticed that only the "first line" of the trade-union forces was called out on strike. They could have taken more drastic action—for instance, by cutting off electric light and gas. As it was, the nation passed safely through a crisis which might easily have led to a revolutionary situation. Unemployment remained a grave social evil until the Second World War, but the method of direct action against the government was not tried again.

Policies of the Conservative and Liberal Parties, 1919–39

The Liberals made their last attempt to regain power on this same issue of unemployment, which their "Orange Book" in 1929 proposed to conquer by heavy expenditure on public works. They had failed, and by 1939 there was no mistaking the collapse of the Liberal Party, which has now but a handful of Members in the House of Commons. The Liberals were caught, after 1918, between two extremes. They could not resist Socialism as definitely and clearly as the Conservatives; they could not offer as much to the masses as the Labour Party with its wide and far-reaching Socialist policy. The Liberal Party was also gravely weakened by a lack of harmony between its two leaders, Asquith (prime minister, 1908–16) and Lloyd George (prime minister, 1916–22). The latter was considered to have driven the former from office. Nevertheless, the virtual disappearance of this once-great party is regretted by many, for it stood for ideals of high and lasting value—freedom, toleration, democracy. But it is, perhaps, true that these Liberal ideals have now been largely adopted by both the Conservative and Labour Parties and are recognized and upheld by British people as a whole.

On looking back, it seems to us that the growth of the Labour Party was the key event of the inter-war period. But although the Conservative governments which mainly held office at this time had no reform programmes comparable to those of 1906–14 and 1945–50, only one of their domestic measures could fairly be described by their opponents as reactionary, and many marked a further step forward. In 1927 the Trade Disputes Act, which tried to limit the right of "sympathetic" striking and substituted "contracting-in" for the "contracting-out" system of 1913, did bear an appearance of revenge for the General Strike of the preceding year. But the first effective housing policy belongs to this period. In 1920 Lloyd George's unemployment scheme, which had been a modest experiment, was made to cover every important industry except agriculture. In 1925 the pensions system was extended to widows and orphans. In 1929 a new Local Government Act, Neville Chamberlain's masterpiece, abolished the Boards of Guardians and largely transformed the system of poor relief which had existed since 1834.

Such measures as the above helped to soften the blow of unemployment. The system of the "dole", as the weekly measure of relief was indignantly termed, was more generous than anything ever heard of in this connection before 1914. But the grave problems, of which a high rate of unemployment was the outcome, in a sense overshadowed the social legislation of the Conservative governments.

25

NEW PROBLEMS FOR BRITAIN

THE rapid, almost breath-taking, advance of science and invention sets difficult problems before the people of every nation. But our own problems since 1900 have been particularly serious, because far-reaching industrial changes (to be described in the next chapter) are taking place at the same time as big changes in our world position; these were beginning before either of the two world wars but have been speeded up and made harder for us by each of them.

Until the end of the nineteenth century, Britain possessed a great and growing export trade and could afford to admit imports freely. In 1891, we spent upon imports a sum equal to one quarter of the entire national income. But other countries, especially the United States and Germany, were rapidly developing their industries and becoming competitors in the race for world trade. The type of goods being manufactured by other countries included the very goods on which Britain's earlier trade had been based, notably textiles. In the 1820's, textiles had represented two-thirds of British exports; in 1860, they were half of the whole; but by 1913 they accounted for only one-third. On the other hand, metal and engineering products, which in earlier years had been relatively small, had increased by 1913 to form nearly a quarter of our total exports; clearly, the future of Britain depended upon the adaptability of our industries to a changing world.

The fact that the world was changing, and changing to our disadvantage, provided the basis for Joseph Chamberlain's famous "Tariff Reform" campaign of 1903–5. He carried a large part of the Conservative Party with him in his twofold claim. He showed by numerous illustrations that British industrialists were being swamped in the home market by cheap goods produced, and exported to us, by foreign competitors such as Germany. A tariff on foreign commodities would check this. Chamberlain also claimed that, if we reintroduced a tariff, we could profitably combine it with a system of Imperial Preferences. Let us encourage the Dominions to give a preference in their markets to our manufactures by giving a preference in our markets to their foodstuffs. But the defeat of his party at the 1906 election showed that Joseph Chamberlain had spoken, if not wrongly, then too soon. The years which followed the election were years of mounting prosperity.

The exports of the United Kingdom were still on the increase, but so were our imports—and, when calculated per head of population the growth of imports was the faster of the two. This was largely ignored at the time because of our other compensating advantages. For Britain had large claims on foreign countries besides the payments due for our exports. As our mercantile marine in the years before 1914 was four times the size of any other, large sums were earned by the carrying trade. As the City of London held the world leadership in all matters of finance, many firms in foreign countries paid large sums for the services of British banks and insurance companies, which they employed to help them conduct their own trade and industry. Thirdly, there was our practice of investing abroad a large part of the new wealth which accumulated in Britain year by year; private investors were well aware that, if the risk involved was higher than at home, so also was the rate of interest. By 1912 the total of these overseas investments was some £3,500 million, nearly half of it being placed inside the British Empire, and the annual investment had reached £180 million. The interest due was, therefore, a further very large item in our *invisible* trade—the things which enabled us to import much more than could be paid for by our direct *visible* exports. Thus the position up to 1914 was that we had big reserves from which to meet the shock of increased competition in the world markets. So far the only sign of serious danger was that real wages, that is, the amount of goods which wages would buy, had ceased to rise in the new century (which was a time of rising prices)—the first time the workers had had this experience since the remote days of the Hungry 'Forties.

Motoring in the summer of 1905—an Edwardian idyll

Effects of the First World War

From the outbreak of the World War in 1914 the country's industries were, of course, largely diverted to serve the demand for armaments, and during the struggle for life against the German submarine campaign in 1917–18 to keep up exports seemed a thing of minor importance. The mercantile marine was quickly rebuilt at the end of the war, but not to its full pre-war superiority over all comers. Otherwise the physical damage—not counting the sacrifice of a million lives—was small, and the Empire emerged with some additional colonial territory in the form of Mandates under the supervision of the League of Nations. We also emerged with an important addition to our force of women workers, since the call for everyone to help to win the war had largely broken down the old class prejudice which identified "ladies" by their abstention from paid employment. City offices, where girl typists had been in growing demand since about 1900, were transformed by this change, and nearly all the professions were also gainers from it. When the Second World War broke out, Britain proved to be second only to Russia in the number and variety of the tasks and responsibilities which its women citizens were prepared to undertake.

But the main effects of the events of 1914–18 on our economic situation were as follows. The sale of part of our foreign assets and investments—perhaps a quarter of the whole—for war purposes abroad had temporarily diminished our "invisible" income. At the same time there was a rise in world prices, which reduced what we could buy with the income that remained. Much more serious, however, was the increased competition of exports not only from the United States, but also from small, efficient European rivals like Sweden, Switzerland, and the new Czechoslovakia and even Poland. There arose, too an aggressive Far Eastern rival in Japan, with its low wages—the one Asiatic country that had rapidly industrialized itself during the latter part of the nineteenth century.

By 1928 we were paying out 50 per cent more than before the war for the imports we bought, and getting in only 33 per cent more for the exports we sold. Cotton goods, now produced on a

London bus-conductress—a novelty of the First World War. The omnibus has solid tyres and the minimum of weather protection

large scale in Indian as well as Japanese factories, made up only one-fifth of our exports. The coal trade was another of our former stand-bys which never recovered. Markets lost during the war were difficult to regain. The changes made in the political map of Europe through the break-up of the old empires and the creation of new states affected the position badly, for the new states were anxious to gratify patriotic feelings and build up their strength by developing their own industries. They therefore adopted heavy tariffs to keep out foreign imports, which increased national jealousies and in time became one of the causes of a second world war. Again, after the Russian Revolution of 1917 that vast country set up a remarkable system of State planning and aimed at becoming entirely self-supporting. And the demand for Germany to pay huge sums in war reparations, which was not finally given up as a bad job until 1932, could only be fulfilled if the Germans (who had once been Britain's best European customer) exported more and imported less than other nations.

October 1929 brought the onset of the greatest economic depression the modern world had known. It began with the sudden collapse of a prolonged Stock Exchange boom, a glorified version of the South Sea Bubble, in America, where "millionaires became beggars in a day". Unemployment in Britain grew with the decline in world trade until, in 1932, it reached the alarming total of 3,000,000. In America unemployment rose to still greater heights —to 12 million—while in Germany the unrest due to the fact that their unemployed numbered over 7 million greatly assisted the rise of Hitler, who promised to find a cure.

Abandonment of the Gold Standard

This world "economic blizzard" of 1929, which did not blow itself out, as we might say, until 1933 or later, had fateful consequences for Britain. In 1925, when Churchill was Chancellor of the Exchequer, a great effort to restore pre-war conditions had been made by bringing back its pre-war value to the £. Gold sovereigns did not replace the treasury notes, to which we had become accustomed since 1914, but large sums of money could once again be changed into gold at pre-war rates. During the world crisis, however, our export trade declined, so that foreigners began to wonder whether we were earning enough to be able permanently to maintain the gold value of the £; their fears were strengthened by the view, expressed in the May Report, that we were spending too much on the relief of the unemployed. In the summer of 1931 there was a run on the bank—foreigners turned their holdings into gold at the Bank of England. The Bank borrowed large quantities of gold from America and France to meet these demands. The Labour Government was replaced by a "National" Government, pledged to stern economy. But foreigners still lacked faith in our future, and on September 21st we were compelled to admit defeat. Since that date the pound has ceased to have a fixed value in gold, and although there are still many parts of the western world which base their trade on sterling (i.e. on the value of British paper money), financial leadership has passed decisively to the Americans.

Other results of our action were these. Gold as the standard of currency was eventually abandoned everywhere, even in America, so that the value of the £ has to be kept up by exchange regulations, which carefully restrict purchases from those countries (such as America) where we have not got a good trade balance, and even limit the sums to be spent there by travellers. Since it was necessary to watch the balance of trade so closely, the National Government had good reasons for abandoning our free trade policy, against which many manufacturing interests had already campaigned for thirty years. In 1932 a general tariff was introduced of 10 per cent, which was later raised to 20 per cent. Most foodstuffs and raw materials still came in free, but wheat imports were restricted to a fixed quota. An Imperial Economic Conference was held in Ottawa later in the same year, at which we struck bargains with the Dominions, reducing the tariff rates in the United Kingdom and the non-self-governing colonies so as to admit imports more easily from the Dominions than from foreign countries, and securing similar concessions for our goods in return. How these imperial preferences would affect British trade in the long run was uncertain: it was an awkward fact that we had always in the past traded much more largely with foreign countries than with the Dominions, the special case of India alone excepted. But up to 1939 our exports were still receiving a stimulus from another result of our abandonment of the gold standard in 1931, namely, the consideration that the fall in the value of the £ made it easier for the foreigner to pay for what he bought in Britain.

Unemployment in what had been our great export industries—such as textiles, the iron and steel trades, and coal-mining—remained the blackest feature in our national life, though the re-armament programme, on which the rising power of Hitler forced us reluctantly to embark, helped to bring down the total of unemployed from 3 to 1½ millions. But when war broke out again in September 1939—and still more the next summer, when we found ourselves standing alone against a triumphant enemy—the economic resources of Britain were strained to breaking-point. In order to share out supplies as fairly as possible an efficient system of food rationing was immediately introduced, followed the next year by clothes rationing. Subsidies were used to keep down the price of most important foods, while the "points" system secured a fair distribution of many semi-luxuries like biscuits and tinned fish. Our resources in manpower also were handled much more carefully than in 1914–18: everybody not required for the armed forces was fully employed, for the most part at good wages. But this time the submarine blockade and the German air offensive between them caused our exports to dwindle away to insignificance, while the havoc of bombing in the industrial areas and principal seaports, besides the immediate suffering it caused, also handicapped post-war recovery.

Our Present Difficulties

Among the main economic results of the Second World War were a heavy loss of British overseas investments, which had been revived with much trouble after the first war; the destruction of property and the difficulty of providing repairs and replacements for buildings, plant and equipment after heavy use during six years of war; world shortages of food and raw materials; and the greatly increased prices of some urgently needed products which Britain must buy from overseas. There were also grave losses from the effects of the war upon our Empire—the independence of Burma, the changed status of India, the disaffection in Malaya, the ending of our old commercial connections with China. Gone were the days when we could say complacently, Trade follows the flag.

The so-called Cold War adds yet another problem. In spite of the work and ideals of the United Nations Organization (U.N.O.), set up by the free nations of the world at the San Francisco Conference of 1944, another armaments drive has become necessary. The wartime alliance with Soviet Russia has not lasted, and unsettled conditions still prevail at many points on the circumference of the now vastly extended empire and sphere of influence of the great Communist Power. Our continued vast expenditure on armaments, though heavily subsidized from America, makes it necessary to limit home consumption in order to release more goods for export; it also calls for manufacturers and workers to produce more goods more efficiently and at lower costs of production. The same set of causes gravely handicaps our efforts by abstracting two years of a young man's working life for military service, a burden we have never borne in peace-time before. Yet on our success as a trading people depends the maintenance of a high level of employment, and therewith our whole standard of life.

Another problem of the present day, though not a result of the war, is the ageing population. This has come about largely because of the advances in medicine and the improved conditions of life which have already been described. People live longer than they did, and so the proportion of old people in the population becomes larger. We have become in fact a middle-aged nation, older on the average by fifteen years. The old people, as well as the very young, are dependents, and have to be maintained by the productive, full-time working people in the middle-age groups of the nation. This problem may become still more prominent with further medical advances, and it is already engaging public attention. It makes all the more important full use of machinery and new sources of power.

In days before pensions, old people commonly remained at work to a high age, and some of them reached the high age because they were still working. It is almost certain that in the next generation we shall need once more to put back the age of retirement in order to increase the proportion of our population which is "gainfully employed". But it is not easy for the large-scale factory or business to cope with the special needs of the older age-groups among its employees.

With the development of science and industry there has been a general tendency towards great size in the industrial or business concern. The cost of installing modern machinery and applying new processes is often so great that only a large undertaking can shoulder it. Again, the economic advantages of large-scale production are so big that only a large concern which takes advantage of them can hold its own. Thus the old days of competition between small units seem to be passing, and industry is more and more dominated by giant firms, some of them owned by the State, others by their shareholders. The effects of monopoly, or a near approach to it, in keeping up the cost to the consumer—but not necessarily the quality—of goods and services, constitute another of the problems of the new age. But this at least is not a problem peculiar to Britain.

26

A NEW INDUSTRIAL REVOLUTION?

THE two world wars have had such a great, and in many respects terrible, effect upon us and upon our country that nowadays people in Britain are inclined to regard August 1914 as the date at which one kind of life came to an end and another, which we are still experiencing, began. But this is only partly true. Victorian social habits were already being affected by such harmless novelties as the bicycle twenty years or so before the war revolutionized them. Our position in world trade had also begun to change for the worse long before the perils of war cost us our best markets. The demand for equality—for more leisure, better education, and generously planned social services—made itself heard as early as 1906, although it needed the common risks and sufferings of two wars to render the demand widely effective. The case is the same also as regards machinery and inventions. War gave the scientists full scope, because no expenditure was too great for keeping ahead of the enemy: but the inventions which have transformed industry were being made or at least foreshadowed by 1900. The use of electric power and of the internal combustion engine both became prominent in the reign of Edward VII (1901–10): the consequences were so far-reaching that perhaps what we see now is still only the first stage of a new industrial revolution which began with the Edwardians.

Electric Power

To the development of electricity men of many nations contributed. Some of the early researches were made in the eighteenth century—about the time that Watt's steam-engine was becoming useful—by the Italians, Galvani and Volta. The Dane, Hans Oersted, had a share early in the nineteenth century. In this country Sir Humphry Davy, Faraday, and Lord Kelvin all made notable contributions to our knowledge and use of electricity. Electric motors and dynamos of a kind were to be seen before 1850. Samuel Morse, the American who invented the morse code of dots and dashes, made the first successful demonstration of telegraphic communication in 1844; the submarine cable between England and America was laid in 1866. Next came the telephone, largely the work in 1872–6 of Alexander Graham Bell of Edinburgh. The German, Hertz, and the Italian, Marconi, experimented in the transmission of electric impulses without wires. In 1901 Marconi sent the first wireless signals across the Atlantic, using the morse code—from that has developed the broadcasting of to-day, with the wireless set a feature of almost every home, and television the latest development.

Thus the development of electricity made possible the telegraph, the telephone, wireless and television. It also made possible electric lighting, when the American Edison, around 1880, besides being the second (but independent) inventor of the incandescent lamp, improved the dynamo into a reasonable means of generating electric power. Since then the use of electricity has steadily increased, replacing gas as a means of artificial light; serving transport in the driving of tramways, underground tube railways, and electric locomotives on railways; and providing a source of power in factories. To-day steel pylons carry the power lines across the countryside from the power stations, most of them dependent on coal, though hydro-electric schemes have been developed on a small scale in the Highlands and Snowdonia. The demand for electricity is growing; even now much of the plant is old-fashioned, and the supply in places insufficient. But the British Electricity Authority is building new power stations and eventually a super-grid will cover the whole country.

To-day an electric motor can be used anywhere to drive any machine, however large or small, at a cost comparable with that of other sources of power. As a result the use of the steam-engine is being increasingly confined to generating the electricity, and driving steam locomotives and ships, for electric power has great advantages. It means that industries can be set up in new areas away from the older sources of power. So it is that there has been a vast growth of light industries driven by electric power around

London. The electric-powered factory, again, is much cleaner; there is an absence of smoke and soot. The factory itself is simpler; it is not encumbered with shafts and belts for driving the machinery, for each machine can be switched on and off as wanted, and the electric wires carrying the power can run conveniently and cheaply to different buildings or sheds, making the design and layout of the factory simpler and cheaper.

The Internal-Combustion Engine

Petrol, the gasolene or "gas" of the Americans, is another new and highly efficient source of power. Early experiments in the invention of the internal-combustion engine were made by N. A. Otto, a German, and he used petrol (refined petroleum) as fuel. Then, in 1885, Daimler, another German engineer, produced a smaller, lighter-oiled engine, which was first applied to a cycle and later to a car. Another German, Dr. Rudolf Diesel, who had worked with Dr. Otto, invented the Diesel engine, which runs on heavy oils: this was successfully used for a big ship in 1912. Meanwhile, in 1896 the Daimler Company was established at Coventry. The date is significant. An old law required the speed of mechanically propelled vehicles in England to be limited to four miles an hour in the country, and to two miles an hour in the towns; and each vehicle to be preceded by a man carrying a red flag, a measure originally designed to warn horse-drivers and riders of an approaching steam roller. This law was repealed in 1896, and in the same year the first motor car appeared in the Lord Mayor's Show in London.

A new transport era had now begun.[1] The new invention had a decisive advantage which enabled it to forge ahead rapidly—the high ratio of power to weight. A steam locomotive in the 1880's weighed about 300 lb. for every horse-power it developed. A modern petrol engine may weigh no more than 1 lb. per horse-power.

The iron roads, as it was once fashionable to call the railways, had drawn all the long-distance traffic, and some of the short-distance as well, away from the macadamized highways. Motor vehicles, however, made them busier than ever before. Besides

[1] See illustration, p. 224.

private motor cars, motor-bus services gave town-dwellers easy means of visiting the countryside, and villagers easy access to towns and shopping centres. Motor lorries and wagons could now carry goods direct to and from the factory or warehouse without any loading and unloading at railway stations, and farmers could now send their produce and their cattle direct to distant markets. But motor traffic created fresh problems in road construction. Wider roads and more reliable and uniform surfaces were needed, as well as the strong foundations recommended by Telford a century earlier. The cost of road-making greatly increased, and the government from 1910 onwards adopted the plan of taxing motor vehicles to form a special Road Fund, from which grants were made to counties and boroughs towards the making and upkeep of roads; local highway rates covered the rest of the expense.

While the light oil or petrol engine thus revolutionized road transport, and the heavy-oil Diesel engine found a use in the most advanced designs of railway locomotives, great changes also took place in the world of shipping. In 1905 two Atlantic liners had been launched, for which the motive power was supplied by turbines, which had been invented by Parsons twenty years before to generate electricity. To the turbine was now added the advantage of oil fuel—cleaner, more easily loaded, more compact, and producing 50 per cent more steam than the same weight of coal. Hence the modern liner and modern warship: nowadays most of the new tonnage built consists of motor vessels.

Air Transport

Above all, the petrol engine also made travel by air possible—since this was a problem of which the solution depended upon the provision of an engine of adequate power, compactness, and reliability. For centuries men had wanted to fly, and even in the Middle Ages and during the Renaissance great scientists and artists (such as Leonardo da Vinci, born 500 years ago) had foreseen that the time would come when men would be able to fly. In the eighteenth century, balloons were used for the purpose, but these could not be steered and were at the mercy of the winds. In 1903, however, the American brothers Wilbur and Orville Wright

fitted a petrol engine to an aeroplane and achieved the first controlled flight. Only six years later the new science of aeronautics
had progressed so far that the Frenchman Blériot could successfully risk the Channel flight from Calais to Dover. Nothing could
now prevent mankind from achieving the kind of world of which
Tennyson had prophesied the coming in 1842, when he

Saw the heavens fill with commerce, argosies of magic sails,
Pilots of the purple twilight, dropping down with costly bales;
Heard the heavens fill with shouting, and there rain'd a
     ghastly dew
From the nations' airy navies grappling in the central blue.

During the First World War small biplanes with their primitive
equipment, better adapted as scouts than as bombers, rather than
the huge but clumsy airships of the German Count Zeppelin, foreshadowed the important part aircraft were to play (as we all know)
in the second war: bombing, happily, was still in its infancy. In
1919 two British airmen, Captain John Alcock and Lieut. Arthur
Brown, made the first Atlantic flight, from Newfoundland to Ireland, in seventy-two hours. About the same time, a daily air
service was started to carry passengers between London and Paris,
and within ten years air services were making regular flights to
India, and thereafter to any part of the world: even the North Pole
was not left unvisited.

In 1938, the year before war again broke out, over 70,000 people
flew from Britain to countries overseas, and ten years later the
number had grown to 914,000. Since then, again, the speed and
availability of services have been enormously improved by the
use of turbo- and jet-propelled air liners and of helicopters.
Urgently needed chemicals, drugs, and machine parts, specimens
for zoological gardens, perishable commodities like fruit, compact
valuables such as diamonds—anything can be transported by
air, though cost still restricts bulk and quantity. That is why
air mail (to which Britain contributed the idea of the special Air
Letter) features so prominently.

The use of the petrol engine and the extension of motor and air
traffic demand vast quantities of oil for fuel. At one time the

presence of oil deposits was regarded as a nuisance; now, to "strike oil" means wealth. A hundred and fifty years ago, a traveller in Persia described Persian oil as "one of nature's ulcers". "A strong, suffocating smell of naphtha", he wrote, "announced something more than ordinarily foul in the neighbourhood." But in our days, the value of the rich Persian oil wells is fully realized, and in 1949 they produced 29 million metric tons of oil. There are other rich oil wells along the Persian Gulf in the Arab Principality of Kuwait, and this has special treaty relations with Great Britain. Even in America, the farmers of Western Pennsylvania were amused when an engineer named Edwin Drake began to sink the first oil well, and they called it "Drake's Folly"! But Americans were quick to realize the potentialities of the vast wealth stored in the earth in the form of mineral (petroleum) oil. To meet this new demand, oil wells were sunk in other parts of the United States—in Oklahoma, in Kansas, Texas, etc.—and these in due course have come to produce about one-half of a total annual world production amounting to 600 million tons of oil. The value of oil imported by Britain in 1950 in the special oil ships, called "tankers", was £149 million; altogether we consume about 18 million tons of petroleum products per annum. In the State of Brunei (north-west Borneo) there has recently been discovered the greatest oil-field in the Commonwealth.

Besides adding oil to the essential items in trade and commerce, the increased use of motors and aircraft demanded also great quantities of rubber for tyres and other parts. The amount of rubber imported into Britain in 1830 was only 23 tons; at the close of the nineteenth century it had risen to 13,200 tons, and, by the middle of the twentieth century, to 225,000 tons. When this demand could not be met by supplies of wild rubber from the forests of Brazil and elsewhere, rubber plantations were developed in Malaya and other regions of the Far East and became of world importance.

Thus, in the early years of the twentieth century, the new revolution in transport made distance vastly less significant. A seventeenth-century sailing ship took nearly three months to cross the Atlantic, whereas a modern liner makes the voyage in five days, and an air-liner can fly from London to New York in a matter of hours. A voyage by sea to Australia still occupies five weeks, but the journey is made by air in fewer than five days. London is now linked with the Western European capitals, Paris, Rome and Bonn far more closely than it was linked with Edinburgh or even Cardiff as long as railways were the fastest means of travel.

Scientists have played a further part in the development of air traffic by perfecting wireless telegraphy, which enables the air pilot to keep in touch with ground staffs, and to receive warnings about fog, bad weather or other possible dangers, and directions for taking off and landing. During the Second World War the device of radar gave ships and shore stations, and to a lesser extent aircraft, a miraculous ability to fix the position of themselves and their enemies; in peace it enables them to defeat the fog.

But modern developments in transport and communication, especially air travel and wireless, impressive as they are as technical achievements, have also their sinister side. They have made the world smaller, so to speak, but they have also made it more dangerous. Trouble in one part of the world becomes known immediately everywhere else, and what might once have been but a local conflict may now become of world-wide concern; a local war may become a world war. If that happens, forces can be moved by air to fight in distant parts of the world, and the weapons at their disposal have been made ever more deadly by modern science. The bomber has already brought death and destruction to cities, far behind the lines, which would have been safe enough in earlier wars. As for the future, the latest atom and hydrogen bombs can threaten destruction, instant, simultaneous, and irreparable, to civilian populations, as well as armies, in any of the main world areas of urban civilization.

Coal

The new Industrial Revolution gives such prominence to electricity and petrol that the question may naturally be raised, what is the place of coal in the national economy of to-day? Although there are now rival sources of power, coal is still vital to our economy and is likely to remain vital to our supplies of power for many years to come. For coal is still the driving force of steam locomotives and ships. When it does not directly drive factory machinery, it drives the generators (the largest consumer of coal) which supply the electric power for the machines. It goes in large quantities to the iron and steel works. It is the source of gas for household and industrial purposes; it supplies household fuel; and it is the raw material for the manufacture of many chemicals. Coal is still, as in the past, the life-blood of British industry.

Nevertheless the coal industry has struggled with considerable difficulties. The export trade fell away after the First World War, and the coal industry, which is in any case a particularly hard and dangerous one, suffered gravely from labour troubles; so the number of men working in it declined. During the years 1939–45 production fell to its lowest level of 183 million tons (1945), with a corresponding fall of employment from a pre-war figure of 782,000 to a bottom level of 697,000, reached in 1950. In the post-war years there have been repeated fuel crises, and supreme efforts have been made to improve the position, with limited success. Everything about the industry remains clouded with uncertainty—except its key importance.

The crises in the coal industry have been due in fact to the great demand for coal. Britain's industrial drive for exports has raised our national production in many industries, increased the use of electric power, and so raised the demand for coal. As a result practically all the coal produced is used at home. The most striking fact in the post-war position is the virtual disappearance of our coal export trade. In 1938 Great Britain was still the largest coal exporter in the world and exported nearly 36 million tons; by 1946 the figure was only 4 million tons. Indeed, we have lately begun to import coal to guard against a possible winter shortage. The position is humiliating: as one commentator puts it, it is as if Britain had to hire a number of foreigners to make up a cricket team with which to challenge the Australians.

Meanwhile the National Coal Board, the new authority for the nationalized industry, continues to struggle with the situation. It is following a policy of mechanization—to develop to the full the use of machine cutters and conveyors to compensate for shortage of men—and seeks to close down the older, unprofitable pits. As things are at present some districts make a profit, but others a

The 415-foot chimney stacks and elevators of the plutonium factory at Windscale, near Workington, on the Cumberland coast

heavy loss. But, for the time being even unprofitable pits must be used, pending a very difficult redeployment of the Labour Force in new areas.

Atomic Power

Though the atom-bomb and the still more deadly hydrogen-bomb menace our civilization and human life itself, the development of atomic power at the same time offers to mankind the opportunity of better life in the future. For atomic power opens out a vista of immense industrial progress. Man has at his possible command a source of untold strength. The heat produced by the disintegration of a given amount of uranium is millions of times as much as that produced by the burning of the same amount of coal. In theory, that heat could be used, as is done with coal, for the production of power. Research is now going on, and experiments are being made, in using the atomic pile as a source of power. At present the capital cost of erecting such a pile, which with its necessary screening walls is a massive installation, is very high. But the avenue for development is there. The Americans have already launched the first atomic-powered submarine. In Britain work has begun on an experimental power station in connection with the plutonium factory at Winscale in Cumberland. It is likely that within twenty years such stations will generate as much power as we at present derive from coal.

Already, in some respects, atomic science is being set to useful purpose in scientific and medical research. Radio-active products from the atomic piles can be used directly in the treatment of disease, and may replace radium. Then there is the "tracer". Substances can be labelled, so to speak, by radio-activity, and thus can be traced, in this way adding to our knowledge of the changes in physical composition which go on inside the body. Experiments with radio-active phosphorus on rats enabled research workers to discover the rate at which the existing phosphorus in the teeth was replaced with new material. It has been suggested that experiments with radio-active substances along such lines may prove to be one of the most wonderful lines of inquiry resulting from nuclear research, and most productive of beneficial results to mankind.

Chemistry and Medicine

During and after the Second World War, very remarkable advances were made in the whole field of chemistry and its relations with medicine. The researches of chemists have produced important new drugs. Paludrine is much superior to quinine for the treatment of malaria in the tropics. The sulpha drugs—of which M. and B. 693 is best known—are highly effective in treating pneumonia. Then there is penicillin—resulting from Alexander Fleming's discovery of a bacteria-killing mould in 1928 and a long process of experiment, which has made possible its production on a large scale. Penicillin has the double advantage of killing bacteria and yet being, in most cases, harmless to the human body. It has proved itself a most remarkable substance which can be taken by the mouth, injected, or applied externally and is invaluable for wounds, skin diseases and many infections.

Not only has modern chemistry helped to cure disease, it has also added greatly to our productive powers. Indeed, in some senses, modern society depends on the chemist as Victorian society depended on the engineer. New industries such as plastics and fermentations offer striking examples of technical innovation resulting from the work of chemists.

Plastics are complex carbon compounds manufactured by chemical processes. They have the useful characteristic that, when moderately heated, they are plastic; they can be moulded, pressed, or rolled into shape, and as they are thus easily worked they form a raw material for a great variety of articles. Among articles made, or which can be made, from plastics are: telephones, fountain-pens, automobile bodies and aeroplane turrets, doors, windows, furniture, and many smaller household articles. Then there are new synthetic fibres made by the chemists. These began half a century ago with the first experiments in the manufacture of artificial silk, but the newest and most fashionable is nylon, of which clothes are already being made in considerable quantities. Nylon has the advantages of being strong, drying quickly after washing, and requiring little or no ironing; and Terylene is an even newer synthetic material, invented in Britain, which looks like wool and has remarkable wearing and crease-resisting qualities. The fermentations industry, developed from brewing, makes scientific use of micro-organisms to carry out chemical changes and gives us acids, antiseptics, and other chemical products.

All these developments in the world of chemistry are a part of the new industrial revolution which electric power and the internal-combustion engine introduced.

27

THE NEW AGRICULTURE

THERE is no space in a little book like this to describe all the efforts which are being made to find new materials, new processes, new manufactures, and new markets, so that we may be able to pay our way as a nation and buy from abroad the things which our island cannot produce for itself. The lead which Britain has established in the building of jet-propelled aircraft offers a dramatic and probably familiar example. The case of agriculture, however, is perhaps the most interesting. The most unobservant townsman, out for a ramble in the country, sees and hears the efforts made to win the utmost from long-neglected soil; and if we know even a very little history we realize that the new agriculture of the 1950's is trying to get back the glories of that golden age of British farming before the inrush of cheap American wheat.

The condition of rural Britain in 1900 was a desperate one. "It would be difficult to paint in too black colours", writes a government report, "the depression of the last quarter of the nineteenth century affecting, as it did, first the corn lands of the south and west and later the pasture districts of the other parts of the country. Bankruptcies among farmers increased to an alarming extent. . . . In some cases land became derelict. . . . While the remuneration for every other class of labour was steadily increasing, the wages of the agricultural labourer actually declined." In thirty years, out of an estimated total of a million such workers, some 300,000 had left the land for the towns or the emigrant steamers.

First Efforts to Revive Agriculture

Both the great political parties, the Conservatives as representing the landed interest and the Liberals as professed champions of the under-dog, had viewed the situation with alarm; but up to

1914 the partial revival of agriculture was due mainly to the efforts of the farmers themselves (or their landlords) to find new sources of profit. The production of prime-quality meat could command a high price in those more fastidious days, because of the slight difference in taste from what was brought in refrigerator ships from overseas. There was also a growing—though nothing like the present—demand for fresh milk, which could be combined with the sale of butter or cheese and eggs; and where labour was readily available (as with the smallholder helped by members of his own family) vegetables, fruit, and even flowers might bring back prosperity.

The government did, however, take two steps. One was to organize scientific help and advice through the Board of Agriculture, founded in 1889 and replaced in 1919 by the Ministry of Agriculture and Fisheries. This helped with agricultural education and research into insect pests and cattle diseases; sampled the quality of fertilizers and artificial feeding-stuffs supplied to the farms; and sent out regional experts to make recommendations about farming problems on the spot. These official activities have since grown enormously. The other step, taken by the Liberals in 1908, was to encourage local authorities to buy land for the use of smallholders, pig and poultry farmers for the most part, people who would be prepared to stay in the country and work hard for their living if they were their own masters. The immediate results of this were disappointingly small: the larger farmers (who influenced every local decision) were prejudiced because small-holdings would reduce their supply of labourers, and the new small-holding was valueless unless there were a house attached to it—in six years local authorities built only 774 smallholders' houses in the whole of England.

The First World War inevitably brought prosperity to the land. In 1914–18 there was ploughing of downland and other inferior soil, which it had not been worth while to cultivate since the overthrow of Napoleon. But between the world wars, especially in the early part of the period the new realization of the importance of agriculture to the national life largely disappeared. There were exceptions, however, in some respects. The growth of the sugar-beet industry continued, so that there were 400,000 acres of beet fields in 1934, when the existing factories were amalgamated into the British Sugar Corporation. The State Forests were being developed: this was a result of the timber famine experienced in 1918. There was also some permanent increase in the number of allot-ment-holders, which a Dig for Victory campaign had brought to a total of 1,400,000 at the end of the war: their activities, however, chiefly affected the use of semi-waste land in or near the towns. But the general position for the farming population was that in the 1920's prices fell, land reverted to rough pasture, and it again became almost impossible to make a decent living from the soil.

Planning

The present-day attitude to agriculture may be said to date therefore from the crisis of 1931, described in an earlier chapter, and the decision of the National Government to reintroduce tariffs. It did not put a direct tax on imported food—such an action would have been too unpopular among the industrial voters—but fixed a series of quotas; these restricted the amounts to be brought into the United Kingdom from abroad, so that our farmers need not be seriously afraid of foreign competition. At the same time the government instituted a series of plans for agriculture.

One reason for these plans was the sharp lesson which was taught us by the general collapse of world trade and our departure from the gold standard: even in peace-time it was dangerous to depend on foreign trade for so large a proportion of the food we ate. Another reason, no doubt, was the break-up of big estates owing to death duties and other forms of taxation. Between one-third and one-half of the farm land had been bought by the farmers who worked it; in hard times these new owner-farmers had no landlord to fall back upon, and could get little help from the bank. But their plight could not very well be ignored, as in the past, if only because the National Farmers' Union (founded in 1908) was now a highly organized body with 200,000 members. Whatever the reasons, the 1930's saw planning applied to wheat, milk, bacon, hops, potatoes, and much else, a good price (subsidized, where necessary, out of the taxes) being guaranteed to the farmer for the food which the planners wanted him to produce.

In 1939 the County War Agricultural Committees, composed of landowners, farmers, and farm workers, were given dictatorial powers; they could even turn a completely inefficient farmer off his own land. In general they carried these pre-war developments one stage further. At the same time the heroic work of the Women's Land Army, the harvest camps of voluntary workers, and the large-scale employment of prisoners of war left no doubt in people's minds that there was a Battle for Food to be lost or won. It was as evident a part of the national war effort as the Battle of the Atlantic against the submarines, of which it was indeed the civilian counterpart. In 1947 an important Agriculture Act made it clear that the national post-war policy this time is to maintain a stable and efficient system of agriculture. The Act helped to stabilize agriculture by giving increased security of tenure to efficient tenant farmers, and at the same time, a policy of guaranteed prices made it easier for the farmer to plan ahead. Not only the risk of war and the uncertainties of international trade, but also the deeper reason that the world as a whole is short of food rather than of manufactures, made such a policy wise. Broadly speaking, industrial exports buy less, in terms of important foodstuffs, than they used to do. It is therefore only common sense to take good care of our agricultural resources.

The success of the new policy, and the strength of the belief that it has come to stay, may be measured by the fact that now, for the first time for over a century, the population in genuinely rural districts shows a substantial increase. Buses, the wireless, and television have practically ended the loneliness of rural life. In matters of water supply, electricity, and housing the village is catching up with the town. Since the passing of the Agricultural Wages Act in 1924, the wages and working hours of farm employees have risen to the standards which trade unions—a late-comer to country life—had established elsewhere. As for the employer, the net annual profits of an English farm nowadays average nearly £1,500, which places the middle type of farmer where he was in the Golden Age a hundred years ago—a man of substance. He works with his hands as well as his head, but has more security and plays a more useful part in the life of the community than many of the black-coated workers who pass him by without a thought, enjoying their week-end leisure in the country and perhaps leaving it to him to close the gates after them.

Science and Farming

The new agriculture, to a greater degree than many industries, depends on science and machinery. Scientists have done much to help the farmer by study and research regarding soil—from which half the food of plants is drawn—and regarding new types of plants, and in the prevention and cure of plant and animal diseases. They are now able to advise farmers just when to drain or water, and exactly what chemical manures they should use to improve the soil. Certain soils are too acid; then the scientists advise "medicine" just as doctors prescribe medicine for human beings. Calcium, in the form of lime, and manganese in the form of basic slag (a by-product in the manufacture of steel) are two great tonics for acid soils. Very important work in field experiments is done at the Rothamsted Experimental Station, near St. Albans, which now has more than a century's experience behind it and is still one of the chief centres in the world for agricultural research. Scientists also study and try to prevent the epidemics from which farm animals suffer, though they have not yet succeeded in preventing or curing foot-and-mouth disease; this is so contagious that an outbreak has to be brought under control by a ban on the movement of farm stock over a wide area and the slaughtering of all infected animals and contacts. Yet another of their activities is the study of the seeds of plants and the mixing of different strains of wheat, etc., to suit differences of soil and climate. This has had results as spectacular as those which followed Bakewell's experiments in cattle- and sheep-breeding in the old days.

But if Bakewell, the Colling brothers, and Coke of Holkham returned to life and visited the Royal Show, what would impress them most would be the mechanization of modern agriculture. They would no doubt notice some further improvement in dairy cattle and nod their heads wisely at the progress achieved along lines they started; but they would shake them in bewilderment at sight of the cooling, cleansing, and sterilizing apparatus of an

Massey-Harris combine
harvester at work

up-to-date dairy. As for power-driven machines to do the actual milking, or the "milking parlour" which visits the fields to save the cows the journey to the old-fashioned stalls—! The men of the eighteenth century might be sceptical about the merits of the "cleaner milk" campaign and deplore the reduction in the dairy maid's traditional labours. What they would certainly approve of, once they understood its complicated mechanism, is the new model of combine harvester, first used in this country in 1928. This single machine does all the work of a team of reapers, threshes and sifts the grain, and drops behind it in the field the filled sack which used to represent the completion of three elaborate processes spread over a long period of time. As for the tractors, used in every season and for almost every laborious operation of the farming year, and already at least seven times as numerous as before the war, they have affected agriculture in much the same way that their military counterpart, the tank and armoured vehicle, has affected war. To work on a farm has for the first time become a likely ambition with the machine-minded, town-bred boy.

One example of the speeding-up of production will illustrate the kind of thing which has been going on wherever machinery has been introduced. A certain measured quantity of wheat could be produced in 1830 by sickle and flail in 57.7 man-hours; to produce the same amount in 1896 with a reaper-and-binder and stationary thresher took 8.8 man-hours; to produce the same amount in 1930 with a combine harvester took only 3.3 man-hours.

What are the results? The output per man in British farming is now by far the highest in Europe, and our farming is the most highly mechanized in the world. We have crops growing on 5 million acres which were not cultivated before the war, and although the total area of agricultural land has gone down rather than up in this age of air-fields, satellite towns, and trunk roads, the food produced on it is 50 per cent more than in 1939. Altogether, the island as farmed at present could provide at need all the food for half the population and the milk and vegetables for everybody. If the total population begins to decline, the gap between what we produce and what we eat will quickly narrow.

28

THE PEOPLE'S SCHOOLS

So far this book has had little to say about schools, although they obviously play a very large part in "making modern Britain". What would be left of our present ways of organizing town life and transport, for instance, if half the people could not read a notice, which was roughly the position less than a hundred years ago? Up to the very end of the reign of Queen Victoria only the elementary schools could be called people's schools. Every other form of education was reserved for the small section of the people who could afford to pay for what they wanted: and this state of affairs was defended by the argument that the masses had no need or use for anything beyond a knowledge of the three R's—Reading, Writing, Arithmetic. Conditions have changed, and improved educational chances now exist for everybody, which means much for the future both of the individual and of our country. But before we consider the connection between education and present-day problems, it may be interesting to trace the story of an institution which affects each one of us closely and inescapably for at least ten important years.

The Need and Demand for Education

The government was slow to help education, and the basic reason was that people did not believe that the government should interfere in such matters. In an age of *laissez-faire* private businessmen built up industries; in the same way it was felt, private enterprise, and voluntary organization, could provide education if it were needed and wanted. And people should pay if they sent their children to school—not expect to have it provided for them by the

State. It was feared, also, that State aid to education might mean government interference with freedom of opinion.

Nevertheless there was a real need for education. It would be impossible to build up a large-scale and complicated industrial system without it. Systems of education have been developed hand-in-hand with industry in all modern states, as demand increased for technicians, engineers, chemists, foremen, clerks, accountants, scientists, doctors, dentists, and trained men of every kind. Elementary education became essential for all, and for increasing numbers of people secondary and higher education were also essential. As a leading authority on the period has said: "The new schools were as necessary as the new machine-tools and the new railways." But it was a long time before governments came to see this.

The demand for education came from reformers, from the prosperous and growing upper-middle class who wanted better schools for their own children, and, to a certain extent, from the working classes. The demand for education was voiced in Parliament itself; in the first thirty years of the nineteenth century there were proposals by some prominent figures, including the Whig leader, Henry Brougham (later Lord Chancellor), for a State system of schools for all children between six and twelve. But nothing of this kind was to come for many years. Among the people's leaders Francis Place was an exponent of education for the working classes, and the Chartists, the Co-operative movement and the trade unions all lent support. Some of the working-class leaders, like the Chartists, William Lovett and Thomas Cooper, worked terribly hard to educate themselves to make up for their lack of schooling. Cooper read voraciously whatever came his way or what he could borrow—novels, poetry, history, theology—early in the morning or when he had finished his work as a shoemaker at eight or nine o'clock at night. Voluntary organizations, usually helped by well-meaning people among the rich, were formed to provide education. Sunday schools taught grown-ups as well as children; adult schools provided elementary instruction alongside religious teaching; Mechanics' Institutes offered lectures and books on scientific matters; and the Society for the Diffusion of Useful Knowledge (founded in 1825 by

Brougham with the support of a number of influential persons) published cheap literature on scientific and many other topics. All these efforts indicated the need felt for popular instruction.

The Public Schools

The need for new means of education, felt by the middle classes as well as by the people generally, showed itself as far as the wealthier elements in the population were concerned in the creation of private schools and particularly in a remarkable revival of the public schools.

The public schools—Eton, Winchester, Westminster, Shrewsbury, Harrow, Charterhouse, Rugby, St. Paul's and Merchant Taylors'—were old schools, and with the exception of the last two, they were boarding-schools. They had fallen into a bad state during the eighteenth century: food and accommodation were poor, the boys were unruly, and discipline could not be enforced in spite of frequent flogging. But they were reformed early in the nineteenth century, first by the great headmasters, Butler of Shrewsbury and Arnold of Rugby, and other heads followed their example. They became thoroughly good schools. So much so that, to meet the growing demand for education for the upper classes, a whole series of new public schools were established—either through the expansion of ancient grammar schools, such as Sherborne and Repton, or as completely new foundations like Cheltenham (1841), Marlborough (1842), and Wellington (1859). Soon afterwards, as a result of commissions of inquiry Acts of Parliament were passed, in 1868 and 1869, to make the older schools broaden their curriculum. Up till then it had been mainly Latin and Greek. But now new subjects began to figure more largely—mathematics, chemistry and physics, history, geography. Some endowments were extended to girls, and girls' schools were also founded and grew in importance.

The principal causes for the revival of the public schools were three: the new middle classes could afford to pay well for the old education, and wanted what the old public schools had provided and the social prestige which was theirs; the railways provided easy access to boarding-schools; and the growth of the Empire overseas meant that parents on service found them convenient for sending sons home to be educated.

Beginning of State Aid

It was in 1833 that the government first made a grant to help the existing elementary schools. These had been built in the previous twenty years by two charitable organizations—the National Society, belonging to the Church of England, and the mainly Nonconformist British and Foreign School Society. The grant began at £20,000 a year—whereas over £300 million are spent on public education at the present day! In 1839 the grant was increased and the first inspectors were appointed to see that the schools, fast growing in numbers, were not too badly conducted. In 1861 an official commission made out that only 4.5 per cent of children received no schooling at all: but they were counting in those who came for a few weeks, to see what it was like or just to fill in time between jobs. Four-fifths of all the pupils had left for good before they reached their twelfth birthday, so it is not surprising that the commissioners set out what seems to us a rather modest set of requirements. The children were expected to learn to write and spell correctly; to be able to make out or check a bill; to know the positions of the countries of the world; and above all to study the Scriptures.

The "National" schools were very strong in country districts, the "British" schools found chiefly in the larger towns: progress was slow and development very haphazard because the two sorts of school represented above all the intense rivalry between Church and Chapel. Elementary education at this time was very closely bound up with Bible reading and religious instruction. Both the Anglicans and the Nonconformists feared that, if the other side controlled the schools, they would bring up the children in their own form of religious worship. The struggle was a bitter one —how bitter is difficult for us to realize to-day. Each side was terribly fearful and jealous of State aid to the other side. For this reason English and Welsh education lagged far behind that to be found in many other countries, including our nearest neighbour, Scotland.

A National System Grows Up

But, in spite of all, the demand for popular education grew stronger. Further proposals were put forward in Parliament. Population was increasing, and more children needed schooling. It was dangerous for England to fall behind other countries; it was pointed out that our ignorant and unskilled men would not be able to compete with educated continental workmen. In war, too, education seemed to count: Prussia with its organized State system of education beat the casual and more backward Austria in 1866. Then again the Reform Act of 1867 gave the vote to working men in the towns. Now, said a prominent statesman, "we must educate our masters". In 1868 the Liberals came into power, and Gladstone put W. E. Forster in charge of education. Forster, a wealthy Quaker, and married to the daughter of Dr. Arnold, was known as an educational reformer. At the same time in Birmingham an organization known as the National Education League, powerfully backed by Joseph Chamberlain, was pressing for education to be unsectarian, free, compulsory, and universal. Something must be done. Forster made a reasonable compromise —appropriate to the possibilities of the time—between the existing system of voluntary schools and the more extreme demands for a universal State system.

W. E. Forster's Education Act of 1870—one of the great landmarks of our social history—laid the foundation of a national system: "Our object", he said, "is to complete the present voluntary system and to fill in the gaps." The Act divided the country into school districts: and where voluntary schools did not provide enough school places for all, a School Board was to be elected by the ratepayers to provide school premises, and could enforce attendance if it thought fit. These board schools received grants from the local rates, and also from the National Exchequer, but the voluntary schools received aid from the Exchequer only. The next step was taken ten years later, in 1880, when education was made compulsory for all children under twelve, and later, in 1891, elementary education was made free: previously there had been a maximum fee of 9d. a week.

The system was very complicated in administration—there were over 2,500 school boards, as well as school managers for each tiny voluntary school, wherever they existed. But so far as elementary education goes, there were now schools for all. All children could learn to read, write, do sums, and acquire a little general knowledge. As yet, however, there was no State provision for secondary education. This was the next big move to be made in building a really national and comprehensive system. Some of the elementary schools, indeed, soon began to provide more advanced work for their senior pupils, and eventually it was necessary to regularize the position and provide for further years of schooling at the secondary level.

The result was the Education Act of 1902. It made other important changes in English education. It abolished the school boards and transferred their functions to the new local authorities. These—county and county borough councils and urban district councils—had not existed in 1870, and now it was obviously convenient that they, together with the borough councils, should administer the schools. The local education authorities were empowered to use the rates to support the voluntary schools as well as the former board schools. This measure aroused tremendous opposition from the Nonconformists, who liked the simple Bible religion taught in board schools and had hoped that Church schools, if denied help from the rates, might die out. But their protest failed and the Act proved its worth.

Most important of all, however, was the provision by the Act of 1902 for secondary education. Counties, county boroughs and boroughs were empowered to provide out of the rates for secondary schools. These schools offered a good education for small fees to the middle and lower-middle classes. They offered "a general education, physical, mental and moral", including as well as Latin all the new subjects—mathematics, science, a modern language, and English, history, geography, and drawing. As time went on the ancient grammar schools, with very few exceptions, sought the financial help of the local education authority, and came to serve the same educational purpose as the county or municipal secondary schools.

The Act of 1902 was of fundamental importance, for it at last created what amounted to a national system of education, with the beginnings of an "educational ladder". The clever child of poor parents could, while at the elementary school, win a scholarship or free place at the secondary school, and from there could win a scholarship or other grant to go on to a university.

In 1907 the School Medical Service began, which provided medical inspection in schools, and this has played a great part in the building-up of national health. Other important developments during the twentieth century have been the longer training of teachers; the greater scope and the lengthening of different stages of education; the gradual reduction in size of classes; the improvement of school buildings; and the development of physical training and of welfare services, such as free milk for schools and school meals. In 1918 a big step forward was taken in the Fisher Act, which gets its name from the distinguished scholar whom Lloyd George put in charge of education. This law fixed five to fourteen as the age for compulsory school attendance and gave Local Education Authorities greater power to improve the provision of schools in their areas. Progress could now be readily judged, as the School Certificate had become the standardized measure for general education in any secondary school.

Schools and Colleges To-day

During the Second World War, another important Education Act (the Butler Act) was passed in 1944, by which our national education system is now divided into three main stages—Primary, Secondary, and Further Education. The Primary Stage includes some nursery schools for under-fives; infant schools for all children from five years to seven years; and junior schools for those between the ages of seven and eleven. At the age of eleven or thereabouts, boys and girls pass on for a minimum period of four years to one of the three kinds of secondary school—to a secondary modern school, giving a general and practical education; or to a secondary grammar school, giving a more advanced academic education; or sometimes to a secondary technical or commercial school for those who desire, or whose parents desire, a special bent to their studies. All this is provided free.

Thus the Education Act of 1944 took two most important

Edwardian education: Standard II receives an object-lesson on oranges.

steps. It raised the school-leaving age to fifteen, an age at which in the past the great majority of children never attended school at all, and it provided secondary education for all. Such steps, however, were in keeping with the spirit of a democratic age, and in line with similar developments in other advanced countries. But it is important to observe that there is, in this country, a process of selection for the different kinds of secondary school. Children at eleven must take an examination and pass certain tests and these determine whether a child will go to a grammar school—which may lead on to the university and the professions—or to one of the other kinds of secondary schools. Some people argue that this is unfair, and that all children should go to the same kind of secondary school—the Comprehensive School. Some schools of this type have been set up by various local education authorities; they tend to be very large—for 2,000 children or more—in order

Education to-day: a Junior School class takes part in a History project.

to make economical provision for the great variety of courses which they require to offer.

For Further Education, after leaving a secondary school, young people may choose to continue their education at some kind of technical college or at a domestic science college or a school of art or some other place of specialized instruction. There are the commercial and technical colleges in London, Birmingham, Glasgow, Liverpool, Manchester, Newcastle, Coventry and elsewhere, which provide advanced training in commerce and technology. There are also municipal and county commercial schools, and numerous evening institutes offering less advanced commercial training and recreational subjects galore: In fact, the opportunities now available are almost endless.

If we take agriculture as an example (since it came in our last chapter) we find that there are regular university degrees and diplomas in the subject, and one university, Reading, in which students of agriculture are the most important element. Then there are the great agricultural colleges, such as the Royal Agricultural College, Cirencester (founded in 1845); Studley College (for women), Warwickshire; Wye College, Ashford, Kent; and colleges for Scotland at Edinburgh and Aberdeen. There are also over twenty county institutes giving a one-year course in the subject. As machinery plays a vital part in modern farming, there is even an Agricultural Engineering Centre at Exeter, where boys, after leaving school, can study up-to-date methods of repairing implements and tractors, oxy-acetylene and electric welding, lathe work and so on; and also receive instruction on the business side of agriculture.

Technical education, as has been noticed already, has always been provided in this country in a somewhat haphazard way, but it is now more completely organized than ever before, although one cannot picture it so clearly as one can an education in the arts or sciences, which will run through consecutive school and university stages. The secondary technical school and the technical college provide for technical training at different levels, and the technical colleges provide advanced courses, often including preparation for an external degree of the University of London. The Universities themselves also provide various technical courses and grant degrees for technical subjects, although not all subjects are to be found everywhere. But, of course, an immense amount of technical education is still learnt on the job, through some form of apprenticeship. This is often combined with "part-time release". The apprentice or young employee is released for a day or a half-day to follow courses at a technical college, or, in some cases, the larger firms provide their own classes and sometimes continuation schools, which provide also for a certain amount of general education.

But no account of the educational ladder would be complete without some reference to its topmost rung—the university. The modern universities, of which London in 1828 was the earliest and Nottingham, Southampton and Hull (which have received their charters since the end of the war) are the latest, have always been honourably distinguished by low fees and facilities for poor students to live at home. They were the people's universities from the outset. But it is a striking change, of very recent years, which has extended the poor man's chance of admission to the Oxford and Cambridge colleges from the select group of those who win entrance scholarships to any qualified person a college chooses to receive. Such Commoner entrants, as they are called, used to be selected automatically from well-to-do families, since they receive no financial help from the college; but since 1945 the State or the L.E.A. will, broadly speaking, find the cost in every case in which the parents cannot afford to support a young man who has obtained admission to such a college by examination and interview. Thus the way is made clear, not merely for the very clever (as of old), but for a much larger number of young men and women without private means to enjoy the advantages of residence at the older universities.

Measuring the Results

What, then, does the nation hope to get in return for expenditure which, in the eyes of the Victorians, even the best of them, would have seemed the maddest extravagance? First, there is a political result to be achieved—the blurring of class distinctions by a system which, when it gets into full swing, will ensure that superior education is the reward of a superior intelligence and hard work, rather than the hall-mark of social superiority helped by the possession of money. Second, economic advantages may be secured which will affect the future of the whole nation. Education may not be able to produce inventive geniuses, but we have suffered for generations in the competition for world trade from weaknesses in our technical education. With ten times the population of Switzerland, we have no centre for technological studies to compare with Zurich. Perhaps this reproach will at last be removed. There is also the prospect that a properly educated nation will be more capable of finding the right solutions for trade problems and making the best use of all its resources. Above all, it is to be believed that an educational system, suited to the needs and capacities of every child, will result in habits of disciplined—self-disciplined—industry, which are the only possible foundation for the all-out national effort so often demanded and so evidently needed.

But while the State has a right to expect to benefit by the education of its future citizens, on which it is expending money with unheard-of lavishness, there are private benefits, too. How do we use our leisure when we are free to choose for ourselves? This is a test of the worth-whileness of education in the light of which the present results of past education are not altogether a matter for national pride. How will the future results of present education face up to the same test?

29

THE PEOPLE'S LEISURE

BEFORE the days of factories hours of work were practically un-limited except by the rising and setting of the sun. But by 1914 the efforts of Lord Shaftesbury and other philanthropists and the steady pressure of the trade unions had fixed and shortened the hours in most industries. In 1908, for example, Parliament had enacted an eight-hour day for coal-miners and in 1912 it instituted the weekly half-day for shop assistants. In recent years this move-ment has gone much further. After the First World War the League of Nations tried to get international agreements for limit-ing hours of work, and in Britain the principle was extended even to such difficult cases as work on a farm. Thus the eight-hour day (with extra pay for overtime), a half-holiday at least on Saturday (or some other day), and—since the Second World War—some provision for an annual holiday (in many cases with pay) have become almost universal in this country.

Working shorter hours and, we must add, under generally easier conditions, people may be assumed to have more energy nowadays when work is finished. At all events their periods of free time are so long that they will not be needed, as they once were, mainly for sheer rest. Another change of social practice, which certainly in-creases the total of spare time, is that only a comparatively small part of the population now devotes much of its leisure to church-going. In Victorian England, and still more in Scotland and Wales, church and chapel services were for very many people their princi-pal interest and activity throughout the Sunday, and often over-flowed into the weekday evenings as well. It is therefore important to ask what is done with all the time which used to be filled with work or kept more strictly than nowadays for religion.

Outdoor sport, which suffered an eclipse when people were first herded into the industrial towns, has gradually recovered from the loss of the village greens and the open countryside, which once were more or less lawfully accessible to the many. Interest in cricket and football has grown until an interest in both has come to be regarded as a national characteristic, although Association football, requiring a less carefully tended ground, has developed more widely as the mass amusement of the people. Time and speed also give the advantage to football. A fast-moving game has a much greater spectacular appeal to the crowds, nor is it easy for so many people to find the time (and patience) to watch a long drawn-out—and perhaps finally drawn—cricket match.

National Games

Cricket and football have become national games in this country and the playing of these games has been carried by British people all over the world, though cricket and rugby football have remained chiefly British games. Some kind of game with bat and ball was played in the Middle Ages. Towards the end of the eighteenth century the Marylebone Cricket Club, with headquarters at Lord's (the land belonged to Thomas Lord), originated; the present ground was opened in 1814. The M.C.C. became the acknowledged authority—thus a private club set the standards and created the tradition which lie behind the national game.

County matches were played in the eighteenth century, and in the following century county clubs were formed. The building of railways aided the growth of cricket, for teams could travel and play away matches. Interest in cricket grew with the county championship matches in the era of the great batsman, Dr. W. G. Grace (1848–1915), and the county championship became the main event of the cricketing season. Matches with Australia began in 1877, and it was in 1882 that we first "lost the Ashes": for after Australia's sensational victory of that year it was said that the "body" of English cricket "will be cremated and the ashes taken to Australia". Since 1894 the term "Test Matches" has been used of international matches, not only with Australia but also with South Africa, the West Indies, New Zealand and India. Though these have become great international events, cricket also flourishes at home as a popular game in schools and universities and

among innumerable amateur clubs in towns and especially villages
up and down the country.

Like the early bat and ball cricket, football was also played in
the Middle Ages. But local mob football was so rough and dangerous that it was sometimes forbidden by law. During the nineteenth
century football developed as a game of skill in the Midlands and
Lancashire. In 1863 the Football Association was formed to stan-
dardize the rules, and "soccer" thus got its name as opposed to
"rugger". Since 1871 clubs have played annually for the F.A. Cup.
From 1888 dates the formation of the Football League, with
special interest attaching to its First Division, and first-class Association football has become predominantly professional. These
professional matches, the league matches, draw the largest crowds.
But there are many amateur leagues, county associations, and
school and university teams, so that on a winter Saturday afternoon thousands of matches all over the country are now played.

Rugby football originated in 1823 with the impulsive act of a
boy called Ellis at Rugby School. Ellis caught the ball and ran
with it. By 1846 the game was standardized at Rugby. It spread
to other public schools, to Oxford and Cambridge, to Black-
heath, Richmond, Guy's Hospital and other early clubs. Rugby-
playing clubs then got together and formed the Rugby Union
in 1871. Two months after its foundation, Scotland beat
England in the first international match. Rugby as played by the
clubs belonging to the Rugby Union has remained an amateur
game. But, in 1895, most of the clubs in the north of England
seceded and formed a professional organization, now known as the
Rugby League. This plays under a different set of rules. Rugby,
unlike Association football, did not quickly become a popular
game abroad. The regular international games are played only
between England, Scotland, Wales, Ireland, and France. But the
Commonwealth countries, especially New Zealand and South
Africa, also produce splendid rugby teams, several of which have
made notable tours in this country. In recent years the rugby game
has spread as far afield as Yugoslavia and the Argentine, while
the international popularity of Association football could even be
seen through chinks in the Iron Curtain that separated us from
the Russians.

Some other games, though they do not have the same mass appeal, are nevertheless played by considerable numbers. Such games are golf, lawn tennis, and bowls. All, in some form or other, are of considerable antiquity. Golf was a popular game in Scotland by the middle of the fifteenth century. In 1834 the King gave the title of Royal and Ancient to the club which had been founded at St. Andrew's in 1754. When golf spread and became popular in England and elsewhere during the nineteenth century, the rules of St. Andrew's were accepted and the Royal and Ancient Club was regarded as the final authority. The British open championship was first played for in 1860. International contests between Britain and the U.S.A. arouse considerable interest to-day, and some of the best golfers in the world are Americans. Similarly with lawn tennis, the game was first developed in England, has spread in popularity, and to-day some of the finest players are Americans and Australians. But the popularity of lawn tennis is comparatively recent. The championships held by the All-England Club at Wimbledon started in 1877. Bowls, though it has not the same spectacular interest, is a very ancient game of considerable appeal to older people.

Many other games and pastimes have developed to fill people's increased leisure time. Boxing, swimming, cycling, running, walking, ballroom dancing, folk-dancing and square-dancing, all have their adherents. Many people play or watch for pleasure, but in all, or nearly all, a professional element has been introduced, and in some this element is most important. Where people will pay to watch a match or game, the promising player is encouraged to specialize and train, and money becomes available to enable him to do so. In this way men come to earn their living by doing things which were originally done for recreation and amusement.

In the case of both football and cricket the number of fairly regular spectators is larger than the number of fairly regular players: this would still be true, if we left out of the calculation those who watch because they are too old to play and those who play because, being at school, they are not allowed to substitute watching for playing as completely as some of them might wish. There is, it is true, an earlier parallel in the crowds which thronged to watch bare-fist boxing and already a century ago had made

Epsom Downs and Aintree famous names in every country where
horses are bred: but it is certainly remarkable that the spread of
education has not resulted in a more individual idea of sport.
What draws us to join the enormous banks of spectators in a huge
amphitheatre like that at Wembley or Hampden Park, on the occasion perhaps of a football "international"? Admittedly we have
come to give vent to feelings of patriotism and pugnacity, as well
as to watch a superb demonstration of physical skill and judgment.
But there is often a third motive, stronger than we care to acknowledge, the desire to join in with the crowd, whatever it may happen
to be doing—active or passive, wise or foolish.

The Open-air Movement

On the whole, then, progress in the use of leisure is not to be
measured by bigger stadiums: but a Victorian would certainly see
a positive gain to health and happiness in the effect which shorter
hours plus better transport have had on the open-air movement.
Apart from such special cases as the anglers by the canal banks,
the growth of industrial towns meant usually a complete break
with the rural enjoyments of the past: even the annual holiday of
the Victorian cotton-worker was a holiday in a town like Blackpool, the bigger the better. The bicycle, as we pointed out in an
earlier chapter, first gave the town population the freedom of the
countryside; from about 1910 onwards the motor-bus, following
the bicycle into the lanes, meant that the direction of a country
walk was no longer confined to the region of a railway line.
Climbing, hiking, and camping all developed. In the 1930's the
open-air movement reached its logical conclusion in the rapid
growth of the Youth Hostels Association, which exists to encourage the young wayfarer by providing simple board and lodging
at the very lowest cost.

There is, however, another association, more appropriate to the
older generation, which tries to ensure that there is something
more on offer to the adventurous than new roads to speed along
to new swimming pools, new fun fairs, and new bathing beaches.
This is the National Trust which, with its many large benefactors
and 33,000 regular members, is busily engaged in securing the

survival in unspoilt condition of castles and houses and gardens—whole villages even—things which speak to us of the past and might be lost for ever. But this is only half of its work, for the National Trust is equally concerned to save from being built upon, and ensure public access to, hills and view-points, woods and commons. In short, the familiar green sign with the oak-leaf emblem is silent propaganda for an active use of leisure and for one which can link us in imagination with the past England of Parson Woodforde or Daniel Defoe.

Boy Scouts and Girl Guides

Another movement which has done much to take young people out into the countryside and teach them something of nature is that of the Boy Scouts and Girl Guides. The founder of this movement was Baden-Powell (1857–1941.) As a soldier he served in India, Afghanistan and South Africa, and showed great gifts for training and leading young men; he distinguished himself in the defence of Mafeking in the South African War, and was eventually promoted lieutenant-general. He used all this experience in planning the Boy Scout movement, which he founded in 1908. The Girl Guides followed in 1910. Baden-Powell aimed at training boys and girls in good citizenship by giving them interesting and useful tasks to perform. Troops and patrols were organized and boys were taken out into the country. They had to learn self-reliance, to march, cook, camp in the open, and look after themselves in every way. They learnt discipline, woodcraft, first-aid, self-defence, and to help other people. The movement made a great appeal to the young, for it spread over the world, and Baden-Powell was recognized as Chief Scout. In its great international rallies or jamborees it brings together the youth of many nations.

The open-air movement, and physical culture in general, also owe much to other, rather older types of organization, such as the Boys' Brigade (founded in Glasgow in 1883) or the Boys', Girls', and Mixed Clubs, of which the prototype is said to have lourished in Bristol nearly a century ago. But it s only recently that their importance to the community has been officially recognized. The Physical Training Act of 1937, for instance, first gave public support to summer camps and recreation centres; and since the War the education law has made it possible to subsidize almost any worthwhile open-air activity which appeals to youth.

Newspapers and Books

The end of the Victorian age was when the modern newspaper really began. Since that time higher wages and the urgency of news during two long periods of war have helped to form a nation-wide habit of newspaper-reading; even in 1900 it would have seemed fantastic to the bold minds of Fleet Street to suppose that this country could ever support five daily papers each with a circulation running into millions. The contents of the press have been restricted since 1939 by scarcity of newsprint, but the eye of a Victorian reader would be surprised and delighted by the better type, varied captions and layout, and, above all, by the photographs which have replaced the often dingy linedrawings of the past. But the tendency for newspapers to fill their columns with "human-interest" stories, novelties, and sensations, to the exclusion of what is important but dull, or interesting—like a parliamentary debate, for instance—but incapable of compression, has unfortunately made just as rapid headway as the technical improvements in production.

Daily Mail report of the Anglo-Egyptian victory at Nakheila, 8th April 1898. The style of the article is bombastic, the lay-out by present-day standards conservative

THE GREAT BATTLE.

STIRRING STORY OF THE SOUDAN VICTORY.

HEROIC DEEDS.

HAIR-BREADTH ESCAPES OF BRITISH OFFICERS.

TERRIBLE CARNAGE.

LIST OF OUR KILLED AND WOUNDED.

SPECIAL TELEGRAMS.

From the fuller details of the Soudan battle, furnished to-day by our war correspondent, one may now gather a just estimate of its value to British arms.

The blow to the dervishes is even more crushing than was at first thought. Twelve emirs, including Wad-el-Bishara, former Emir of Dongola, were slain, 3,000 to 4,000 dervishes killed, and 4,000 prisoners are the fruits of the victory.

The battle, too, was rich in those incidents which show the mettle of the British race, its stubborn valour and cool intrepidity.

THE DERVISH ROUT.

HOW THE BRITISH WON NAKEILA

(From Our War Correspondent.)

UMDABIA, April 8.

The details I have already despatched give but a meagre idea of the brilliancy of the attack on Mahmud's position. I therefore supplement them by the following :—

The force left here at six o'clock on Thursday evening, and halted from seven till one a.m., but the troops slept little, being told off to water.

They then marched till dawn.

Sunrise revealed the four brigades in position, the guiding—as, in fact, all the staff work throughout the whole battle—being wonderfully accurate.

The dust raised by our army had dimmed the sun, but presently the light, also revealed the enemy's position. It appeared a line of bushy dom palms—a grey streak in front with flags of yellow, white, pale brown, and blue indicating the zariba; undulating gravel, tufted with coarse grass, stretched out in front.

The whole army advanced

IN A MAJESTIC LINE

till within 600 yards, when they halted, and watched the artillery bombardment begin.

At the opening of the bombardment blacks were seen strolling inside. Few of them returned the fire, and soon all was

A less mixed blessing, which is also connected with the growth of reading habits among the masses of the people, is the development of the Public Library. Boroughs were allowed to build libraries as early as 1850, but the amount of the ratepayers' money which they might spend on them was severely restricted. In spite of the munificent gifts of the Scottish-American millionaire, Andrew Carnegie, public libraries long continued for the most part to be cheerless institutions, giving a rather limited service to those sections of the population which could not afford to patronize the subscription libraries. Their transformation has been among the conspicuous successes of the more truly democratic policy of most county and borough councils in the period since the First World War. To-day the shelves, offering the heritage of every art and science, present a positive challenge to members of a library: can they, will they, use their leisure for reading in a manner and to an extent which match what is so lavishly and attractively set before them?

Triumph of New Entertainment

We have left the biggest changes of all to the last. Suppose one had asked a late-Victorian social worker to prophesy—such a person, say, as one of the Salvation Army officers, whose new methods and enthusiasm were then just beginning to penetrate into the worst slums. Had he been told that in the new century wages and leisure would both increase, and then been invited to prophesy the social consequences, his answer would have been that, failing a great increase in religion, there would be a great increase in drunkenness, which was then, and long had been, the curse of the poorer quarters of the industrial towns. Yet a large decline in church attendances (which must reflect some decline in religion) has been accompanied by a very large decline in drunkenness. To see a drunkard in the street on a Saturday night is now a rare sight: forty years ago in some parts of some towns it would have been a rarer sight to see a street without one. The cynic says that it is the result of the high taxes on beer and spirits, but these have to be considered in relation to the increase in earnings. The truth is that, together with improved housing (which will be considered in the next chapter) new forms of entertainment have provided great new interests, whereas drinking was a refuge for people to whom no interests seemed to be available.

The vogue of the cinema began just before the First World War. The early films were silent, the reels discontinuous, the image on the screen jerky and blotched. But to audiences which in many cases had never had the chance to see anything better than a cheap travelling repertory company or a music-hall turn, the new medium appeared marvellous from the outset, and the early "stars" like Chaplin and Mary Pickford evoked an enthusiasm which is almost pathetic. After twenty years of experiment in film technique and constant improvement the sound apparatus arrived, bringing with it the type of film with which we are familiar nowadays. For its social influence it is enough to point to the statistics which show that the average person makes a weekly attendance at the cinema, for better or worse. There are bad films, just as there are bad books, and the film having cost our admission-money is less easily laid aside. About the effects of the other two inventions—broadcasting and television (large-scale broadcasting started soon after the First World War and television became widespread soon after the Second)—it is impossible to speak precisely: reports on the size of listener audiences at least can never guarantee that more than a fraction of attention is given to the radio set, which is often left on all day, for company or just to save the bother of switching it off. But it would be agreed that here again we are faced with a nation-wide expenditure of money, time, and interest.

As for the value of the content—what is in the picture or the talk—it is worth noticing that one of the most serious Victorian writers and philosophers, John Stuart Mill, urged the importance of allowing every sort of view to be put forward, so that we might all of us have liberty to choose the best. His book *On Liberty*, published in 1859, never envisaged the power, persistence, and variety with which these new inventions can, if they choose, present false ambitions and ignoble ways of life for us to imitate. In practice they set before us both the best and the worst. This is perhaps not a bad thing provided we are not passive recipients, waiting only to be entertained and too lazy to make the effort to criticize what we hear and see. For it is surely important that our use of leisure, even when we are sitting still in a comfortable chair, should be an active use.

30

THE PEOPLE'S STATE

THE events of the last ten years are too close to us to be recounted in this history, except where a reference to them might add point to the account of an earlier period. But the political changes have been too vast, and have had too big an effect on social and economic development, for us to ignore them entirely.

The immensely popular war-time leader, (Sir) Winston Churchill, lost power in July 1945 at an election held just before the campaign in the Far East had been finally concluded. The Labour Party could never have obtained a sweeping majority in such circumstances if there had not been among the voters, including the millions still under arms, a desire for fundamental change. The programme was to catch up with arrears of social progress from the 'twenties and 'thirties and, in particular, to eliminate the possibility of large-scale unemployment being allowed to waste and ruin the lives of one section of the community as it had done in Durham and South Wales and elsewhere before the war.

The Labour Party introduced and passed a number of important and highly controversial Socialist measures—nationalization of the Bank of England, the mines, railways and other forms of transport, gas and electricity. But by now people were accustomed to the idea of state control of industry, and the changes came about quietly. They no longer seemed as revolutionary as the very suggestion of them had once appeared to be. The Labour Government also carried through the measures for National Insurance and the Health Service which make so important a part of the new Welfare State. Here, however, the Labour Party took over ideas which had been worked out (and publicized) during the war by Lord Beveridge, who had been a civil servant in the earlier period of Liberal social reforms and was now one of the leading figures in the dwindling Liberal Party.

After two general elections, held in 1950 and 1951, the Conservatives came back to office in time to prevent the nationalization of the iron and steel industry and to restore road haulage to private transport firms. But their parliamentary majority was too small for any more drastic reversal of the changes, amounting almost to a social revolution, which their predecessors had enacted. Moreover, the upheavals of war-time, and the mere fact that Labour ministers had been in power, as well as the actual policies they had carried out, had combined to alter the balance of classes, perhaps permanently and certainly for a long time to come. The upper and middle classes had lost power; the working class was gaining it. This is clearly illustrated by the authority, amounting sometimes to tyranny, which the trade unions now exercise, irrespective of which political party happens to be in power; also by the extreme reluctance with which the strongest of private employers or even the government itself embarks on any attempt to override their wishes.

Trade Unions To-day

The trade unions, like the Labour Party of which they are the main source of support, have changed much since the early periods of social struggle and class conflict. Gone are the days—which lasted all through the nineteenth century at least—when numerous powerful employers could refuse to engage "union labour". Instead, powerful unions can forbid employers to engage anything else. Modern Britain contains 700 trade unions with a total membership which exceeds 9,000,000.[1] Many of the smaller ones are craft unions of the type which began to flourish about a century ago. But the representative union of to-day is the giant, such as the National Union of Mineworkers, the National Union of General and Municipal Workers, or the Transport and General Workers' Union. The last of these has well over a million members and as a "general" union is typical of a further great change, which has been gradually taking shape ever since the Dock Strike of 1889. The link between the members of such a union is not the possession of a common skill or training, the value of which they

[1] See Table, p. 157

seek to cherish and enhance. Instead, the giant union tries to get members from as many occupations as possible, in the knowledge that numbers—with discipline—will give bargaining-power.

The salaried officials of the big unions are nowadays national figures, men of long experience and a sense of responsibility in the handling of big resources in men and money. Other things being equal, they are anxious to avoid strike action: yet the situation is always full of peril. The unions had a hard struggle to win their present position and the rights and privileges which they have established for their members. They are thus unwilling to admit new ideas and new, more economical methods into industry. Restrictive practices persist—union rules may prevent men working when they are willing to work, may prevent overtime, prevent redundant workers being moved elsewhere or dismissed, and resist the admission of new workers into an industry. The large size of the unions puts the leaders and officials out of touch with the rank and file. Thus there has been a tendency towards unofficial strikes. The shop steward (chosen in the factory) may stir up trouble, leading to a strike not recognized by the union. And it is not yet clear what is the position of the trade unionist in a nationalized industry. Does he incur a special obligation to his fellow-citizens, because he is working for them—to work more conscientiously; or is the obligation all on their side as paying his wages—to pay more generously?

The Approach to Social Equality

We are now perhaps in a better position to study the biggest of all the changes which have come to Britain in the last fifty years, namely the introduction of the Welfare State. People's State is perhaps a better name, because what is new is not that the state aims at welfare—the Victorian state did this according to its lights, when it concentrated on giving each individual the greatest possible freedom in which to struggle for his own welfare. What is new is that the whole people now controls the state and uses its control deliberately to raise the standard of life of that depressed and submerged 20–30 per cent of our population whose fate the Victorians almost completely ignored. At the same time, though less deliberately, we lower the standard of life of a smaller minority—the 5 per cent or so who in the days of low taxation enjoyed all the amenities of large houses, numerous servants, and lavish entertainment. There has been an astonishing process of levelling up and levelling down. The main instrument in achieving this tremendous change, which all political parties now accept as the undoubted will of the people, is the spread of Social Services. They are financed by income-tax at a standard rate of nearly half the income (after allowances have been deducted) and Sur-tax, rising for the biggest incomes to a total levy of 19s. 6d. in every £; and the annual expenditure already averages more than £10 per head of population and tends to increase.

Thus, it may be reckoned that about three-quarters of the households which make up the nation are better off than their type of household was before the war. Prices have gone up enormously, so that it takes £1 now to buy what could be bought for about 7s. before the war, and the wage-earner now pays heavier taxes. Nevertheless, because wages have risen faster than prices and because every would-be wage-earner nowadays can find a job, the wage-earning households—which are also the homes which derive most benefit from new social services—are definitely better off than ever before. The opposite is the case with the other one-quarter of households, corresponding roughly to the upper and middle classes, who live on salaries and, to some extent, on investments, and who were not greatly affected by unemployment in the old days. Their earnings for the most part have not risen much faster than the rise in prices, and their incomes, which used to be so much larger than those of the wage-earning class, have been rapidly reduced by the need to levy heavier taxes to pay for the new social services.

The tremendous change which has taken place in our social life amounts to a bloodless social revolution, and this astonishing change has come about so gradually and silently that even now we are hardly aware of it. To-day we are a more average, equal kind of people than ever before. We have largely abolished poverty at one end of the social scale and luxurious and complete idleness at the other end. We are almost without unemployment, which between the wars varied between one and over three millions; indeed, so great has been the demand for labour that we have drawn into paid employment more than half a million married women and mothers. Not only are all these people employed but they are earning higher wages than before, getting many new privileges such as holidays with pay, and enjoying the insurance cover and the benefits of the social services.

This change is, in many respects, an excellent thing. Most people are better off; three-quarters of the nation enjoy what was formerly regarded as a middle-class standard of life. They enjoy more leisure, there has been a great increase in travel, there are wider educational facilities; people spend more on their homes, on radio, on games and entertainment—though this includes increased expenditure on what may be considered unprofitable amusements, such as betting and football pools. With this vast spread of a more settled, middle-class way of life people as a whole are becoming more settled and middle-class in their outlook, less given to extremist views on social and political questions. Indeed it is often difficult to say clearly what the differences are to-day between our two great political parties.

But there is also a danger. Because, as a result of the war, we are a debtor instead of a creditor nation, we are forced to make a supreme effort to export, in order both to pay our debts and to pay for the goods we have to import. The social changes in themselves do nothing to increase the total output of consumable goods available for the people of this country—the social revolution is merely transfer of wealth by taxation and other means from one group of our citizens to another. Before we can really feel safe about maintaining for the future what we have now achieved we must increase our total of consumable goods available. That means the greatest possible effort to raise our national efficiency and productivity, which calls for continuing effort by all classes as well as full use of the mechanization and scientific methods which our scientists are developing.

Social Services

Our Social Services have been described as "the modern expression of a long tradition of humanitarianism and mutual aid".

During the Second World War Sir William (now Lord) Beveridge drew up a model plan for these services, and declared that their object was "the destruction of Want, Disease, Squalor, Ignorance and Illness". Three years later, in 1945, Family Allowances of 5s. a week (since increased to 8s.) for each child after the first were introduced to meet the obvious needs of young families, which have always pressed hardly upon the wage-earner. And in 1946 the National Insurance Act put the coping-stone on the slowly built-up structure of services, requiring everybody to pay contributions towards a nation-wide provision of help in the event of sickness, unemployment, bereavement of women and children, and for old age. Thus a person's minimum needs are met. For further help in cases of necessity, National Assistance replaces the old Poor Relief: the name of "pauper"—a term of reproach and not of pity—has legally disappeared.

How Social Services Began

Our public social services are rooted in the voluntary social services of older days. In the Middle Ages monks and nuns cared to some extent for the poor, the sick and the aged. The medieval guilds helped their less fortunate members and the widows and orphans of deceased members; they also endowed schools and almshouses. In the Tudor Age, as the charitable work of the guilds and monasteries disappeared, a poor law system was created for those who could not, or would not, work, and Elizabeth's great Poor Law Code (1601) remained the law of the land for more than two centuries. Friendly Societies, too, have certainly been in existence since the eighteenth century, probably longer; these provide subscribing members with assistance in sickness and other benefits, and (as we know) the example was followed by many trade unions.

For some time the only social services provided by public authorities were those connected with the poor law and with education. During the greater part of the nineteenth century public opinion resented too much activity on the part of the State, on the ground that it undermined the independence of the individual citizen; in an age of rapid progress it was thought that there was no excuse for anyone, unless actually disabled, who was not self-supporting. However, a great extension of State activities did gradually take place. Besides housing and sanitary reforms, parks and recreation grounds were opened in many towns; libraries and swimming baths were built. Then came the great work of Asquith and Lloyd George. But it was the emergencies and suffering of the two world wars of the twentieth century which gave the greatest impetus to social reform. In particular, the devastation of big towns by air attack in 1940–1 and 1944 created a situation in which the State had daily to find first aid, food, homes, and even employment for people who had suddenly lost everything. The evacuation of mothers and children from slum areas into country districts also gave many people first-hand knowledge of slum conditions, so that public opinion was prepared to welcome big developments in social services after 1945.

Some important social services are concerned with employment, ranging from the work of the factory inspectors, who ever since 1833 have administered an increasingly effective code of laws to protect workers against accident, disease and overstrain, to that of the Labour Exchanges (started by Mr. Churchill in 1909) and their more recent offshoot, the Juvenile Employment Bureaux. But the most obvious necessity is the health services, which try to produce a fit nation. For unless people are fit the most perfect system for organizing employment will fail.

The Health Services

The most important modern developments in the health services came with the National Health Service Act of 1946. This Act aimed at providing a universal health service by means of doctors (both general practitioners and specialists), hospitals, and eventually health centres, free to all. It meant that everyone could get, according to need, free medical and dental treatment, and free provision of drugs, dentures and spectacles. It will take some years before the scheme can be fully developed. Doctors have been overworked by the large number of patients coming for free treatment, and the cost was found to be very heavy. Already certain modifications have been necessary: a dentist charges a standard

£1 fee, and there is a nominal charge of 1s. by the chemist for each prescription he makes up.

Health services also arrange for the welfare of the blind and deaf and crippled, and for mental defectives and others who are unable to lead a normal life. Institutions provide lodging and medical care. Blind people receive a pension at the age of forty, but many thousands of blind people have been trained and placed in suitable employment. Books in Braille type, which can be read with the fingers, are provided for them. Local authorities are responsible for teaching and training blind and deaf children; and some combine over a wide area to provide training for crippled children. Further, various centres have been established at which men and women disabled in the World Wars are trained to some occupation such as watch and clock making, light metal work, weaving and so on—by which they can earn at least part of their livelihood.

Public money is used on a considerable scale to enable mothers and children to obtain milk and certain other vital foods at prices within their means. Local Food Offices (and Infant Welfare Centres, as described below) supply cheap orange juice and free cod liver oil. During the Second World War the government for the time being extended this principle of subsidy to the benefit of the ordinary consumer—at a vast cost—in order to keep down the prices of certain necessary articles of food, such as bread, butter, meat, milk and eggs. Milk is now supplied to all children under five at less than half-price, and there is a free daily distribution of one-third of a pint in every school. Schools also provide a midday meal at a low price.

Social services play a very important part in the health of young citizens. When a baby is born a trained health visitor calls at the home and gives any advice necessary. Considerably more than half the children under one year of age are brought to Infant Welfare Centres, where they are weighed and examined, and where the mother can obtain advice and arrange to get milk, orange juice and other foods free or at a reduced price. There may be an opportunity for a child to attend a nursery school, but in any case it will go to an infant school at the age of five. Then it will not only be educated, but will come under the care of the school doctor, nurse

Mobile child welfare clinic at work near Aberdeen

and dentist. All children are medically examined at least three times during their school life and more frequently by the school nurse. This school medical service, with its open air schools for invalid children, has greatly improved the health of the children, and the average height and weight have increased at every year of age.

The hospitals of Britain include about one thousand which were founded by voluntary benefactors, together with those provided by public authorities, including many former Poor Law institutions. Apart from the great teaching hospitals, which have a special position in the training of doctors, all hospitals now partake equally in the work of the national health service under the control of Regional Boards. Special dispensaries and sanatoria exist to deal with tuberculosis; although the first government grants to aid such institutions were only made in 1911, an almost nation-wide service now exists. Deaths from tuberculosis had fallen in 1938 to a third of the number in 1900; and other scourges of past times, such as cholera and smallpox, have almost disappeared. Typhoid fever, which accounted for 1,228 deaths per million people living in 1838, was responsible for only 174 per million in 1900, and only 5 per million in 1938. Most impressive of all is the fall in the death-rate among infants under one year, which in 1900 was 156 per thousand in England and Wales and 130 in Scotland—a terrible total and one which had actually got worse during the preceding quarter of a century. This figure has now been reduced by 75 per cent. Families are smaller; the total population will soon perhaps be ceasing to grow at all, for the first time presumably since the Black Death in 1348; children are increasingly valuable. But the chief credit for the change is due to the wide scope and efficiency of the health services.

Housing

If people live longer than they used to, then it is all the more important that they should somehow be provided with good homes as the natural basis for a satisfactory home life. At the close of the First World War a disgracefully large number of slums still remained in large towns, while the fact that private building comes to a standstill in wartime meant that there was also much leeway to make up in the quantity of housing normally built to accommodate the wage-earners. Nothing daunted, the then Prime Minister (Lloyd George) promised the returning soldiers "homes for heroes". After the war the Housing Act of 1919 directed local councils to build houses which might be let to suitable tenants,

"The Lawns"—a section of Harlow New Town,

while subsidies were offered to encourage private building, and as a result some hundreds of thousands of houses were built, but this was not nearly enough. Then in the 1930's the Ministry of Health, which had replaced the Local Government Board in 1919, encouraged big schemes, under which large estates of well-spaced "council houses" made their appearance, together with blocks of up-to-date flats to serve the central areas of large cities, where slum clearance schemes made ground available. The great achievements of these years went a long way towards removing the worst evils of overcrowding and bad housing conditions; the chief remaining problem was how to re-house more people within reasonable distance of their place of work.

But then came the Second World War and the vast destruction of property by enemy bombing in London and many other great cities. Official schemes for rebuilding our cities were under consideration as early as 1940. At the present day the Ministry of Housing and Local Government still faces a huge task in dealing with the layout of new towns and large building estates, and with the problems of proper drainage, sufficient water supplies, open spaces, and other necessities for healthy conditions. It is estimated

Essex, on which work began in 1947

that one-third of the entire population of Great Britain has been re-housed since 1918, and our view of one of the new satellite towns, seven of which are being built to try to relieve pressure on accommodation in London, is a reminder of the more imaginative and more generous way in which this great question of the housing of the people is now being tackled. But there is still a lamentably large gap between demand and supply, between the dream and its fulfilment.

Social Services and the National Life

Social services may add indirectly to the cost of our exports, the sale of which is essential to the life of Britain—we cannot even complete a housing scheme without imported timber. But short of such a catastrophe as national bankruptcy or a third World War, it is safe to prophesy that these services have come to stay. Four of the greatest forces of our time are among their supporters. There is the old and honourable force of philanthropy, which seeks to complete the work begun by Lord Shaftesbury more than a hundred years ago. There is the scientific spirit which likes to see people's lives directed by a well-informed plan, whether for the dietary of infants or the layout of a community centre. Then there is the power of the trade unions: one citizen in every six is a trade unionist nowadays, and the largest and strongest unions are those of the once "submerged" unskilled workers. Their newly acquired ability to negotiate with employers on rather more than equal terms largely depends upon the maintenance of the unemployment and other benefits provided by the State.

Finally, we must not forget that social services represent the special aspirations of the two most newly enfranchised classes of citizens. The manhood suffrage law of 1918 gave the vote to millions of the ill-paid and underemployed, who had been the worst sufferers from the old Poor Law system and the lack of a comprehensive health service. The equal franchise law of 1928 gave the vote to all women (not merely those over thirty, as by the 1918 Act), and women were the most keenly aware of the deficiencies in the national provision for child welfare.

Nevertheless, like every good thing in life, the social services have their dangers. The people's state does so much for us that we must beware of the danger of slowly losing the capacity for strenuous work, the habit of manly self-reliance, the readiness to run risks and pioneer new ventures. These were the qualities that made the modern Britain of which we have been tracing the development; even the men who originated the social services sought security chiefly for others, not for themselves. The People's State, the ideas it stands for; its wealth, and its possessions, have all been created by long centuries of individual effort. It is as true to-day as it was in the time of Cromwell's Ironsides. that

> *The same arts that did gain*
> *A power, must it maintain.*

APPENDIX I

Social History in Contemporary Verse

1. *The publication of* THE VILLAGE *by George Crabbe in 1783 marked a revival of realism in the attitude of poets to the lives of humble people, with their long hours of work and, even in the wretched poor-house (a less highly organized predecessor of the Victorian workhouse), the "doleful hum" of compulsory spinning.*

The Village Life, and every care that reigns
O'er youthful peasants and declining swains;
What labour yields, and what, that labour past,
Age, in its hour of languor, finds at last;
What form the real picture of the poor,
Demand a song—the Muse can give no more.

Go then! and see them rising with the sun,
Through a long course of daily toil to run;
See them beneath the dog-star's raging heat,
When the knees tremble and the temples beat;
Behold them, leaning on their scythes, look o'er
The labour past, and toils to come explore;
See them alternate suns and showers engage,
And hoard up aches and anguish for their age.

Theirs is yon house that holds the parish-poor,
Whose walls of mud scarce bear the broken door;
There, where the putrid vapours, flagging, play,
And the dull wheel hums doleful through the day;—
There children dwell who know no parents' care;
Parents, who know no children's love, dwell there! . . .
The lame, the blind, and, far the happiest they!
The moping idiot and the madman gay.
Here too the sick their final doom receive,
Here brought, amid the scenes of grief, to grieve . . .
Here, sorrowing, they each kindred sorrow scan,
And the cold charities of man to man.

2. THE BOROUGH (*1810*) *gives Crabbe's account of the tiny seaport of Aldeburgh in Suffolk, his native town, where he struggled in vain to establish himself as a doctor or apothecary, for which he had been educated. The descriptions of a Friendly Society and of local schools are typical of the everyday scenes pictured in the twenty-four Letters composing the poem.*

Of manufactures, trade, inventions rare,
Steam-towers and looms, you'd know our Borough's share—
'Tis small: we boast not these rich subjects here,
Who hazard thrice ten thousand pounds a year;
We've no huge buildings, where incessant noise
Is made by springs and spindles, girls and boys . . .
Still common minds with us in common trade,
Have gain'd more wealth than ever student made.

The poor man has his club; he comes and spends
His hoarded pittance with his chosen friends;
Nor this alone—a monthly dole he pays,
To be assisted when his health decays;
Some part his prudence, from the day's supply,
For cares and troubles in his age, lays by;
The printed rules he guards with painted frame,
And shows his children where to read his name.

To every class we have a school assign'd,
Rules for all ranks, and food for every mind:
Yet one there is, that small regard to rule
Or study pays, and still is deemed a school;
That, where a deaf, poor, patient widow sits,
And awes some thirty infants as she knits;
Infants of humble, busy wives, who pay
Some trifling price for freedom through the day.
At this good matron's hut the children meet,
Who thus becomes the mother of the street . . .
Though deaf, she sees the rebel heroes shout—
Though lame, her white rod nimbly walks about.

To learning's second seats we now proceed,
Where humming students gilded primers read . . .
"Reading made Easy", so the titles tell;
But they who read must first begin to spell:
There may be profits in these arts, but still
Learning is labour, call it what you will.

"But is it sure that study will repay
The more attentive and forebearing?"—Nay!
The farm, the ship, the humble shop have each
Gains which severest studies seldom reach.

3. *Shelley's* MASK OF ANARCHY, *of which these are the central stanzas,
was written on his receiving news in Italy of the Peterloo Massacre
(August 1819). It was sent to the Radical periodical,* THE EXAMINER,
*but though it advocated no more than passive resistance, this "flaming
robe of verse", as Leigh Hunt called it, remained unpublished until 1832.*

What is Freedom?—ye can tell
That which slavery is, too well—
For its very name has grown
To an echo of your own.

'Tis to work and have such pay
As just keeps life from day to day
In your limbs, as in a cell
For the tyrants' use to dwell,

So that ye for them are made
Loom, and plough, and sword, and spade,
With or without your own will bent
To their defence and nourishment.

'Tis to see your children weak
With their mothers pine and peak,
When the winter winds are bleak—
They are dying whilst I speak. . . .

'Tis to let the Ghost of Gold
Take from Toil a thousandfold
More than e'er its substance could
In the tyrannies of old. . . .

And at length when ye complain
With a murmur weak and vain
'Tis to see the Tyrant's crew
Ride over your wives and you—
Blood is on the grass like dew.

4. THE LAY OF THE LABOURER, *like the better-known* SONG OF THE SHIRT, *was written by Thomas Hood in the early 'forties, when nearly 10 per cent of the entire population were paupers and agricultural wages for eighteen southern counties averaged 8s. 5d. a week.*

A spade! a rake! a hoe!
A pickaxe, or a bill!
A hook to reap, or a scythe to mow,
A flail, or what ye will—
And here's a ready hand
To ply the needful tool,
And skill'd enough, by lessons rough,
In Labour's rugged school.

To hedge, or dig the ditch,
To lop or fell the tree,
To lay the swarth on the sultry field,
Or plough the stubborn lea;
The harvest stack to bind,
The wheaten rick to thatch,
And never fear in my pouch to find
The tinder or the match.

To a flaming barn or farm
My fancies never roam;
The fire I yearn to kindle and burn
Is on the hearth of Home;
Where children huddle and crouch
Through dark long winter days,
Where starving children huddle and crouch,
To see the cheerful rays,
A-glowing on the haggard cheek,
And not in the haggard's blaze!

To Him who sends a drought
To parch the fields forlorn,
The rain to flood the meadows with mud,
The lights to blast the corn,
To Him I leave to guide
The bolt in its crooked path,
To strike the miser's rick, and show
The skies blood-red with wrath.

A spade! a rake! a hoe!
　A pickaxe, or a bill!
A hook to reap, or a scythe to mow,
　A flail, or what ye will—
The corn to thrash, or the hedge to plash,
　The market-team to drive,
Or mend the fence by the cover side,
　And leave the game alive.

Ay, only give me work,
　And then you need not fear
That I shall snare his worship's hare,
　Or kill his grace's deer;
Break into his lordship's house,
　To steal the plate so rich;
Or leave the yeoman that had a purse
　To welter in a ditch.

Wherever Nature needs,
　Wherever Labour calls,
No job I'll shirk of the hardest work,
　To shun the workhouse walls;
Where savage laws begrudge
　The pauper babe its breath,
And doom a wife to a widow's life,
　Before her partner's death.

My only claim is this,
　With labour stiff and stark,
By lawful turn, my living to earn,
　Between the light and dark;
My daily bread and nightly bed,
　My bacon, and drop of beer—
But all from the hand that holds the land,
　And none from the overseer!

5. *A contrasting picture from the same period as the preceding one—the meeting of the Maidstone Mechanics' Institute at Park House, the home of Tennyson's friend. Edmund Lushington, on 6th July 1842, which he used as the setting for* THE PRINCESS *(1847).*

Sir Walter Vivian all a summer's day
Gave his broad lawns until the set of sun
Up to the people: thither flocked at noon
His tenants, wife and child, and thither half
The neighbouring borough with their Institute
Of which he was the patron.

There moved the multitude, a thousand heads:
The patient leaders of their Institute
Taught them with facts . . . and here were telescopes
For azure views; and there a group of girls
In circle waited, whom the electric shock
Dislink'd with shrieks and laughter: round the lake
A little clock-work steamer paddling plied
And shook the lilies: perch'd about the knolls
A dozen angry models jetted steam:
A petty railway ran: a fire-balloon
Rose gem-like up before the dusky groves
And dropt a fiery parachute and past:
And there thro' twenty posts of telegraph
They flash'd a saucy message to and fro
Between the mimic stations; so that sport
‑Went hand in hand with Science; otherwhere
Pure sport: a herd of boys with clamour bowl'd
And stump'd the wicket; babies roll'd about
Like tumbled fruit in grass; and men and maids
Arranged a country dance . . .

                              And overhead
The broad ambrosial aisles of lofty lime
Made noise with bees and breeze from end to end.
Strange was the sight and smacking of the time.

6. *An extract from Tennyson's hymn to Victorian prosperity, written for the opening of the International Exhibition at South Kensington in 1862. There were twice as many exhibitors as in 1851, which seems to justify both Gladstone's Free Trade budgets and the poet's elaboration of what he calls the "myriad horns of plenty at our feet".*

Lo! the long laborious miles
Of Palace; lo! the giant aisles,
Rich in model and design;
Harvest-tool and husbandry,
Loom and wheel and enginery,
Secrets of the sullen mine,
Steel and gold, and corn and wine,
Fabric rough, or fairy-fine,
Sunny tokens of the Line,
Polar marvels, and a feast
Of wonder, out of West and East,
And shapes and hues of Art divine!
All of beauty, all of use,
That one fair planet can produce.

7. *W. H. Davies, before he found success as the author of* THE AUTO-BIOGRAPHY OF A SUPER-TRAMP *(1908), experienced for many years the hardships of existence in doss-houses on 8s. a week. His verses therefore show London, then the richest city in the world, as it appeared to the generally inarticulate "submerged tenth" of its population.*

My song is of that city which
Has men too poor and men too rich;
Where some are sick, too richly fed,
While others take the sparrows' bread:
Where some have beds to warm their bones,
While others sleep on hard, cold stones
That suck away their bodies' heat.
Where men are drunk in every street;
Men full of poison, like those flies
That still attack the horses' eyes.
Where some men freeze for want of cloth,
While others show their jewels' worth
And dress in satin, fur or silk;
Where fine rich ladies wash in milk,
While starving mothers have no food
To make them fit in flesh and blood;
So that their watery breasts can give
Their babies milk and make them live.

Where one man does the work of four,
And dies worn out before his hour;
While some seek work in vain, and grief
Doth make their fretful lives as brief.
Where ragged men are seen to wait
For charity that's small and late;
While others haunt in idle leisure,
Theatre doors to pay for pleasure.

8. THE DEAR OLD VILLAGE, *John Betjeman's modern version of Crabbe,
should not be taken too seriously. Nevertheless, there is a sting in its tale.*

Behind rank elders, shadowing a pool,
And near the Church, behold the Village School,
Its gable rising out of ivy thick
Shows "Eighteen-Sixty" worked in coloured brick.
By nineteen-forty-seven, hurrah! hooray!
This institution has outlived its day.
In the bad times of old feudality
The villagers were ruled by masters three—
Squire, parson, schoolmaster. Of these, the last
Knew best the village present and its past.
Now, I am glad to say, the man is dead,
The children have a motor-bus instead,
And in a town eleven miles away
We train them to be "Citizens of To-day".
And many a cultivated hour they pass
In a fine school with walls of vita-glass.
Civics, eurhythmics, economics, Marx,
How-to-respect-wild-life-in-National-Parks;
Plastics, gymnastics—thus they learn to scorn
The old thatch'd cottages where they were born.
The girls, ambitious to begin their lives
Serving in Woolworth's, rather than as wives;
The boys, who cannot yet escape the land,
At driving tractors lend a clumsy hand.
An eight-hour day for all, and more than three
Of these are occupied in making tea
And talking over what we all agree—
Though "Music while you work" is now our wont,
It's not so nice as "Music while you don't".
Squire, parson, schoolmaster turn in their graves.
And *let* them turn. We are no longer slaves.

APPENDIX II

Books For Further Reading

I. VILLAGE LIFE IN THE EIGHTEENTH CENTURY

Introductory

R. BAYNE-POWELL, *English Country Life in the Eighteenth Century* (Murray): pp. 96–111—an account of Woodforde.

Authorities

G. M. TREVELYAN, *English Social History* (Longmans): c. XIII—country-house life.

C. HOLE, *English Home Life, 1500–1800* (Batsford): Part II—illustrations of domestic interiors, etc.

Contemporary

J. WOODFORDE, *The Diary of a Country Parson* (O.U.P.): selections, edited by J. Beresford.

2. TOWN LIFE IN THE EIGHTEENTH CENTURY; LONDON

Introductory

R. J. M. MITCHELL and M. D. R. LEYS, *A History of England* (Longmans): pp. 455–66—houses and furniture.

K. BARNE, *Elizabeth Fry* (Methuen).

D. LINDSAY and E. S. WASHINGTON, *A Portrait of Britain, 1688–1851* (O.U.P.): cc. 11 and 12—life in Johnson's England.

Authorities

A. S. TURBERVILLE (editor), *Johnson's England*, 2 vols. (O.U.P.): Vol. I, c. VII —London, by M. D. George; c. VIII—provincial town-life, by G. D. H. Cole; pp. 329–34—philanthropy, by J. L. and B. Hammond.

M. D. GEORGE, *London Life in the Eighteenth Century* (Kegan Paul): Introduction and cc. I, II and IV—the life of the poor.

P. PRINGLE, *The Romance of Medical Science* (Harrap): c. VIII—vaccination.

Contemporary

D. DEFOE, *A Tour through England and Wales*, 2 vols. (Everyman): Letter V, on London; notices of other towns, as indexed.

3. EIGHTEENTH-CENTURY PEOPLE AT WORK

Introductory

C. R. FAY, *Great Britain from Adam Smith to the Present Day* (Longmans): Introduction.

Authorities

L. W. MOFFIT, *England on the Eve of the Industrial Revolution* (King): for the period 1740–60, especially in Lancashire.

J. H. PLUMB, *England in the Eighteenth Century* (Penguin Books): cc. I and II —for the period 1714–42.

Contemporary

A. E. BLAND, etc., *English Economic History Select Documents* (Bell): pp. 482–500.

4. WHAT WAS THE INDUSTRIAL REVOLUTION?

Introductory

T. K. DERRY, *Outlines of English Economic History* (Bell): c. XIII.

Authorities

T. S. ASHTON, *The Industrial Revolution, 1760–1830* (O.U.P.): cc. I and II.

J. L. and B. HAMMOND, *The Rise of Modern Industry* (Methuen): cc. I–IV—origins; cc. V–XI—main aspects of industrial change.

W. H. B. COURT, *A Concise Economic History of Britain from 1750 to Recent Times* (C.U.P.): c. I—population.

G. T. GRIFFITH, *Population Problems of the Age of Malthus* (C.U.P.): cc. I, II, X, XI.

M. C. BUER, *Health, Wealth and Population in the Early Days of the Industrial Revolution* (Routledge): cc. IX–XVI—health factors.

Contemporary

ADAM SMITH, *Wealth of Nations* (Everyman).

5—6. HOW THE GREAT CHANGES CAME

Introductory

FAY, op. cit., c. VII.

H. HAMILTON, *History of the Homeland* (Allen & Unwin): c. XV—commerce and the flag.

Authorities

P. MANTOUX, *The Industrial Revolution in the Eighteenth Century* (Cape): Pt. III, c. II.

COURT, op. cit., c. V.

R. SAW, *The Bank of England* (Harrap): cc. I–VIII—on the period 1694–1821.

Johnson's England: Vol. I, pp. 256–9—banking.

Contemporary

C. R. FAY, *Huskisson and His Age* (Longmans): c. XI—material for the Truck Act of 1831.

7. THE REVOLUTION IN TEXTILES

Introductory

M. and C. H. B. QUENNELL, *A History of Everyday Things in England*, 4 Parts (Batsford): Part III, c. III.

Authorities

MANTOUX, op. cit., Pt. II, c. II and pp. 225–239—for Arkwright.

ASHTON, op. cit., pp. 70–78.

A. P. WADSWORTH and J. DE L. MANN, *The Cotton Trade and Industrial Lancashire, 1600–1780* (Manchester U.P.): cc. XXI–XXIII—machine spinning.

E. LIPSON, *A Short History of Wool* (Heinemann): c. VII.

S. LILLEY, *Men, Machines and History* (Cobbett): c. VI.

Contemporary

J. GALT, *Annals of the Parish* (Everyman): cc. XXIX–LI—the development of the factory system, etc., in a Scottish parish, 1788–1810.

8. THE REVOLUTION IN TRANSPORT

Introductory

G. D. H. COLE, *Persons and Periods* (Penguin Books): pp. 78–98.

Authorities

W. T. JACKMAN, *The Development of Transportation in Modern England*, 2 vols. (C.U.P.): Vol. I, c. IV—roads; c. V—canals.

Johnson's England: Vol. I, c. VI.

C. HADFIELD, *British Canals* (Phoenix House): pp. 1–141.

S. and B. WEBB, *The Story of the King's Highway* (Longmans): pp. 114–191.

9. THE REVOLUTION IN FARMING

Introductory

QUENNELL, op. cit.: Part III, c. I.

C. S. and C. S. ORWIN, *Farms and Fields* (O.U.P.): pp. 61–85.

Authorities

LORD ERNLE, *English Farming Past and Present* (Longmans): cc. VIII–XI.

J. L. and B. HAMMOND, *The Village Labourer, 1760–1832* (Longmans): cc. III–V—enclosures.

Johnson's England: Vol. I, c. X—by C. S. Orwin.

E. HALÉVY, *A History of the English People in 1815* (Benn): pp. 192–224—the system of large estates.

M. D. GEORGE, *England in Transition* (Penguin Books): c. V—the village in transition.

H. HAMILTON, *The Industrial Revolution in Scotland* (O.U.P.): cc. II and III—agricultural improvement.

Contemporary

J. BYNG, VISCOUNT TORRINGTON, *The Torrington Diaries* (Eyre & Spottiswoode): selections edited by C. B. and F. Andrews.—enclosures (index).

BLAND, etc.: op. cit., pp. 528–541.

10–12. COAL, THE STEAM ENGINE, AND IRON

Introductory

J. S. RANSHAW, *Great Engines and their Inventors* (Burke): cc. I and II; c. III—Trevithick.

Authorities

T. S. ASHTON and J. SYKES, *The Coal Industry of the Eighteenth Century* (Manchester U.P.): cc. II, III, IX, X.

W. H. B. COURT, *The Rise of Midland Industries* (O.U.P.): Bk. II, cc. I–III, VI—coal, iron, power.

MANTOUX, op. cit.: Pt. II, c. IV, pp. 385–390—Boulton.

T. S. ASHTON, *Iron and Steel in the Industrial Revolution* (Manchester U.P.): cc. II, III, IV, VI.

LILLEY, op. cit.: c. VI.

13. POTTERY AND SHIPPING

Introductory

S. E. ELLACOTT, *The Story of Ships* (Methuen): pp. 47–66.

Authorities

R. H. THORNTON, *British Shipping* (C.U.P.): cc. I–V.

B. CABLE *A Hundred Years History of the P. & O.* (Nicholson): cc. I–XVII.

G. M. YOUNG (editor) *Early Victorian England*, 2 vols. (O.U.P.): Vol. I c. VIII—the mercantile marine 1830–65.

MANTOUX: op. cit., pp. 391–7—Wedgwood.

Johnson's England: Vol. I, pp. 232–4—pottery.

14. THE FACTORY TOWNS

Introductory

QUENNELL: op. cit., Pt. III, c. V.

Authorities

J. L. and B. HAMMOND, *The Town Labourer, 1760–1832* (Longmans): c. III.

Early Victorian England: Vol. I, c. IV—life in the new towns.

HALEVY: op. cit., pp. 289–95—Luddism.

A. REDFORD, *Labour Migration in England*, (Manchester U.P.) cc. III, IV.

Contemporary

B. DISRAELI, *Sybil* (World's Classics): description of industrial conditions in early 'forties based on official reports.

15. WOMEN AND CHILDREN; THE FACTORY ACTS

Authorities

I. PINCHBECK, *Women Workers and the Industrial Revolution* (Routledge): cc. IX and XI—work in factories, mines, and the metal trades.

J. L. and B. HAMMOND, *Lord Shaftesbury* (Constable): cc. II–IV, VII–XI.

A. HUTCHINS and A. HARRISON, *A History of Factory Legislation* (King): cc. II–IV.

M. G. JONES, *The Charity School Movement* (C.U.P.): pp. 142–154—Sunday Schools.

Contemporary

W. A. BARKER, etc., *Documents of English History, 1832–1950* (Black): II—industrialism.

BLAND, etc.: op. cit., pp. 502–25, 592–614—factory legislation.

16. BRITAIN AFTER WATERLOO

Authorities

A. BRYANT, *The Age of Elegance* (Collins): cc. VIII–X—the rulers and the ruled; the underworld.

D. THOMSON, *England in the Nineteenth Century* (Penguin Books): cc. I and II—Britain in 1815; the forces of change.

E. L. WOODWARD, *The Age of Reform, 1815–1870* (O.U.P.): pp. 1–38—England in 1815.

Contemporary

W. COBBETT, *Rural Rides*, 2 vols. (Everyman): visits to 27 counties.

17. THE COMING OF THE RAILWAYS

Introductory

O. S. NOCK, *The Railways of Britain Past and Present* (Batsford).

O. S. NOCK, *British Trains Past and Present* (Batsford).

J. THOMAS, *The Story of George Stephenson* (O.U.P.).

E. GARNETT, *The Master Engineers* (Hodder and Stoughton): the Brunels.

Authorities

JACKMAN, op. cit.: Vol. II, c. VII.

J. H. CLAPHAM, *An Economic History of Modern Britain*, 3 vols. (C.U.P.)
Vol. I, c. IX.

C. H. ELLIS, *British Railway History, 1830–76* (Allen & Unwin): pp. 77–149—
covering the period 1830–45.

R. B. LLOYD, *Railwayman's Gallery* (Allen & Unwin): c. II—the navvy.

Contemporary

R. S. SURTEES, *Plain or Ringlets?* (Methuen): cc. XXXIII and LXI—a novel-
ist's picture of railway stations in the 'fifties.

18. THE COMING OF FREE TRADE

Introductory

A. BRYANT, *English Saga* (Collins): pp. 84–119.

Authorities

FAY, op. cit.: cc. II–IV.

COURT, op. cit., pp. 310–316—origins of the free trade policy.

WOODWARD, op. cit.: pp. 68–70, 114–19, 159–61, 172–75.

J. MORLEY, *Life of Richard Cobden* (Unwin): cc. VI–XVI.

Contemporary

BLAND, etc., op. cit.: pp. 692–711—the Corn Laws.

19. TRADE UNIONS AND CO-OPERATIVE SOCIETIES

Introductory

W. CITRINE, *British Trade Unions* (Collins): pp. 1–37—history, with illustrations.

QUENNELL, op. cit.: Part IV, pp. 155-7—co-operatives.

Authorities

G. D. H. COLE, *A Short History of the British Working-Class Movement,
1789–1947* (Allen & Unwin): Pt. I, cc. V and VI, Pt. II, cc. III, V, VI and
VIII.

FAY, op. cit.: cc. XIX and XX.

S. and B. WEBB, *A History of Trade Unionism* (Longmans).

W. H. CHALONER, *The Social and Economic Development of Crewe* (Manchester U.P.): c. IX—a local co-operative movement, 1845–1923.

Contemporary

G. WALLAS, *The Life of Francis Place* (Allen & Unwin): c. VIII—extracts
from Place's writings about the repeal of the Combination Acts.

E. C. GASKELL, *Mary Barton* (Everyman): a novel by a resident describing
industrial life in Manchester in 1842-3.

20. THE WORKSHOP OF THE WORLD

Introductory

A. WILLIAMS-ELLIS, *Men Who Found Out* (Howe): c. V—Faraday; c. VIII—
Lister.

A. WILLIAMS-ELLIS and E. COOPER-WILLIS, *Laughing Gas and Safety Lamp* (Methuen): Davy and Faraday.
QUENNELL, op. cit.: Part IV, c. II—the farmer and his work.

Authorities
J. DEARDEN, *Iron and Steel To-day* (O.U.P.): cc. I–VII—history of techniques.
CLAPHAM, op. cit.: Vol. II, pp. 47–72—iron and steel; shipbuilding.
COURT, op. cit.: pp. 161–84—Victorian agriculture and industrial enterprise.
ERNLE, op. cit.: pp. 358–382.
G. E. FUSSELL, *The English Rural Labourer* (Batchworth): cc. VIII–XI.

Contemporary
S. SMILES, *Self-Help* (Murray).
J. RUSKIN, *Unto This Last* (Everyman): four essays on the nature of wealth, which aroused great controversy in 1860–2.

21. NEW TRENDS IN GOVERNMENT

Introductory
T. K. DERRY, *British Institutions of To-day* (Longmans): c. II and cc. VIII–X —parliamentary reform acts; local government.
F. G. KAY, *Royal Mail* (Rockliff).

Authorities
J. A. R. MARRIOTT, *England Since Waterloo* (Methuen): pp. 98–9, 350–54, 417, 491–2—parliamentary reform.
H. J. LASKI, W. I. JENNINGS, and W. A. ROBSON (editors), *A Century of Municipal Progress, 1835–1935* (Allen & Unwin): c. II—the social background, by J. L. Hammond; c. III—the municipal revolution of 1835, by W. I. Jennings.
A. BRIGGS, *History of Birmingham*, 2 vols. (O.U.P.): Vol. II, c. IV.
E. T. CRUTCHLEY, *G.P.O.* (C.U.P.).
H. ROBINSON, *Britain's Post Office* (O.U.P.).

Contemporary
J. L. GARVIN, *The Life of Joseph Chamberlain* (Macmillan): Vol. I, pp. 179–214—some contemporary material for the reforms in Birmingham.
R. H. TAWNEY (editor), *The Life and Struggles of William Lovett*, 2 vols. (Bell): on the struggle for the 1832 Reform Act (c. IV) as well as for the history of Chartism.

22. TOWN LIFE AND HEALTH

Introductory
C. WOODHAM-SMITH, *Lady-in-Chief* (Methuen): Florence Nightingale.
P. PRINGLE, *The Romance of Medical Science* (Harrap): cc. IX and XI.
QUENNELL, op .cit.: Part III, c. V—sanitation; Part IV, c. VI—public health.

Authorities
J. L. and B. HAMMOND, *The Bleak Age* (Penguin Books): cc. V and XII—towns and public health; cc. VI and XIII—parks, etc.
F. S. TAYLOR, *A Century of Science* (Heinemann): cc. III and IV.
H. WILLIAMS, *A Century of Public Health in Britain* (Black): pp. 263–301—the architects of social medicine.

Contemporary

P. QUENNELL (editor), *Mayhew's Characters* (Kimber): pp. 85, 157, 169—examples of London poverty.

C. KINGSLEY, *Two Years Ago* (Macmillan): novel describing a cholera outbreak in a Cornish village.

23. VICTORIAN COMFORT

Introductory

A. BOTT, *Our Fathers* (Heinemann): lavishly illustrated social history of 1870–1900.

A. BOTT and C. CLEPHANE, *Our Mothers* (Heinemann): as above.

QUENNELL, op. cit.: Part IV, c. XI—amusements and holidays.

D. M. STUART, *The English Abigail* (Macmillan): cc. VIII and IX—domestic service.

Authorities

Early Victorian England: Vol. I, pp. 90–103—the daily round in a country house.

TREVELYAN, op. cit.: c. XVIII—the later Victorian period.

CLAPHAM, op. cit.: Vol. I, pp. 8–9 and Vol. II, pp. 517–18—growth of coastal resorts.

Contemporary

F. A. WALBANK, *England Yesterday and To-day* (Batsford): pp. 1–23—extracts from representative Victorian novels.

24. A NEW ERA IN POLITICS

Introductory

W. G. HALL, *The Labour Party* (Collins).

Authorities

J. A. SPENDER, *Great Britain, Empire and Commonwealth* (Cassell): pp. 763–803—comments on economic changes.

D. C. SOMERVELL, *British Politics Since 1900* (Dakers) pp. 20–34—origins of the Labour Party.

Contemporary

VISCOUNT SNOWDEN, *An Autobiography*, 2 vols. (Nicholson): Vol. II, cc. XLIV, XLV—the first Labour Government; c. LVI—the General Strike.

G. LANSBURY, *My Life* (Constable).

C. R. ATTLEE, *As It Happened* (Heinemann).

25. NEW PROBLEMS FOR BRITAIN

Introductory

D. LINDSAY and E. S. WASHINGTON, *A Portrait of Britain, 1851–1951* (O.U.P.): cc. 17 and 18.

Authorities

CLAPHAM, op. cit.: Vol. III, pp. 511–554—epilogue, covering 1914–1929.

C. L. MOWAT, *Britain Between the Wars* (Methuen): cc, 5 and 8—economic problems and solutions.

Contemporary

A. SALTER, *Recovery* (Macmillan): a survey by an economic expert in 1932.

26. A NEW INDUSTRIAL REVOLUTION

Introductory

W. SHEPHERD, etc., *The Wonderful Story of British Industry* (Ward, Lock): cc. 3, 5 and 8—light industry, the chemist, the scientist in the factory.

L. E. SALT, etc. (editors), *Oxford Junior Encyclopaedia* (O.U.P.). Vol. III, Industry and Commerce—e.g. "Plastics".

Authorities

LILLEY, op. cit.: cc. VIII–X.

A. W. HASLETT, *Science in Transition*: cc. V, X, XI.

PRINGLE, op. cit.: cc. XV, XVI.

27. THE NEW AGRICULTURE

Introductory

E. HOLT, *The Farmer* (E.S.A.).

Authorities

T. B. HUTCHESON, *Machinery on the Farm* (Blackie).

C. S. ORWIN, *A History of English Farming* (Nelson): cc. III, IV—covering 1850–1945.

LORD ERNLE, op. cit. (revised edition, 1936): c. XVIII onwards.

Contemporary

A. G. STREET, *Farmer's Glory* (Faber): Parts I and III—farming in 1906–1931

28. THE PEOPLE'S SCHOOLS

Introductory

K. LINDSAY, *English Education* (Collins): with illustrations.

Authorities

A. D. C. PETERSON, *A Hundred Years of Education* (Duckworth).

T. L. JARMAN, *Landmarks in the History of Education* (Cresset Press): pp. 209–13—Education and the Industrial Revolution; cc. XIV–XVIII—development in England.

Contemporary

WALLAS, op. cit.: c. I—early struggle for education.

TAWNEY, *Lovett* (op. cit.): pp. 3–10, 21–22, 35–37—as above.

THOMAS HUGHES, *Tom Brown's Schooldays* (Everyman): based on recollections of Rugby in the 'thirties.

29. THE PEOPLE'S LEISURE

Introductory

V. OGILVIE, *Our Times—A Social History 1912–1952* (Batsford): c. XI—leisure.

N. WYMER, *Sport in England* (Harrap): cc. VII–XIV.

Oxford Junior Encyclopaedia, Vol. IX, Recreations—historical articles.

Authorities

R. C. K. ENSOR, *England 1870–1914* (O.U.P.): cc. V, X, XV.

MOWAT, op. cit: cc. 4 and 9—the condition of Britain in the 'twenties and in the 'thirties.

Contemporary

H. LLEWELLYN-SMITH (editor), *The New Survey of London Life and Labour* (King): Vol. I.

T. CAUTER and J. S. DOWNHAM, *The Communication of Ideas* (Chatto and Windus): pp. 23–202—interests of the people of Derby.

C. B. FRY, *Life Worth Living* (Eyre & Spottiswoode).

P. WARNER, *Long Innings* (Harrap).

30. THE PEOPLE'S STATE

Introductory

W. A. BARKER, etc., *General History of England, 1832–1950* (Black): c. X—the welfare state.

LINDSAY and WASHINGTON, op. cit.: c. 22—the social revolution 1939–50.

Oxford Junior Encyclopaedia, Vol. X—e.g. "Social Insurance".

Authorities

D. L. HOBMAN, *The Welfare State* (Murray): cc. II–IV.

G. NEWMAN, *English Social Services* (Collins): health services, etc. up to 1939.

Contemporary

W. H. BEVERIDGE, *Report on Social Insurance and Allied Services* (H.M.S.O.): the Report of 1942.

M

INDEX

303